I0418910

THE FRICKS COLLECT

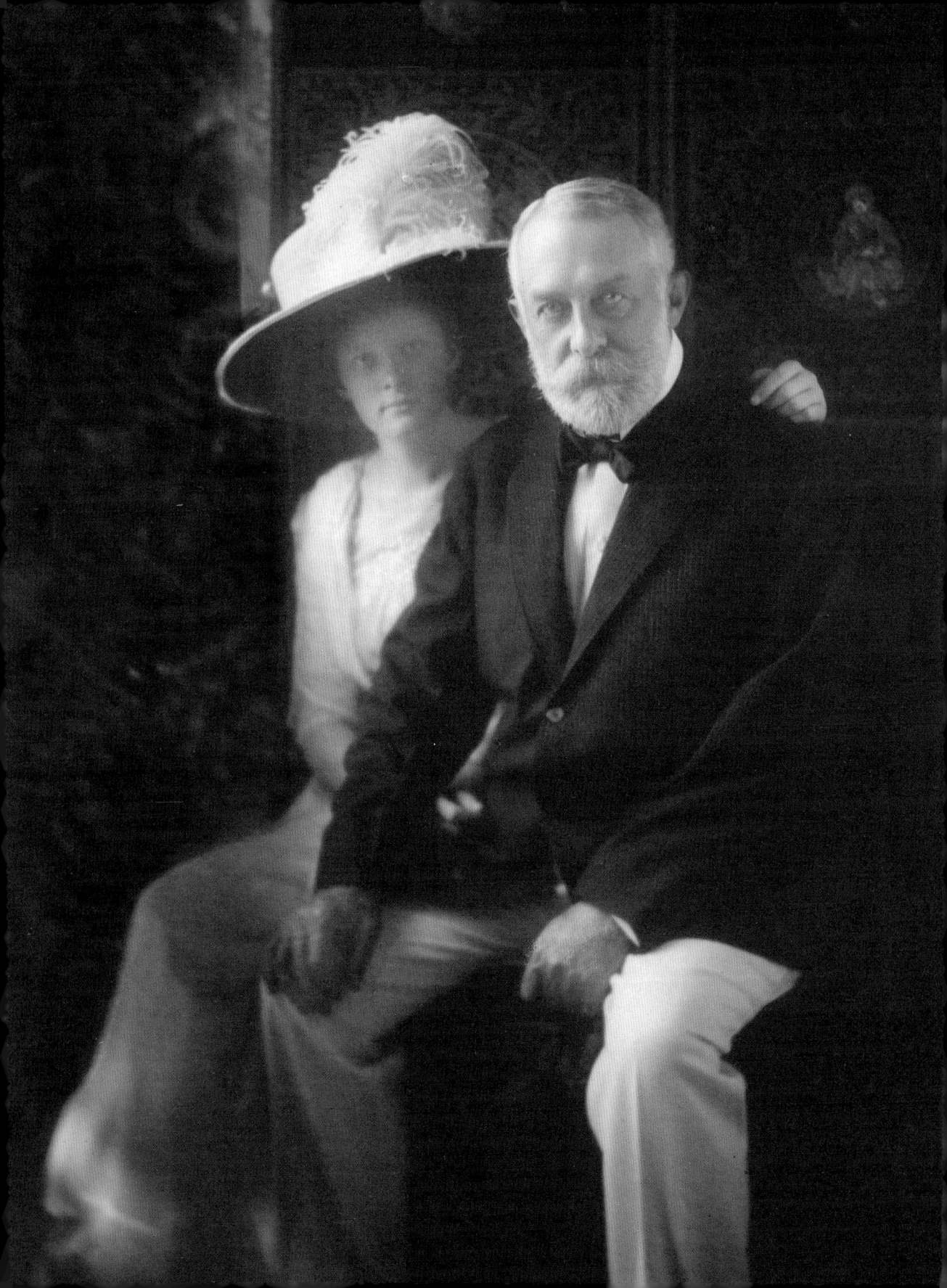

THE
FRICKS
COLLECT

AN AMERICAN FAMILY
AND THE EVOLUTION OF TASTE
IN THE GILDED AGE

Ian Wardropper

Foreword by Julian Fellowes

Rizzoli|**Electa**   THE FRICK COLLECTION

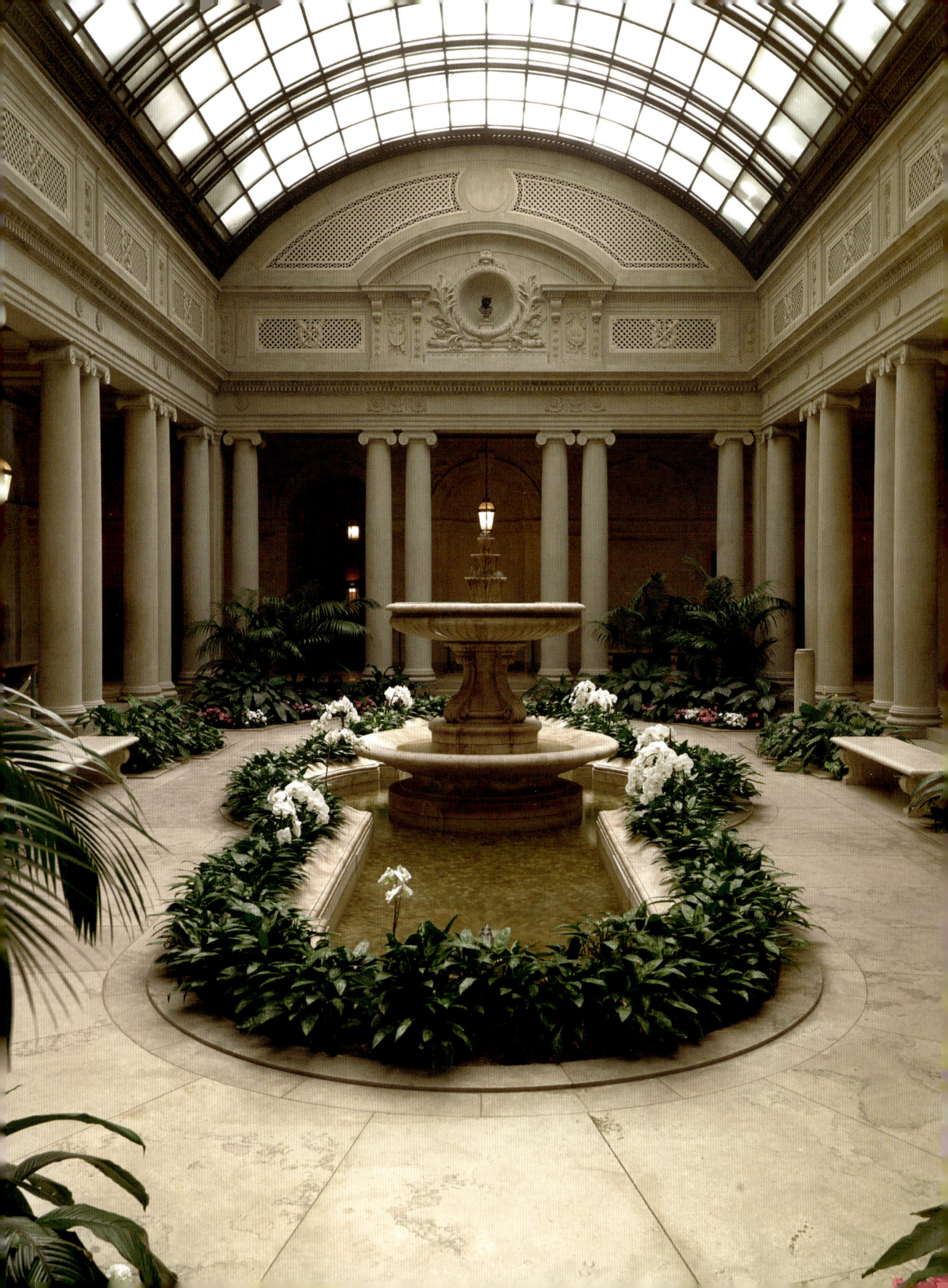

FOR SARAH, CHLOE, GORDON, AND WILLA

CONTENTS

FOREWORD

The Frick Collection changed my life, or at any rate, it opened me to a new perception of American history, long before that interest led me to write the series dealing with the Gilded Age.

About half a century ago, when I was still fairly new to the United States, I was staying at an apartment on the corner of Fifth Avenue and East 62nd Street, with an ancient former girlfriend of one of my father's more disreputable cousins, when she suggested that I stroll up the avenue and visit the Frick. I have always favored smaller museums, where you can enjoy the items on display without feeling submerged and overwhelmed—the Wallace Collection in London, the Musée Nissim de Camondo in Paris, the Mauritshuis in The Hague—and the moment I stepped into the Frick, I knew I had found just such a refuge in the heart of New York City. Perhaps it is because they were all family houses before they began their careers as museums that they seem to have a sense—one that none of the huge national galleries can claim—of the lives being lived around these beautiful and rare objects.

And what lives. Before the Civil War, the leaders of American society usually descended from younger sons of gentry families—from England or Scotland or the Netherlands—so much so that where such descent was missing, it was frequently invented, as in the case of the two presidents from the Adams family who were supplied with a false Welsh aristocratic lineage that was published and widely believed, despite being completely untrue. But the Civil War changed all that. Huge fortunes were amassed by former butchers and bakers and candlestick makers who wanted no part of an invented noble European background. They were Americans, and they needed a high society that was American in tone, with room for new families as well as old. And that is what had emerged after the war, under the tutelage of Mrs. Astor, by the time the Fricks moved to New York in 1905 and, in 1912, started to build their house at 1 East 70th Street, where they would hang their growing collection of wonderful paintings.

Henry Clay Frick was an interesting, maybe even iconic, example of the so-called robber barons. Born in Pennsylvania in 1849, the son, perhaps tellingly, of a failed businessman, he vowed at twenty-one to be a millionaire by the time he was thirty, and he more than achieved his goal. We cannot hide from the fact that he was a ruthless man in his professional dealings, working for much of the time alongside Andrew Carnegie, most notoriously at the Homestead Strike of 1892, in which Pinkerton detectives opened fire and eight strikers died before the state troops arrived and something like order was restored. It was an angry fight between angry men, and it left the reputations of Carnegie and Frick in tatters. How extraordinary, then, that these days Carnegie is remembered as the benevolent provider of public libraries and concert halls, and Frick is valued for having assembled one of the finest art collections in America.

I suppose, in the end, it was that vivid combination that fired my imagination: limitless quantities of money and splendor, coupled with powers of patronage that rivaled the princes of the Renaissance, all linked indissolubly with the violence and bullish strength of an emergent economy, building the new great nation that would push away Russia and Austria and France and Britain and all the other empires that had shaped the world since the dawn of time, to dominate the twentieth century from the start.

As to whether they were heroes or villains, these self-made giants, cleverer people than I have wrestled with that one. The answer must surely be both, but The Frick Collection remains a vibrant testimony to where they did well with their money and power, however they gained them, making America one of the main custodians of high culture in the modern world.

JULIAN FELLOWES
2024

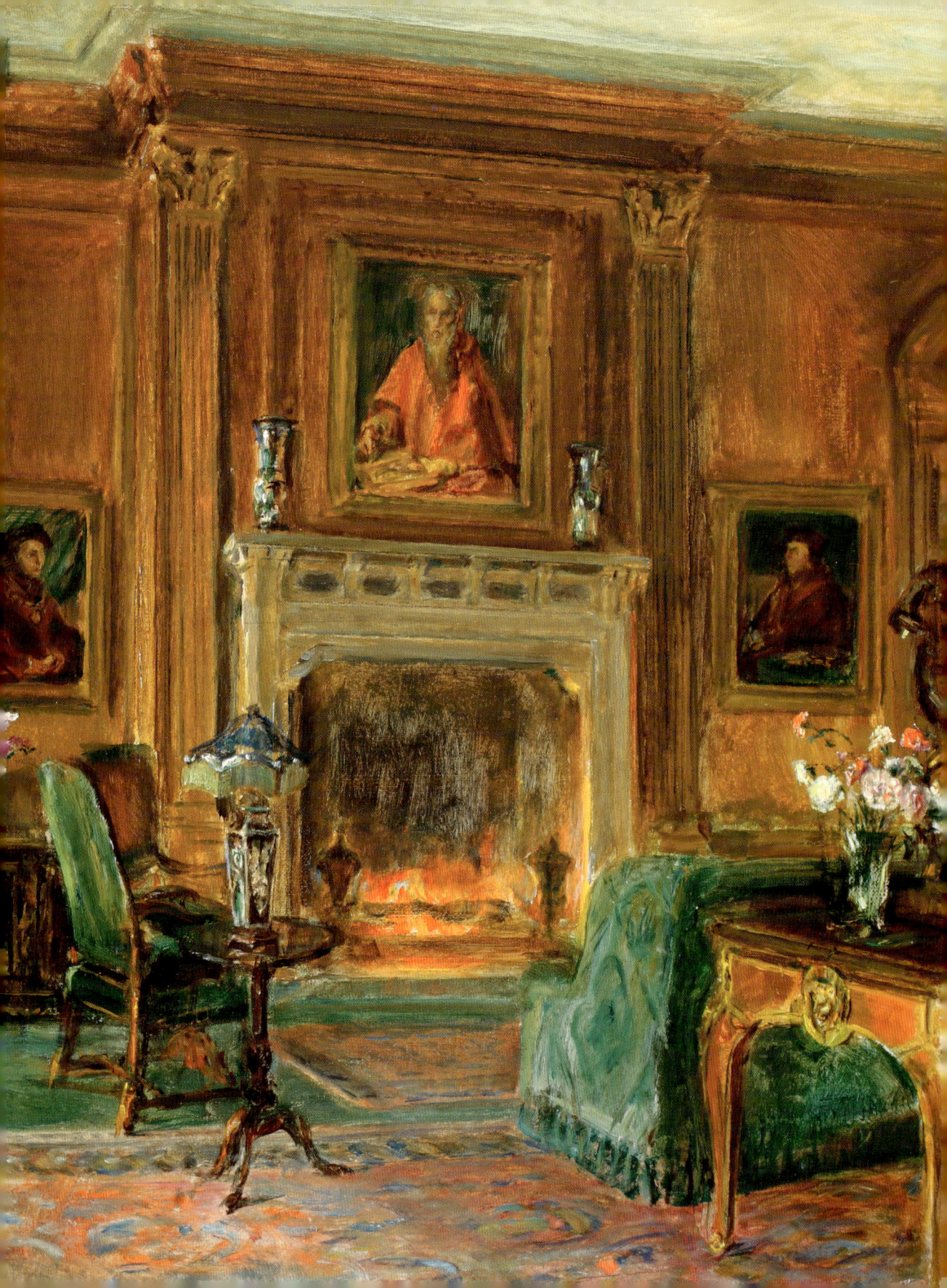

PREFACE AND ACKNOWLEDGMENTS

Visitors to The Frick Collection often ask how Henry Clay Frick (1849–1919) became a collector. How did such a rough-and-tumble businessman learn about art? Did he have advisors, or did he make his own choices? Why did he decide to leave his private collection, and the beautiful Gilded Age house that contains it, to the public? This book sets out to answer those questions.

The Frick family has helped to steward the collection since its inception. I am most grateful to those family members who have served on the board of trustees during my tenure as director. Helen Clay Chace, chair emerita and great-granddaughter of the founder, has always entertained me with stories of her relatives and inspired me with her clear sense of the purpose of the museum and library. As chair of the committee of acquisitions and, later, of buildings and grounds, the late Peter P. Blanchard III, Frick's great-grandson, taught me about the quality of art and architecture that are at the core of The Frick Collection. Of that generation, Emily Frick, wife of Henry Clay Frick II, Frick's grandson, has always been a stalwart; the younger generation, including Martha Loring, J. Fife Symington IV, and Suzzara Durocher continue to engage with the museum and connect the family to its future. The institution has been fortunate in the many civic-minded individuals who have served on the board. I have learned from and been supported by them all, especially Margot Bogert and Betty Eveillard, past and present chairs, respectively.

Founded in 1920, the Frick Art Research Library (FARL) has been an indispensable resource for this book. Andrew Mellon Chief Librarian Stephen J. Bury and his staff ably administer a library that was created to support scholarship on the collection. No research on the museum's history, particularly its collecting, would be possible without extensive consultation with the library archives. Under the leadership of Sally Brazil, the Barbara G. Fleischman Associate Chief Librarian for Archives and Records Management, these records are perfectly preserved and made accessible. I am particularly grateful to Archivist Julie Ludwig, a font of knowledge of the Frick family's history. Always forward-looking, FARL is a leader in digitization, meaning that I and other researchers have an easier time finding documents. I am personally grateful to the late Vartan Gregorian, who, as president of the Carnegie Corporation of New York, responded to a request for funds to digitize Henry Clay Frick's collecting papers. Ease of access to these documents was hugely helpful to me and would be to others interested in the subject. It is appropriate that the foundations of Frick's closest friend, Andrew W. Mellon, and his business partner, Andrew Carnegie, continue to support the library.

The Center for the History of Collecting, based at FARL for a number of years, became an advocate for studies in this relatively new field. Its founder, Inge Reist, along with Esmée Quodbach and Samantha Deutsch, oversaw numerous symposia, publications, and research fellowships that brought attention to and deepened understanding of many subjects in this history. Each also lectured on and authored important essays on The Frick Collection's collecting.

Deputy Director and Peter Jay Sharp Chief Curator Xavier F. Salomon suggested that I write this book, and I appreciate both his urging me on and his careful reading of my text. John Updike Curator Aimee Ng and Associate Director of Development and External Affairs Angie Calderwood helped me organize a Director's Trip to Pittsburgh for a group of the museum's friends; research and preparation for this visit enriched my understanding of the Frick's history there. I have learned much from former Frick curator Charlotte Vignon, an expert on the Duveen Brothers and their dealings with American collectors. Anne L. Poulet Curatorial Fellow Geoffrey Ripert became indispensable in helping me find, and secure permissions for, the illustrations of this book. His contribution has greatly enhanced its visual appeal. Conversations with Associate Museum Educator Caitlin Henningsen, whose book on the Frick mansion servants is forthcoming, were helpful. Editor in Chief Michaelyn Mitchell oversaw the production of the book and carefully edited my text in the midst of the extraordinary production of publications she has overseen at the Frick for the past eleven years. She was ably assisted by Assistant Editor Gemma McElroy. I would get little done at the Frick without Executive Assistant Blanca del Castillo, who made sure I found time to work on the book and also contributed to it in many ways. Through an exceptional period in the Frick's history—moving to Frick Madison and orchestrating the return to the mansion on Fifth Avenue—the entire staff has been a part of this enterprise. For their dedication to the job, I owe them all my thanks, and to many of them goes my gratitude for conversations that helped me form ideas for this book.

Colleagues at The Frick Pittsburgh have been helpful with this project: Executive Director Elizabeth Barker, Chief Curator and Director of Collections Dawn Reid Brean, and Director of Learning and Visitor Experience Amanda Dunyak Gillen. My thanks also to the chairman of the Frick Center Board of Trustees, Robert M. Hernandez, and former chairman Cary Reed, as well as to Ned Danes and other Frick family members on the board.

Discussions with David Cannadine, Cynthia Saltzman, and Ross Finocchio were particularly helpful to me, as were their respective publications. David's biography on Andrew Mellon was a bedrock of history for my project. Cynthia's extensive research and publications on American collectors of the Gilded Age were fundamental resources. And Ross's unpublished dissertation and articles on the early collecting of Frick are full of insight. I also acknowledge Frick descendant Martha

Frick Symington Sanger, who has published several well-informed books about the family and its houses.

I feel fortunate that Julian Fellowes, who has done so much to promote a wider interest in the period of the Gilded Age in America—not to mention his brilliant programs about the British aristocracy—agreed to write a foreword for this book. I thank Philip Reeser, at Rizzoli, our publishing partner, as well as Jesse Kidwell, the book's designer.

Finally, a book about the history of a family could not have been written without a sense of family dynamics. My wife, Sarah McNear, and our children, Chloe Wardropper, Gordon Granger, and Willa Granger—accomplished writers and storytellers all—taught me what it means to be a family. I am grateful for their support throughout my time at the Frick.

IAN WARDROPPER

Anna-Maria and Stephen Kellen Director
The Frick Collection

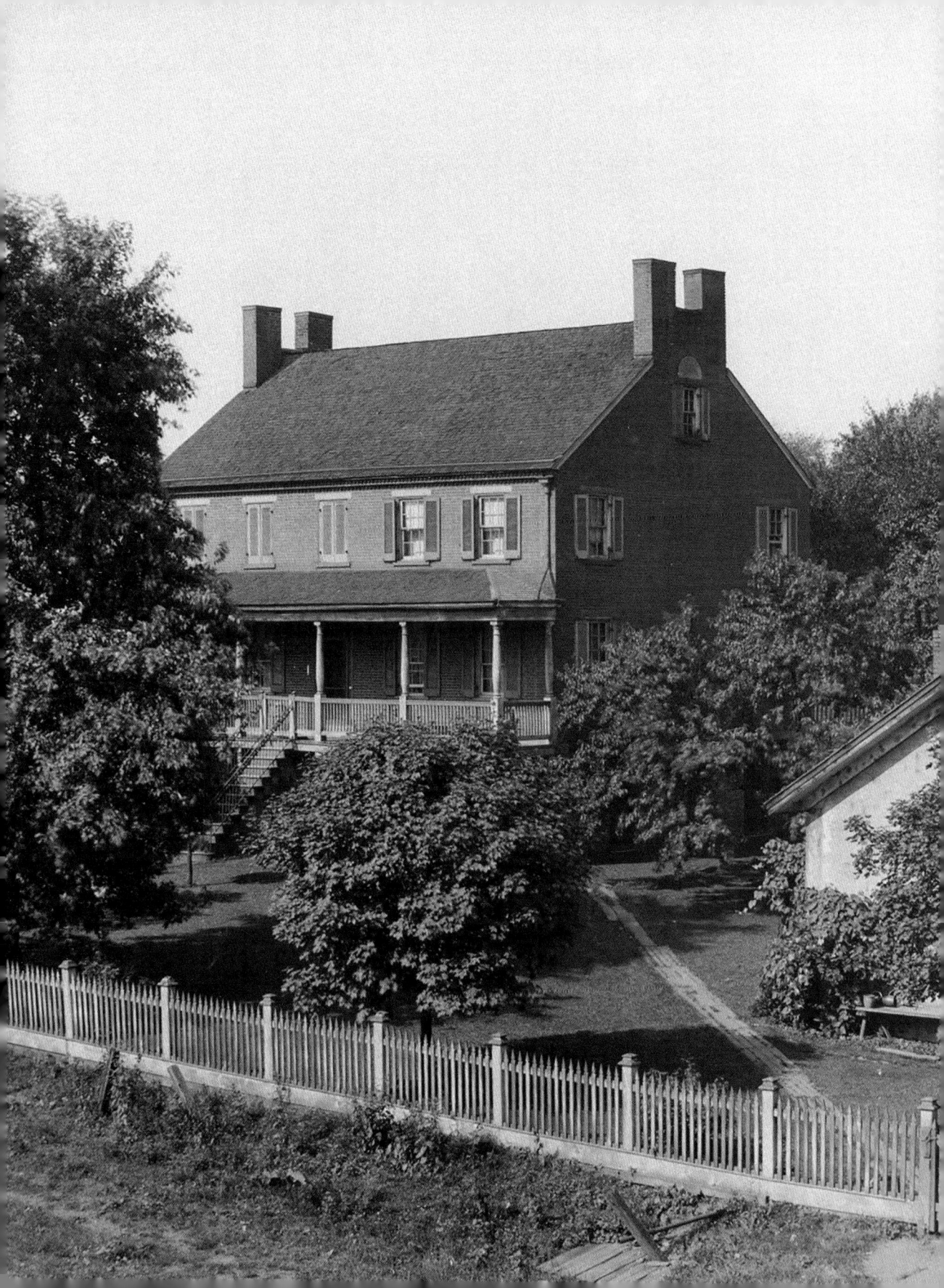

THE FRICKS OF PENNSYLVANIA

The Frick name is today synonymous with one of the most important collections of Old Master art ever assembled by a private family in the United States. Over the 166 years of their combined lifetimes, Henry Clay Frick (1849–1919) and his daughter Helen Clay Frick (1888–1984) pursued and acquired some of the greatest works of European art—paintings, sculptures, and decorative arts—first with an eye to satisfying their personal ambitions, interests, and tastes, and then with a shared vision of establishing a public institution that would be open to "all persons whomsoever." The story of this partnership—and the creation of the New York museum that bears the family name—spans the last quarter of the nineteenth century and reaches well into the twentieth century, but it begins in 1849 in the rural western Pennsylvania town of West Overton with the birth of Henry Clay Frick. In order to fully understand the story of the Fricks—father and daughter—as collectors, it is necessary to summarize both the origins of their wealth and the societal and familial circumstances that spurred them in their shared passion for collecting.

Frick's father, of Swiss-German Mennonite stock, was a farmer, and his mother's family, the Overholts, were prosperous and well respected in the community, owning a whiskey distillery established by Frick's grandfather Abraham (fig. 1). Named after the Kentucky statesman Henry Clay (1777–1852), Frick was often called Clay by his familiars. As a child, he was somewhat frail, suffering from indigestion and rheumatism and requiring care and supervision. In maturity, he became robust and athletic, though he never completely escaped his ailments. While Frick had schooling through one term of college, his extended family offered him early employment: he worked as an accountant at the Overholt Distillery, and later an uncle recommended him as a clerk at Eaton's hardware store in Pittsburgh.

When Frick was a young man, he and a group of friends and relatives had the foresight to recognize the importance of coke, an industrial fuel derived from coal, to the burgeoning iron and steel industries. A cousin, Abraham Tinstman, owned coal lands and took Frick, only twenty years old, and two others into partnership to begin

FIG. 1
The Overholt Homestead, n.d.

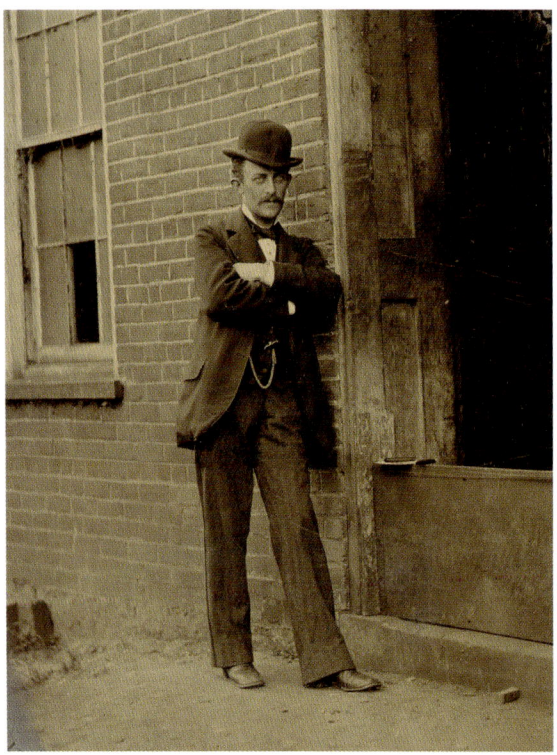

a coke business. Frick's investment came through loans, likely made possible by the death of his grandfather Abraham Overholt in 1870, the year before the coke company partnership. The coal needed for making coke—created by baking it in ovens—is essential in the production of steel and iron and is bountiful in this region of Pennsylvania. Started with family funding and continued with loans from the T. Mellon and Sons Bank in Pittsburgh, the company grew rapidly. While Frick's family gave him early assistance, it was his own drive and intelligence that led to his success. Industrious and good with numbers, Frick was the force behind expansion and in short order bought out his partners (fig. 2). Within a decade, H. C. Frick & Co. operated more than a thousand ovens and had a monopoly on the world's supply of coke, supplying 80 percent of it (fig. 3). By the age of thirty, Frick had become a millionaire.

In his twenties, Frick was fully committed to growing his business. Little time was left for social engagements. Yet he had friends, and by 1880 he was established and wealthy. Introduced to Adelaide Howard Childs, from a Pittsburgh family involved in manufacturing and importing shoes and boots, he soon proposed, and they wed on December 15, 1881 (fig. 5). After their honeymoon in Boston and New York, they returned to Pittsburgh to begin married life in Frick's apartment in Monongahela House, the foremost hotel in the city. The following year, they purchased their first home, called Clayton, and, after remodeling, moved in by 1883.

As a youth, Frick had enjoyed the love and support of his family; he, in turn, became devoted to his wife and their four children: Childs, born in 1883, Martha Howard in 1885, Helen Clay in 1888, and Henry Clay Frick Jr. in 1892 (fig. 6). With a growing family, Henry and Adelaide had embarked on plans to enlarge and renovate Clayton in 1891–92. Tragically, Martha died in 1891, following a long illness; soon after, Henry Clay Frick Jr. died in infancy. The deaths of two children affected the parents enormously; both long grieved their deceased children.

In the meantime, Frick's business was expanding further. The even larger Pittsburgh iron and steel firm founded by Thomas and Andrew Carnegie needed a steady supply of coke. In 1882, Carnegie Brothers and Company Ltd. brought the reformulated H. C. Frick Coke Company into partnership. Frick's appetite for expansion and his managerial skills made him a natural leader of the iron and steel company. As he learned the business, he consolidated its component industries and by 1889 became chairman, acquiring a stake in the company second only to that of Carnegie and partner Henry Phipps Jr. Through the 1880s, the firm and its partners prospered enormously. However, the cost accounting at which Frick excelled, maximizing profits, brought him and the company into conflict with the growing labor union movement. Negotiations and disputes with the unions came to a head in July

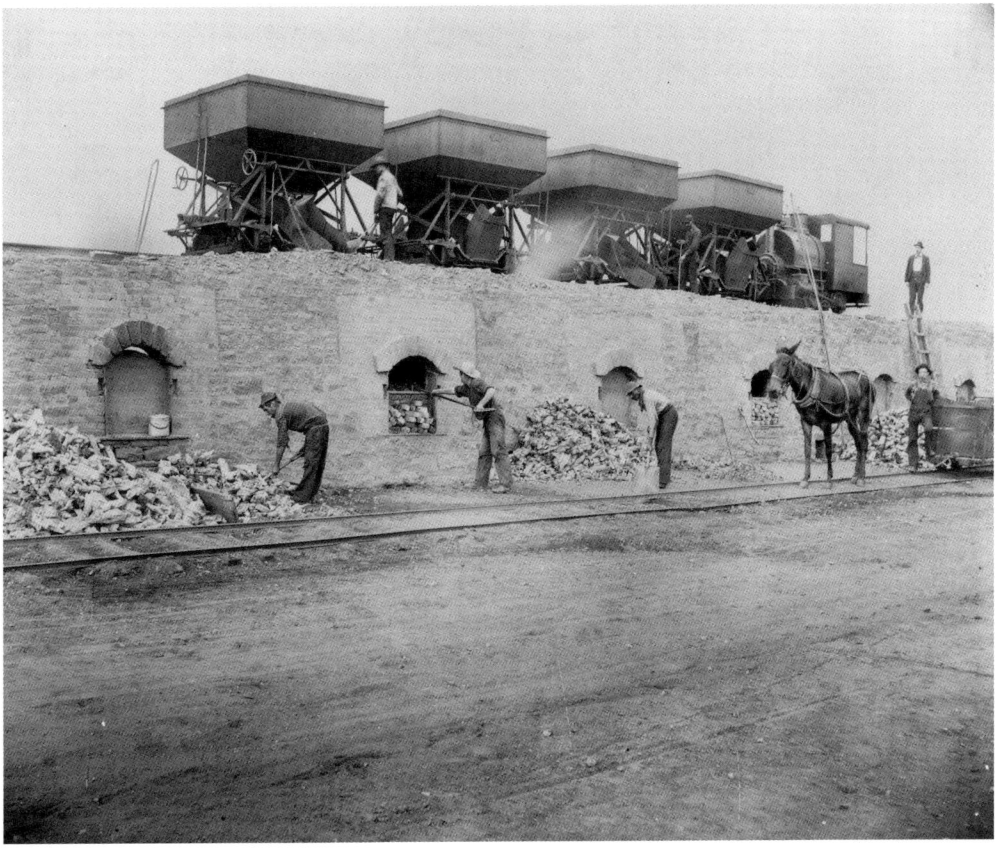

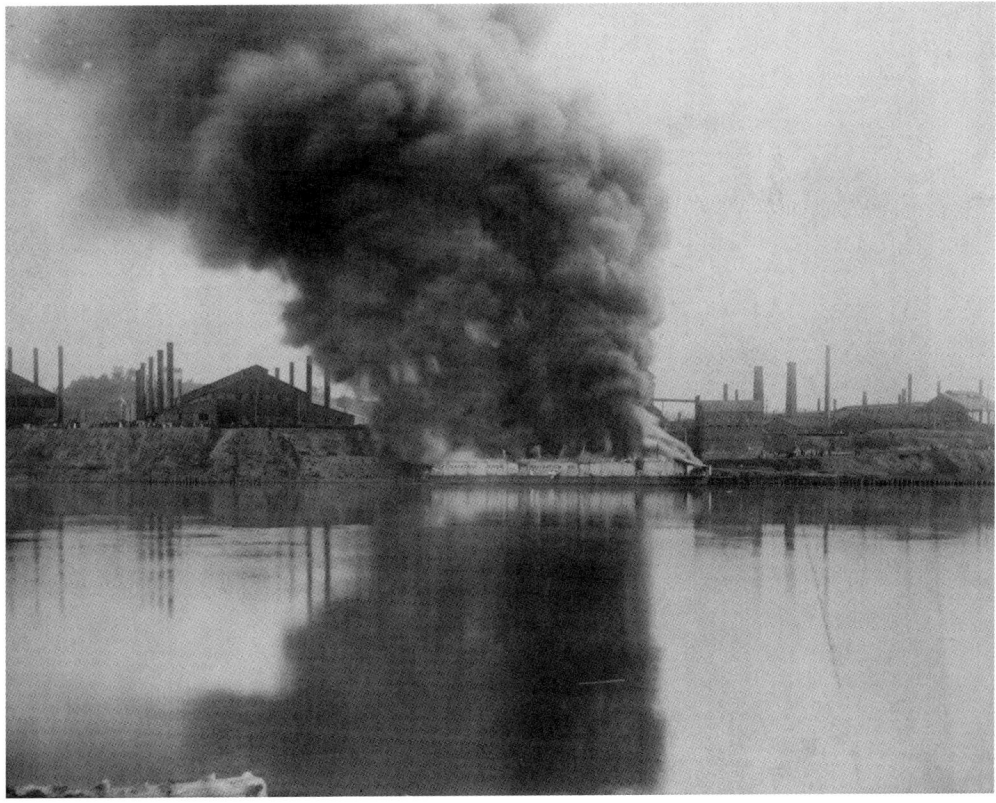

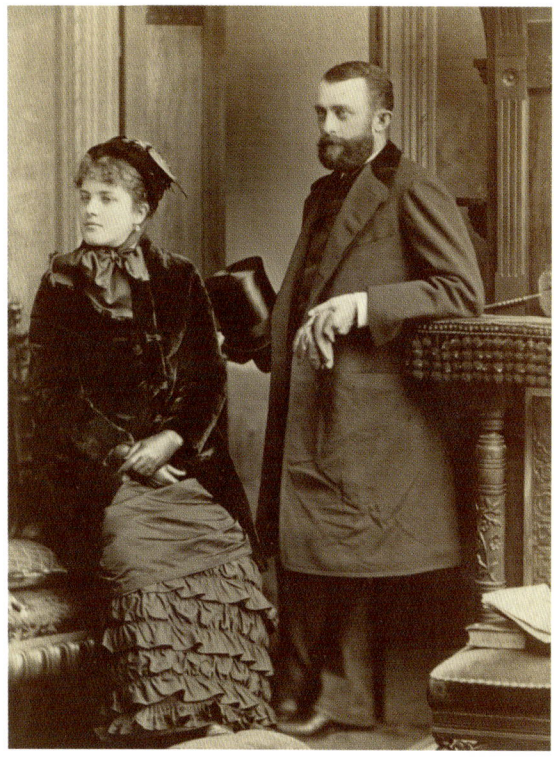

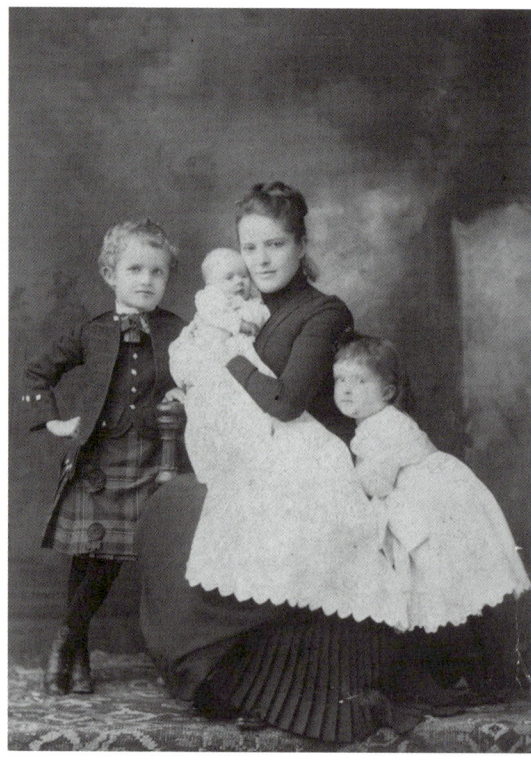

FIG. 5
Henry Clay Frick and
Adelaide H. C. Frick, taken
in Boston during their
wedding trip, 1882.

FIG. 6
Adelaide H. C. Frick with
her children, Childs, Helen
Clay, and Martha Howard,
1888.

1892, when the Amalgamated Association of Iron, Steel, and Tin Workers voted to strike at the Homestead Steel Works, the huge plant on the Monongahela River serving Carnegie Brothers and Company. Vacationing in Scotland, Carnegie left it to the chairman to manage the crisis. After failing to persuade the governor of the state to bring in the National Guard, Frick hired Pinkerton detectives to make the strikers back down. In an ill-advised venture, boats filled with armed men tried to approach the factory stealthily (fig. 4). The Pinkertons were discovered, and in the resulting shooting and fire, some eight lives were lost. Frick was widely condemned for these actions; many called him "The Most Hated Man in America."[1] On July 23, 1892, a professed anarchist named Alexander Berkman traveled from Worcester, Massachusetts, to Pittsburgh to assassinate him. Berkman shot Frick twice and stabbed him three times, but a company officer, other employees, and the victim himself wrestled the assailant to the ground. With characteristic calm, Frick dictated a cable to his mother and a second to Carnegie that read "Was shot twice but not dangerously. There is no necessity for you to come home. I am still in shape to fight the battle out."[2]

By November, Frick had settled the strike and restored the factory to business. By 1900, the company was producing more than 30 percent of the nation's steel and had made an astronomical profit of $40 million (equivalent to almost $1.5 billion in today's terms). A rift, however, had opened between Frick and Carnegie. In the 1890s, Frick twice threatened to resign. Eventually, his role was reduced, and further damage to his relationship with Carnegie ensued when he engaged in discussion of the sale of the company without informing Carnegie. Frick was forced off the board and brought a lawsuit, which was resolved in his favor in 1900.

Frick gradually withdrew from business activity in Pittsburgh as his interests shifted to investing. He served on various boards and became the largest stockholder of railroads in the United States. In 1905, the family left Clayton for New York. They lived initially in rented quarters, the William H. Vanderbilt House. They began plans for their own mansion further north, on Fifth Avenue at East 70th Street, which broke ground in 1912. In the meantime, they built Eagle Rock, a large summerhouse near Gloucester at Pride's Crossing, Massachusetts. With the Frick mansion complete in 1914, the family took up residence in its own New York home. The first floor of the house was designed to accommodate the art collection and facilitate entertaining. Frick conducted his many business affairs from his office next to the Picture Gallery. The couple's luncheons and dinner parties included Henry's business associates, as well as his and Adelaide's friends.

On October 18, 1919, their grandchild Henry Clay Frick II was born. Despite a cold and a bout of inflammatory rheumatism, which plagued him throughout his life, Frick insisted on traveling to his son's house on Long Island (today the Nassau County Museum of Art) to meet the new grandchild. This proved to be a mistake, as he returned exhausted and, within days, died. He left an estate worth $145 million. Most of it—$117 million—was given to public charities. His Fifth Avenue house and art collection went to the City of New York along with a $15 million endowment; there were gifts to Princeton University, Harvard University, and the Massachusetts Institute of Technology; donations to the Educational Commission of Pittsburgh (for training public-school teachers); and land plus an endowment to create the Frick Nature Preserve. The balance of the estate went to his family, with his daughter Helen Clay receiving the lion's share. Adelaide continued to live in the house until her death in 1931; Frick's wish, as stated in his will of 1915, to turn the house and its collection into a public institution following Adelaide's demise, was then put into effect. The Frick Collection opened in 1935. Frick's children played major roles in the creation and evolution of their father's museum: Childs served as president of the board of trustees from 1920 to 1965, while Helen Clay was head of the Acquisitions Committee until 1961, decisively shaping the future of the art collection.

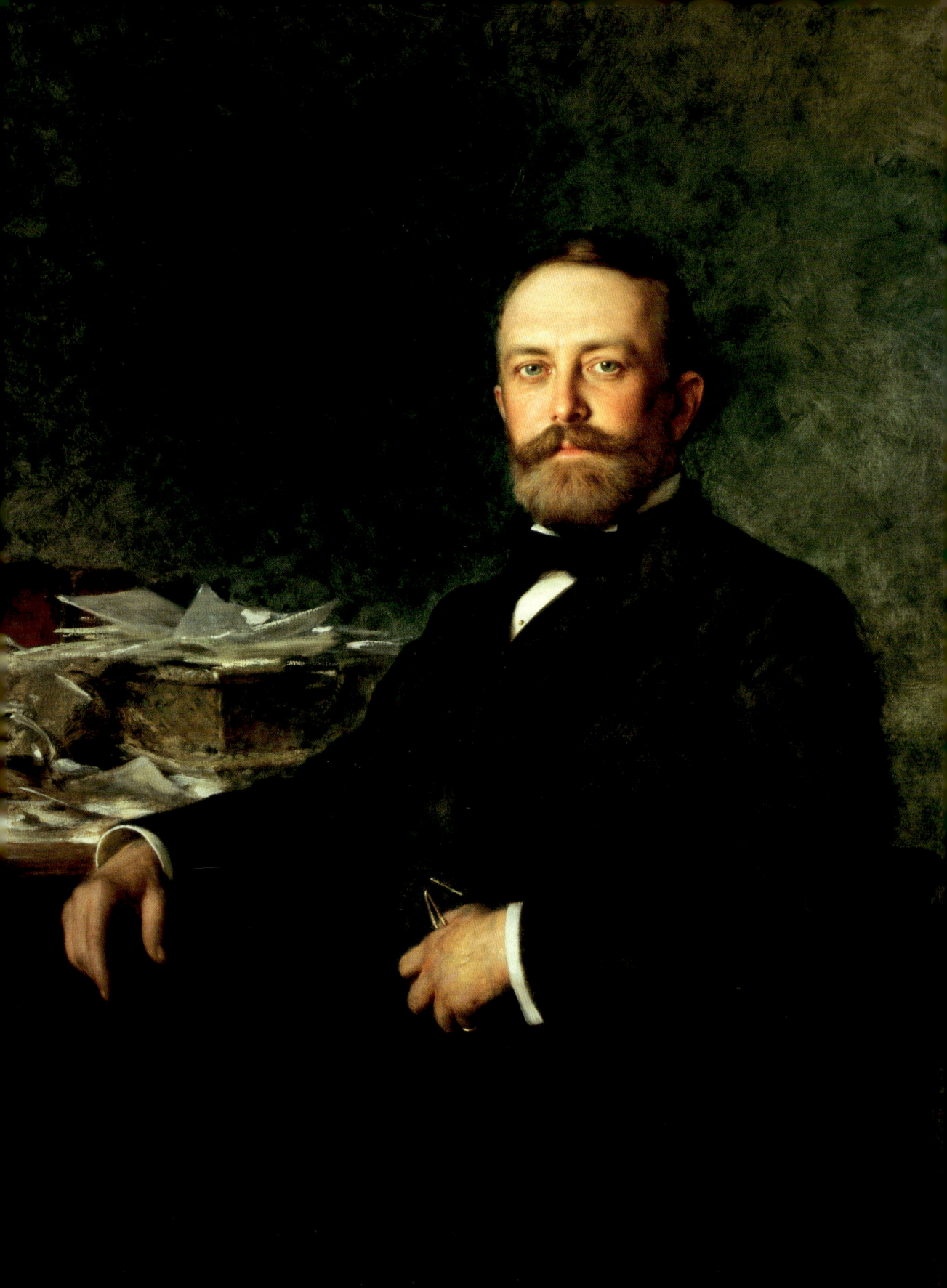

HENRY CLAY FRICK, BECOMING
A COLLECTOR

"[Henry Clay Frick] may be a little too enthusiastic about pictures"
JAMES B. COREY,
T. MELLON AND SONS, 1870

An often-told anecdote hints at Frick's beginnings as a collector.[3] As he started his coking operations, he applied for a loan from the Pittsburgh bank T. Mellon and Sons. When a bank representative raised concerns, Thomas Mellon dispatched an experienced mining partner, James B. Corey, to prepare a report: "Lands good, ovens well built; manager on job all day, keeps books evenings, may be a little too enthusiastic about pictures but not enough to hurt; knows his business down to the ground; advise making the loan." Though never verified in the archives, this quotation rings true, the side remark on art adding color to the commentary and evidence of a site visit during which Frick probably spoke about his first acquisitions.

What was it that Frick hung on the rough walls of his factory office in the 1870s? Most likely, they were framed prints. Three years earlier, when he clerked in a dry-goods store, a print and lithography shop shared space in the building. Reproductions of art circulated widely in the era; they could be a source of income for artists, and they also introduced their work to a large audience. The French art dealer Goupil & Cie partnered with American publishing houses after 1846, sending such illustrations of paintings throughout America. Prints were not an absorbing interest for Frick later in life. He did, however, acquire superb etchings by Rembrandt and Whistler, as well as a set of prints after paintings in the W. H. Vanderbilt collection, which he framed and hung at Clayton in the 1890s (fig. 7). Many of the engravings after Vanderbilt paintings were of nineteenth-century European renderings of genre scenes set in earlier eras, subjects Frick avoided later in his collecting career. Such reproductions—an affordable way for a young man to decorate an office and a means of learning about art—may have sparked Frick's interest in collecting, as well as ignited his ambition to own the real thing. In the late 1890s, he bought superb drawings by artists of the Barbizon School—a nineteenth-century movement among French painters who specialized in landscapes in a realist mode—among them pastel and Conté-crayon sheets by Jean-François Millet that are still in Pittsburgh (fig. 8). Some sketches may also have hung among his earliest artworks.

Detail of FIG. 15.

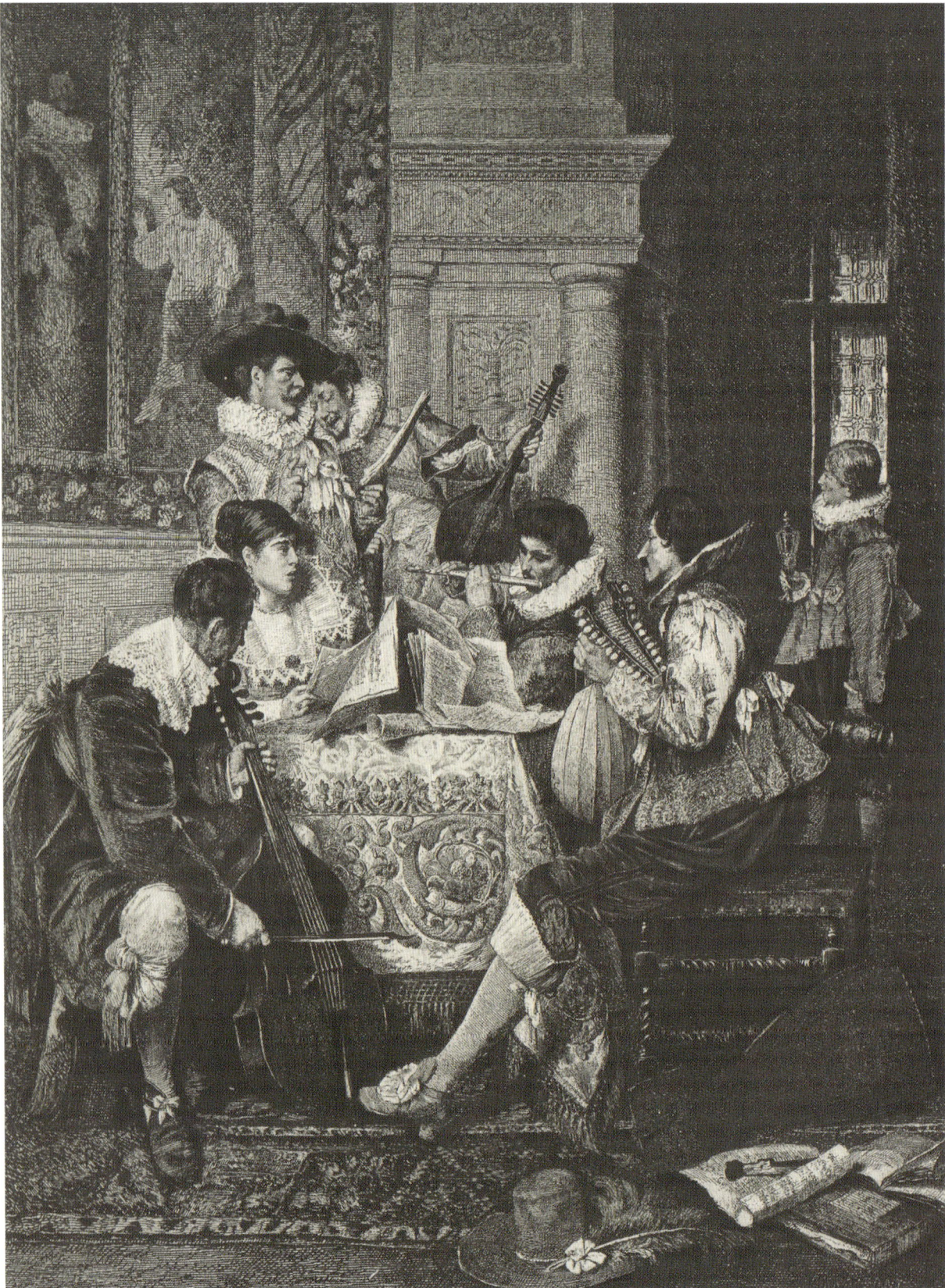

It remains unknown, however, what caused Frick, who was so fully engaged with his business as a young man, to pause and first consider a picture on purely aesthetic grounds. While the New York collection of W. H. Vanderbilt may have served as an aspirational model, his collecting interest took root and grew in Pittsburgh, a city built on industrial wealth and affluence. The influences there were many, and as Frick's social register expanded, so did the evolution of his taste.

PITTSBURGH ART COLLECTIONS

In the mid-nineteenth century, Pittsburgh was one of the most dynamic cities in America, its location at the confluence of the Allegheny and the Monongahela Rivers making it a strategic point for transportation and trade. The mineral riches of the Allegheny Mountains, particularly coal, became the basis of much of its industry. The smokestacks of its steel and iron factories covered the area with clouds of soot. "Hell with the lid off" was *Atlantic Monthly* writer James Parton's 1868 characterization. Iron and steel production were accelerated to meet the need for weapons in the Civil War and to establish the railroads and erect the buildings that fed the growth of the United States. Entrepreneurial talent led to the foundation of some of the most consequential companies in the country, such as the Westinghouse Electric Company and the Heinz Company. Between 1870 and 1910, the city's population grew from 86,076 to 533,905.

Around 1850, Pittsburgh art collections, such as those of C. H. Wolf and John and Mary Shoenberger, were relatively modest, focused primarily on the output of local painters, with some work by printmakers and sculptors rounding out their

FIG. 7
After Ferdinand Victor Léon Roybet, *The Musical Party*, 1885.

FIG. 8
Jean-François Millet, *Shepherd Minding His Sheep*, ca. 1863–66.

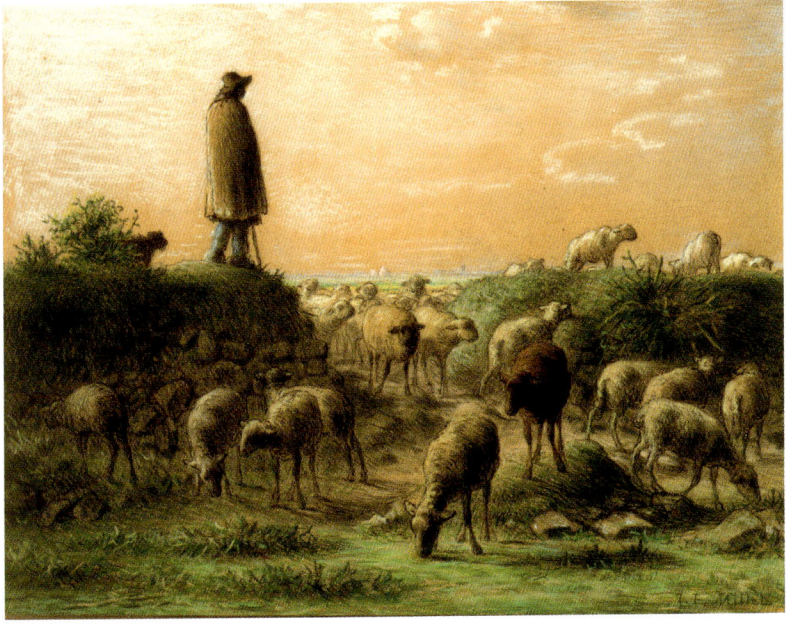

holdings. As an up-and-coming businessman, Frick would have been intrigued by the art he saw on the walls of his associates in commerce.

By the 1890s, when Frick was hitting his professional stride, Pittsburgh's private collections had become more serious, expanding beyond American artists to European ones. Especially popular in Pittsburgh was the Barbizon School. In time, Frick's collection became the most prominent, but a look at other major city collections reveals that his wish list was largely the same as those of his neighbors.

Iron manufacturer Alexander McBurney Byers and his wife, Martha, were noted for the quality of their holdings, even outside of the state. Sourcing works from local exhibitions and galleries, New York dealers, and trips abroad, the couple gravitated toward contemporary French artists such as Charles-François Daubigny and Jean-Baptiste-Camille Corot, but by the end of the decade, they turned to earlier British artists such as Thomas Gainsborough and Joseph Mallord William Turner. Another iron and steel magnate, Charles Lockhart, owned Barbizon School works, as well as those of other popular artists of the decade, such as William-Adolphe Bouguereau and Ernest Meissonier (fig. 9). The lawyer David Watson and his wife, Margaret, traveled abroad frequently. Among their ninety-odd works were numerous Barbizon and English paintings. Less expected in the Watsons' collection is *Beggar Boy* by the seventeenth-century Spanish artist Bartolomé Esteban Murillo. It was purchased in London in 1905, the same year Frick wrote to Watson, wishing to take him to see a collection in New York. This was a year after Frick acquired his only Murillo, a rare self-portrait, which suggests that Watson was inspired by Frick's purchase. Clearly, Frick knew these prominent Pittsburgh businessmen, some, like him, manufacturers of iron and steel. Like many collectors, they sought what was popular and what they could show off to those who would understand and value what they saw on visits to their friends' grand houses. In this regard, Frick was no different, but he was somewhat more adventurous in his tastes. Ultimately, what would set him apart was his exacting requirement for art of the highest quality.

Aside from Frick, the most noted Pittsburgh collector at the turn of the nineteenth century and into the twentieth was Andrew Mellon. In 1881, the two young men—both eligible bachelors—attended parties together, and at one of these, it appears that Mellon introduced Frick to his future wife. Mellon remained a close friend of Frick throughout his life and was an honorary pallbearer at his funeral in 1919. Like Frick, Mellon began collecting contemporary art somewhat sporadically but, over time, concentrated on Old Masters. It was through the European trips the two friends made together, first in 1880 and later in 1896–98, that Frick initiated Mellon into the pleasures of art. The later trips coincide with Mellon's first serious purchases. Mellon's early forays into collecting were conventional and inexpensive, as he bought the work of Barbizon artists such as Henri Harpignies, Constant Troyon, and Jean-Charles Cazin. The second director of the National Gallery of Art, John Walker, dismissed these as mediocre, a harsh judgment but apt in the context of what Mellon later acquired. The experience of seeing Frick's great collection assembled in his New York mansion and visiting other collections, such as Henry Huntington's eighteenth-century English portraits in the house at San Marino, California, ignited Mellon's passion for collecting. When he introduced Mellon to Joseph Duveen, Frick told the dealer that one day his friend would become "the greatest collector of us all" (fig. 10).[4]

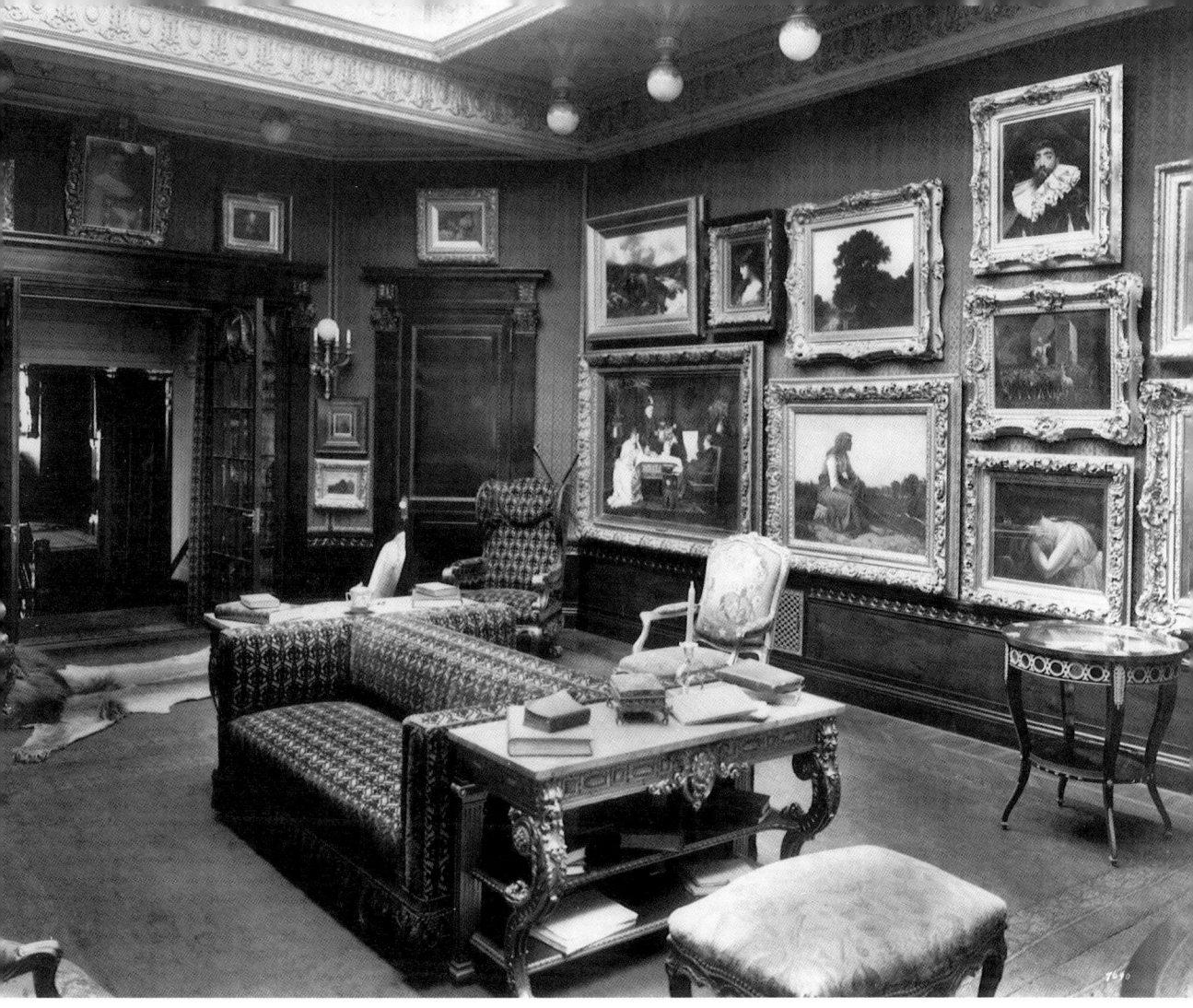

FIG. 9
Charles Lockhart's gallery,
ca. 1880.

Through the efforts of dealers such as Duveen and Roland Knoedler, this pre-diction became true when Mellon began to select the best Old Masters available. Ultimately, Mellon's collection surpassed Frick's, but the latter's method of carefully selecting the finest works by the best artists was undoubtedly the model. Similarly, Mellon's great collection ended up not in Pittsburgh but on the East Coast and became the foundation of a major institution, the National Gallery of Art in Washington. When, in 1930–31, the cash-poor Soviet Union authorized the sale of paintings from the Hermitage Museum in St. Petersburg (then Leningrad), Mellon was primed to negotiate for the greatest group of paintings sold during the century. Because of this, masterpieces by Raphael, Titian, Rembrandt, Velázquez, and others became the core of the nation's collection in Washington. Not coincidentally, the same architect, John Russell Pope, was commissioned in the 1930s to design classically inspired buildings to house both the Frick and Mellon collections. Pope's expansion of the original Frick mansion predated the construction of the National Gallery of Art; while the Washington edifice is considerably larger than the New York one, they share elegantly

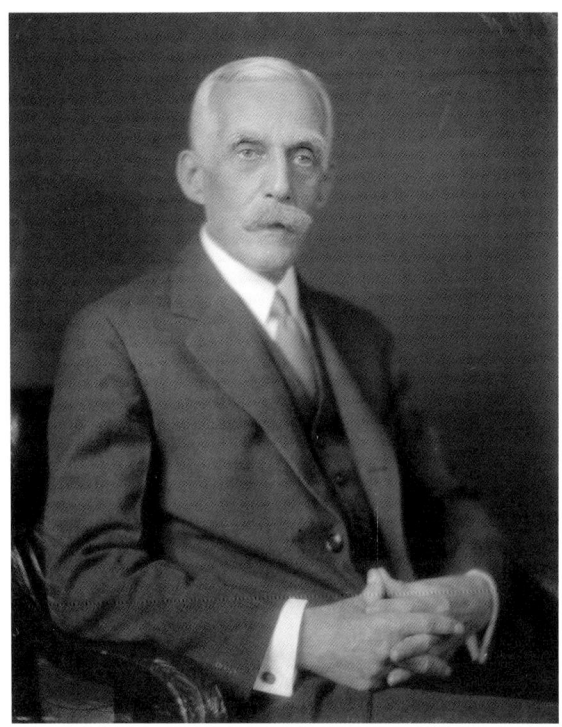

FIG. 10
Andrew W. Mellon, 1905.

FIG. 11
George Hetzel, *Landscape with River*, 1880.

proportioned galleries and garden courts. Mellon's son Paul wrote eloquently of the influence on his father "from early European travels until well into middle age of his great friend Henry Clay Frick."[5]

ARTIST INFLUENCERS

Frick's earliest documented purchase of a painting is a landscape by the Pennsylvania artist George Hetzel, acquired for $260 in 1881 from Pittsburgh dealer S. Boyd & Co. (fig. 11). Calling on Pittsburghers such as C. H. Wolf, who, by the evidence of an 1873 inventory, had one of the largest collections in the city, he would have seen works by local artists David G. Blythe, Joseph R. Woodwell, and Charles D. Linford, as well as Hetzel. Frick had easy relationships and developed some true friendships with painters, who clearly influenced his taste in art as his interests developed.

Foremost among these was Woodwell (fig. 12). Helen Clay recalls, "When my father and I took walks together, we nearly always headed in the direction of [Woodwell's] studio and spent hours there looking over his most recent pictures and listening to the tales he told of his early years as a student in Paris."[6] Frick was close enough to Woodwell to ask if the visiting French painter Théobald Chartran could borrow his studio to complete a portrait of Thomas Mellon, Andrew Mellon's father, that Frick commissioned in 1896. Henry and Adelaide spent parts of their summers with the Woodwells near Gloucester, and their pleasant experiences there induced them to build their country house, Eagle Rock, nearby. Frick was generous with gifts of art to his friends and, in 1895, gave Woodwell a painting by John J. Hammer of Gloucester Harbor, a subject that would interest this Gloucester resident.

Naturally, Frick bought some of Woodwell's paintings. More important, the advice of this trusted friend helped to turn his attention to contemporary artists from Europe. In an 1897 letter to Knoedler, Frick writes, "Mr. Woodwell was over yesterday evening, and I never saw him more enthusiastic over a picture. I had made up my mind not to buy anything, but am rather glad I changed it in this case, as it seems to me that it is just what I needed in my collection."[7] This concerned a painting by Narcisse-Virgile Diaz de la Peña (fig. 13) and confirmed his inclination to the Barbizon School. Lectures and articles spread Woodwell's influence throughout the city. He lectured on French and Italian artists at the Carnegie Institute in May 1898 and, in an 1899 article titled "Masters of Modern French Art," praised Corot and Meissonier, two artists Frick favored.

Another instance of Frick's rapport with artists is Chartran, an academic painter famous for *Vanity Fair* caricatures of notable figures of the day. Frick became aware of Chartran's work through Knoedler and took the initiative to invite the

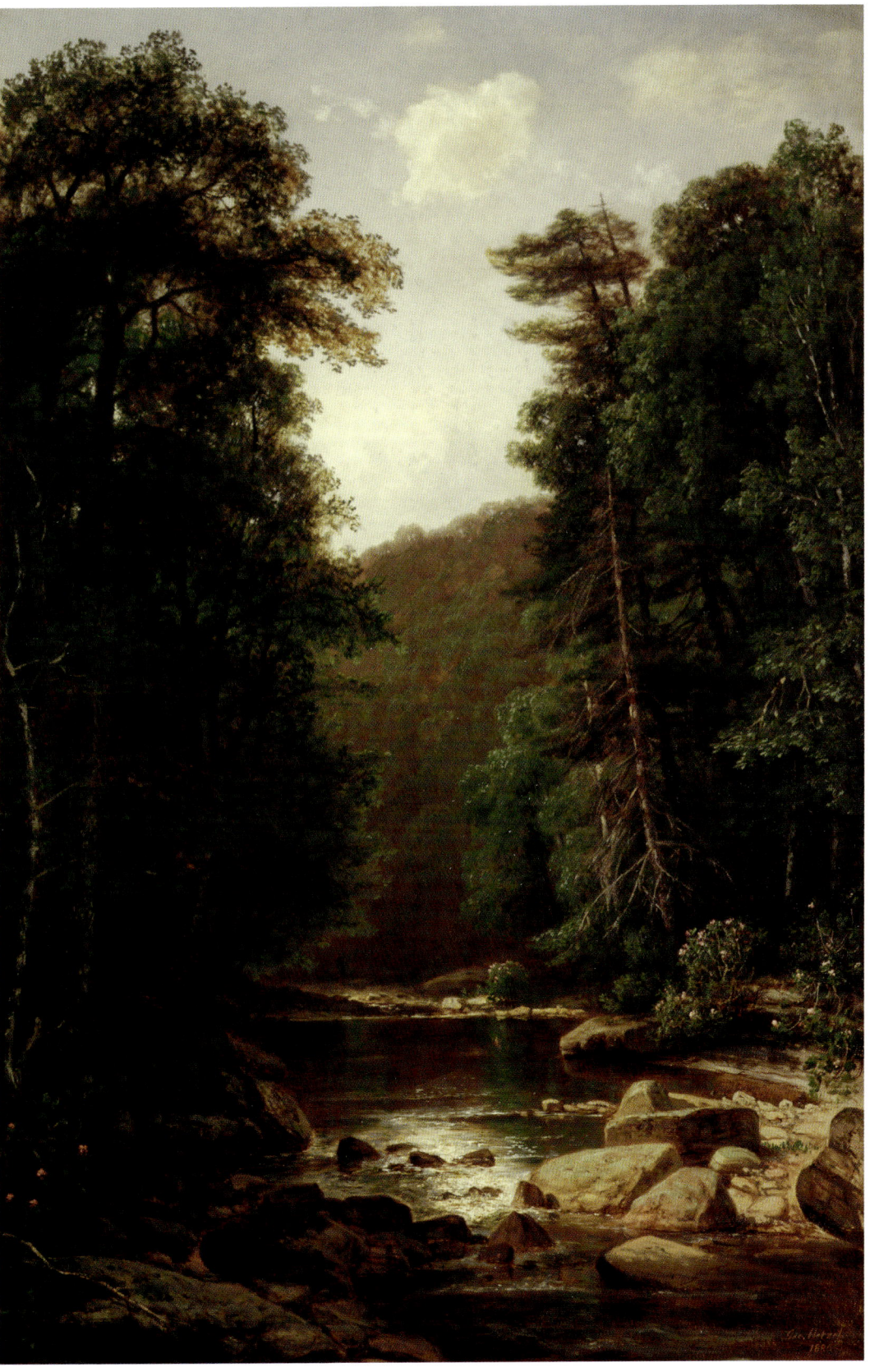

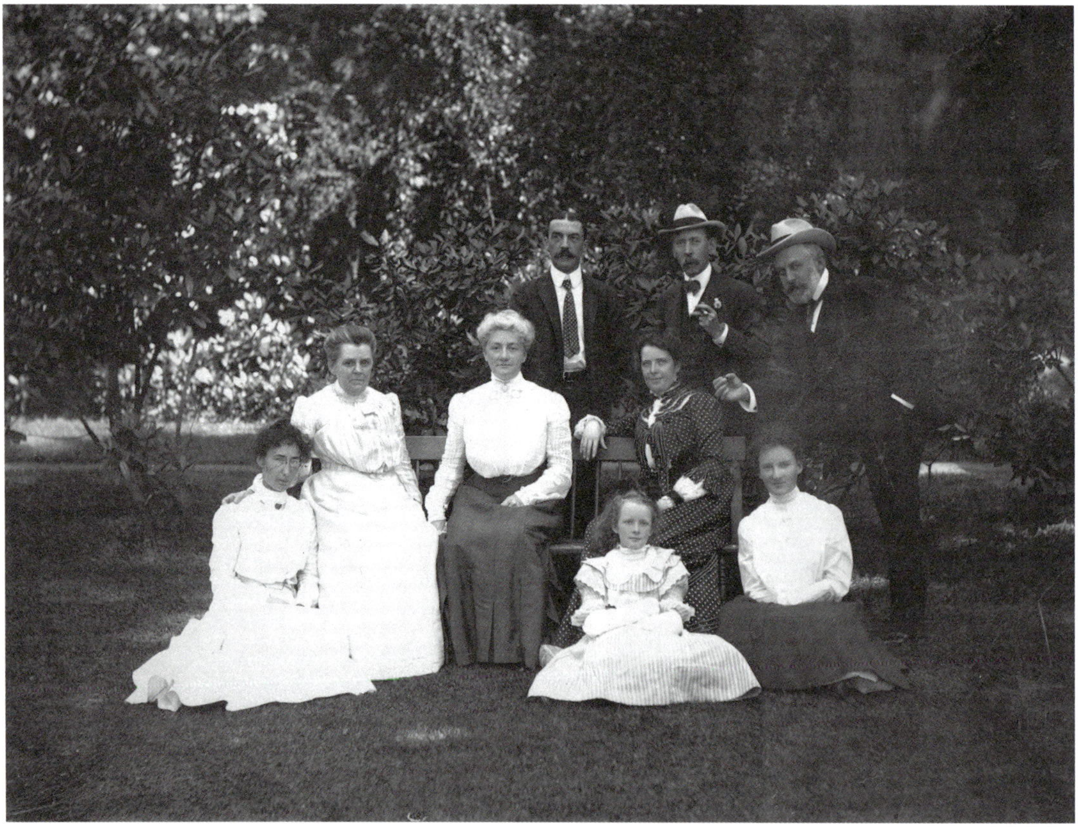

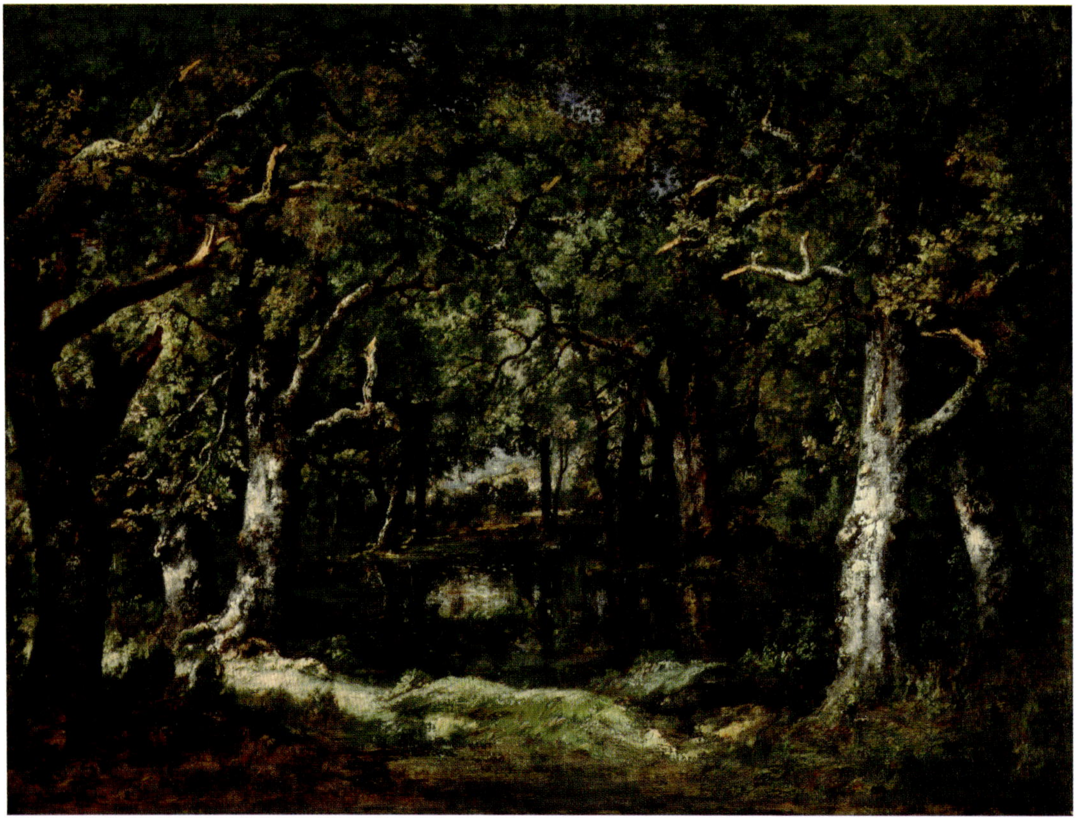

artist to Pittsburgh, where he promoted his work. The inscription on a photographic portrait of Chartran—"To my charming friend, Frick, after the Poker, 11 July morning, 1898, 2 o'clock, Chartran"— hints at the pair's closeness and at how personal Frick's introduction of the painter to Pittsburgh society was (fig. 14). In 1896, a year after he commissioned Chartran for a portrait of Andrew Carnegie, Frick commissioned one for himself. Comparing the two paintings is telling: Carnegie, as the visionary, sits placidly, while Frick, the practical man, gazes intently at the viewer, his desk spilling over with papers (figs. 15, 16). Frick's efforts to introduce Chartran to Pittsburgh society led to a number of portraits of people close to him, such as Thomas Mellon and his wife, though he criticized the depiction of Mellon as too rushed. He went on to commission Chartran to portray a political event, the treaty concluding the Spanish-American War, overseen by President McKinley. Titled *Signing of the Peace Protocol between Spain and the United States, August 12, 1898*, the painting was offered to the United States; accepted by President Theodore Roosevelt, it still hangs in the Treaty Room of the White House.

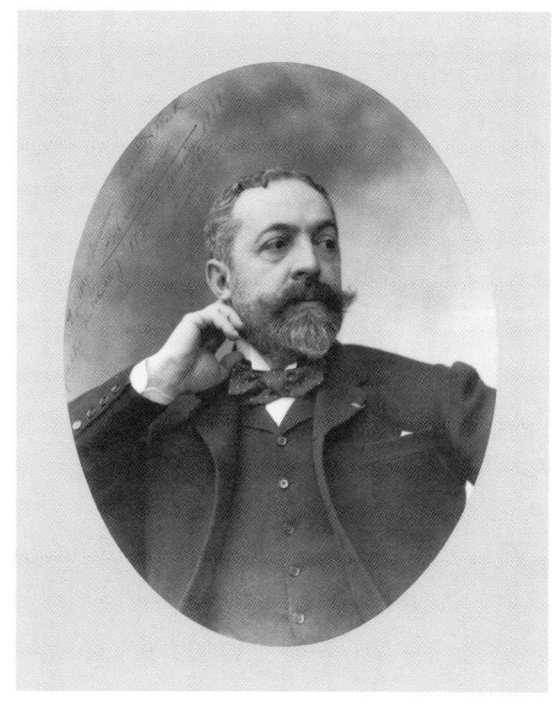

Frick's exchanges with artists were not purely about aesthetic matters. By paying for portraits of colleagues, he cemented relationships and furthered his business interests, even as far as Washington. In the case of Chartran, he began to act as tastemaker, pushing forward a favored artist. In return for promoting their careers, he received an education in art and access to up-and-coming artists in America and Europe. Clearly, too, he enjoyed their company as a distraction from the pressures of business.

AMERICANS ABROAD

In the post–Civil War period, travel abroad became popular among wealthy Americans. Just as the Grand Tour had been essential for the education of British aristocrats in the eighteenth century, so trips to the British Isles and the Continent became desirable for broadening the horizons of Americans in the nineteenth. Touring the capitals of culture also provided entrée to society and increased social standing back home, and a number of wealthy American debutantes returned with marriage proposals from English nobles. For many tourists, travel included visits to palaces and churches, as well as museums (a new activity). These ranged from palaces that had opened to the public, such as the Musée du Louvre, to purpose-built museums such as the Glyptothek in Munich in the beginning of the nineteenth century, to Sir John Soane's Museum in London, a private collection turned public that opened its doors in 1837. Seeing private collections, artist studios, exhibitions, and the annual

FIG. 12
Top row, William Nimick Frew, Joseph Woodwell, Henry Clay Frick; middle, Margaret Woodwell, Emily Frew, Adelaide Frick; bottom, Marika Ogiz, Helen Clay Frick, Virginia Frew, ca. 1900.

FIG. 13
Narcisse-Virgile Diaz de la Peña, *Pond of Vipers (La Mare aux Vipères)*, 1858.

FIG. 14
Théobald Chartran, 1898.

salons of art in Paris and London rounded out these experiences. Isabella Stewart Gardner and her husband, Jack, for example, made eleven extended trips abroad between 1867 and 1897. Early on, these trips included Egypt, Greece, the Middle East, and Asia, while later, the Gardners concentrated on Europe.

On Frick's first trip to Europe in 1880, with his best friend Andrew Mellon, they were joined by Frank Cowan, a lawyer, doctor, and an entertaining storyteller, and A. A. Hutchinson, a potential investor in Frick's company. The four of them sailed first to Ireland, stopping in Dublin and Belfast; next to Scotland—Edinburgh and Glasgow; crossed the channel to Paris; and then made a "dash across the continent to Venice" (fig. 17).[8]

This transatlantic trip was evidently a success, since after this, Henry and Andrew frequently traveled together. It is telling that Frick made his first documented purchase of a painting, albeit by an American, the Hetzel landscape, the following year. Seeing so much art in Europe may have sparked an interest in owning paintings himself. Another factor was his move from the "half-office and half-living room in a clapboard shack" at the coking operation to rented quarters in Monongahela House. The grandeur of what he had seen in London and Paris may have motivated him to improve the decor of his living arrangements.

Following Frick's marriage, and then the births of the couple's children, his trips were no longer bachelor excursions. These now-family vacations sometimes included business meetings, if in informal settings. In July 1887, Henry and Adelaide sailed to Europe with their two children and Adelaide's mother and sister. His partner,

FIG. 15
Théobald Chartran,
Henry Clay Frick, 1896.

FIG. 16
Théobald Chartran,
Andrew Carnegie, 1895.

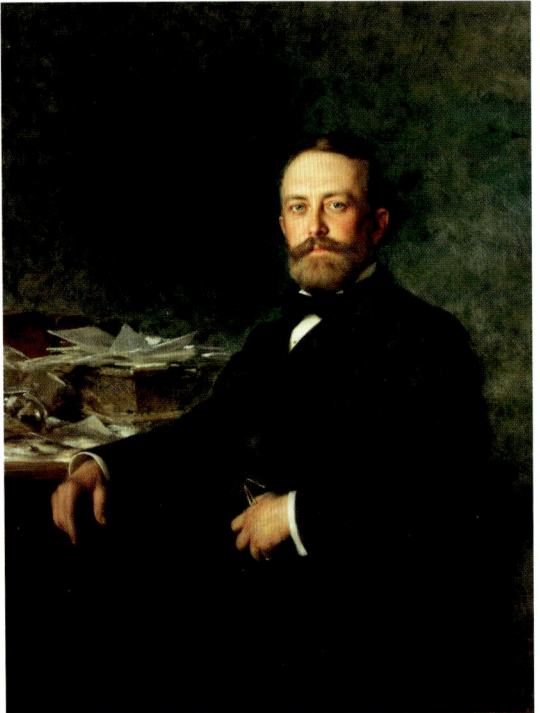
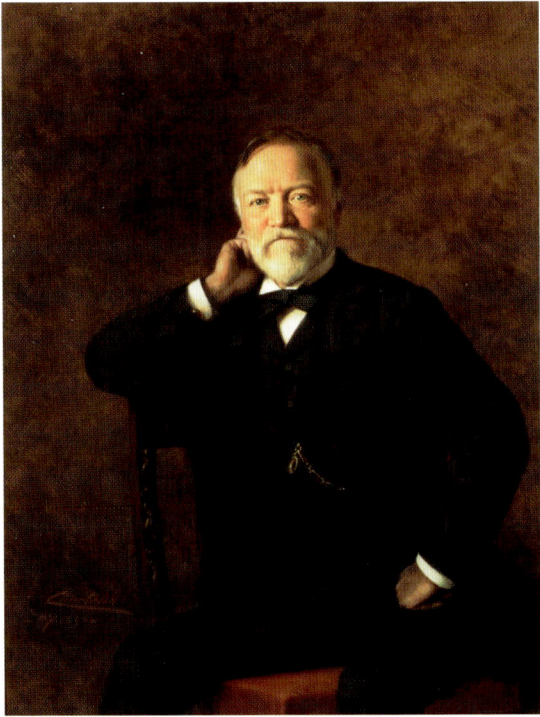

Carnegie, invited them to stay at Skibo Castle, his manse in Scotland, writing, "Come and see what one gets in Scotland these summer days" (fig. 18).[9]

The family would also visit artist studios, increasingly an attraction for tourists. In 1895, the Fricks stopped by Bouguereau's Paris studio (fig. 21), carrying away a print of the artist's painting *L'Espieglerie* inscribed to Helen Clay. In London, they saw the work of Lawrence Alma-Tadema; the following year, the artist's *Waiting and Watching* (Frick Pittsburgh) hung on the walls of Clayton. On a later trip, Frick saw private houses converted into public institutions, which may have planted the seeds for The Frick Collection. Notable among them was Hertford House, which Richard Wallace's widow gave to the nation in 1895, opening to the public in 1900. Another was the Museo Poldi-Pezzoli in Milan, a private residence that opened in 1881. With its mix of paintings and decorative arts, it is one of the closest European correlates to the Frick.

As Frick showed more inclination to collect, especially after 1895, when he made more than a dozen purchases, dealers began to accompany the family on their travels. A postcard to Helen Clay in 1904, following a luncheon at Chartran's villa, is signed by the dealer Charles Carstairs, among others (fig. 23). They would arrange for access to private collections, while at the same time signaling works of art available for purchase. Various members of the Knoedler firm were their most frequent companions. In time, decorators played a role in these trips, too. In 1914, Elsie de Wolfe convinced Frick to postpone a round of golf to see the John Murray Scott collection—parts of which were inherited from Sir Richard Wallace—on the rue Laffitte in Paris (he turned up in his sporting attire). In a sale handled by the Germain Seligman firm, Frick spent $400,000 over the course of a month on fine examples of French furniture.

There is one trip that Frick was most fortunate to postpone. After visiting Florence, he went straight to Egypt, as Frick wrote Philander Knox: "Up the Nile, then to Syracuse on the Island of Sicily." Returning to Paris, the couple planned to sail on the *Titanic*, but Adelaide sprained her ankle, and they decided to wait for another ship. Among the many lives lost in the *Titanic*'s sinking on April 15, 1912, were those of fellow collectors George Widener and his son Harry.

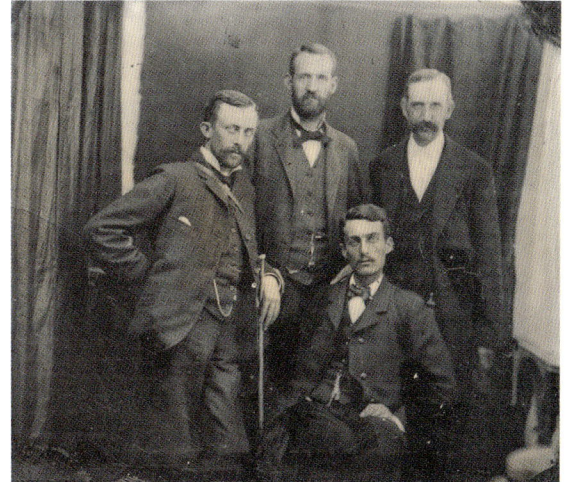

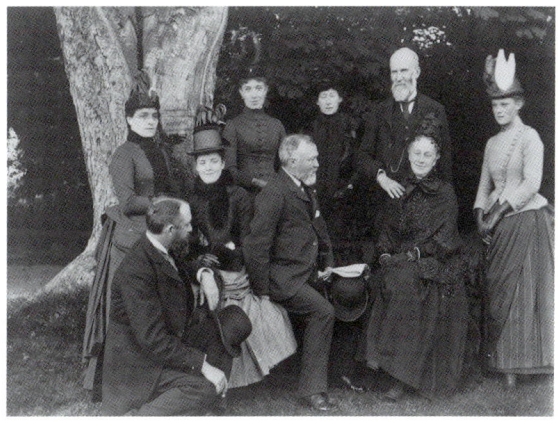

FIG. 17
Henry Clay Frick (left), A. A. Hutchinson (top left), Frank Cowan (top right), and Andrew Mellon (bottom right) on board the steamer *Abyssinia*, 1880.

FIG. 18
Henry Clay Frick with his wife, Adelaide; Andrew Carnegie; and others in Kingussie, Scotland, ca. 1895.

ART FAIRS AND EXHIBITIONS

Andrew Carnegie was never as serious a collector as Frick, but he played a major role in establishing institutions for the arts in Pittsburgh. In the 1890s, he gave a million

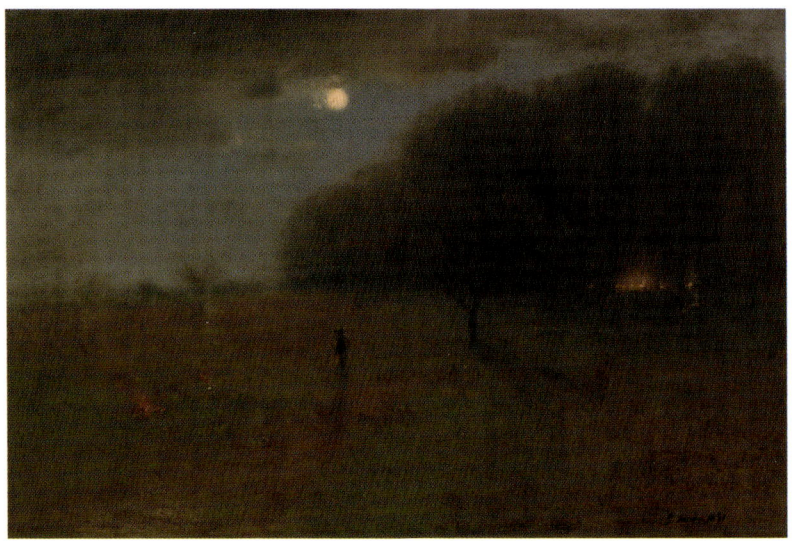

dollars for a cultural center—including a library, art gallery, music hall, and a museum of natural history—that would become the foremost museum in the city. In those same years, when dealers' shops and private collections were virtually the only venues where art could be seen, the library's art gallery and an offshoot, the Carnegie International art fair, introduced American and European art to Pittsburgh and enhanced the city's reputation as a center for art.

The New Carnegie Art Galleries exhibitions (a precursor of the public museum) also established a platform for local artists and encouraged collectors to purchase their work (fig. 20). From the outset, Carnegie envisioned this as a showcase for contemporary painters "likely to become Old Masters in their time."[10] He wrote, "The Gallery is for the masses of the people primarily, not for the educated few." Over time, the gallery acquired art of the day and exhibited it, though this meant that Pittsburgh only slowly gathered significant holdings of earlier art. Landscape painter John W. Beatty, who had served as secretary of the Art Society of Pittsburgh and organized one of its exhibitions, became the first director of the New Carnegie Art Galleries in 1896 (fig. 22). Frick knew Beatty and purchased his *Harvest Scene* (Frick Pittsburgh) in 1895, even at the moment when his allegiance was shifting from American to European art. The collector was even more smitten by the visionary American landscape painter George Inness, buying eight of his canvases (fig. 19). Beyond that, Frick served as treasurer of the Carnegie Library and Museum. He did his best to ensure its success, lending no fewer than twelve paintings to its loan exhibition of 1895. In an interview the year before, he modestly stated that his collection was not newsworthy. Following his significant acquisitions of 1895, however, he now thought his works by artists such as Diaz, Daubigny, George Frederic Watts, Inness, Millet, and Jean-Léon Gérôme could elevate the standards of the Carnegie exhibitions. Frick was becoming a serious collector and publicly acknowledged the fact with loans to exhibitions.

The Carnegie International, now the longest-running exhibition of international contemporary art in North America, was established in 1896. Beatty scouted

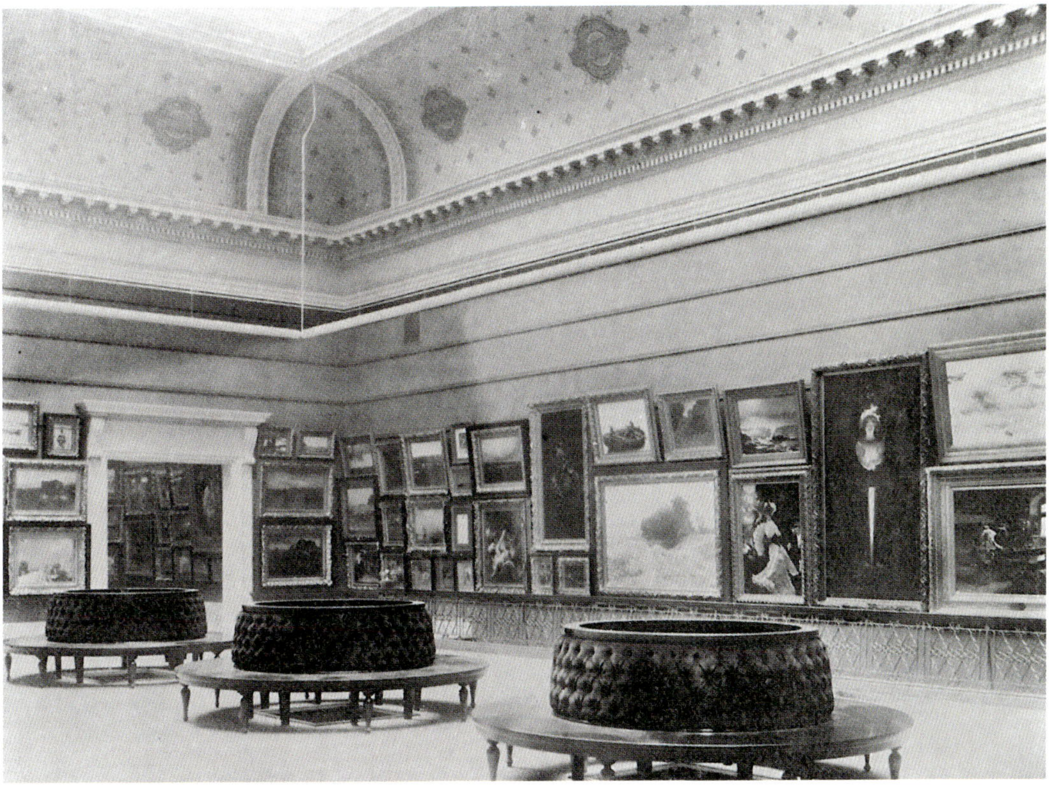

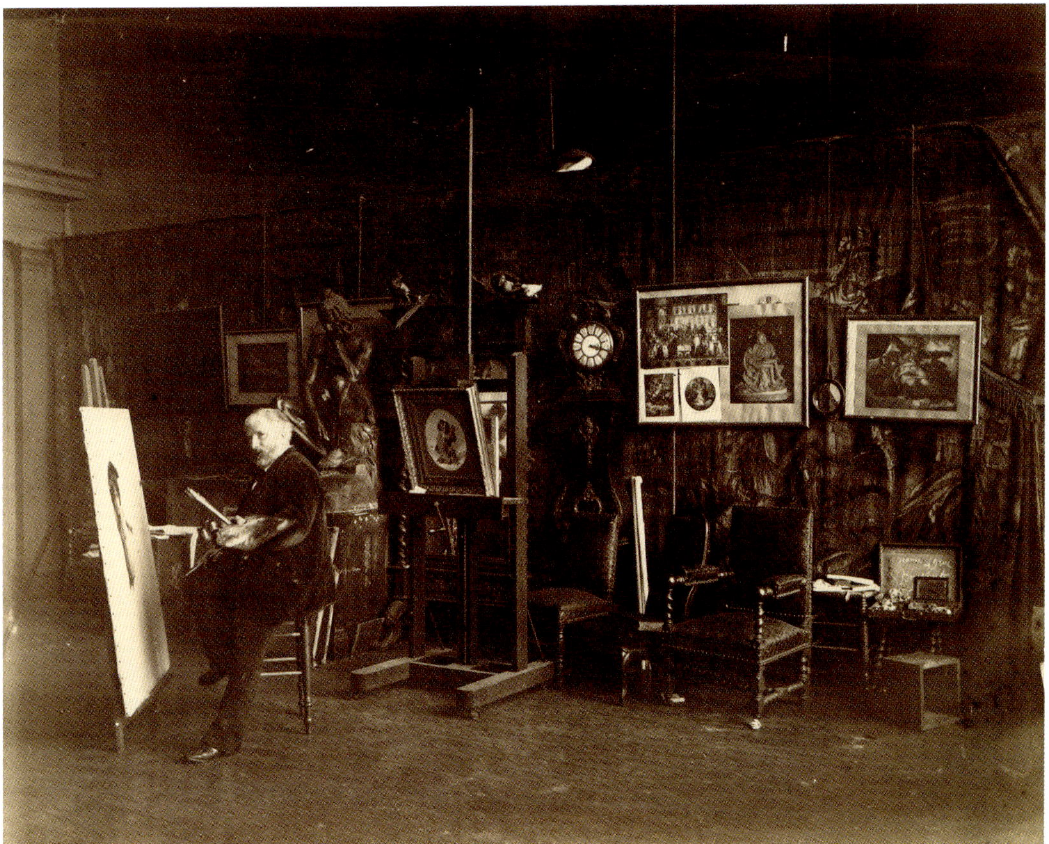

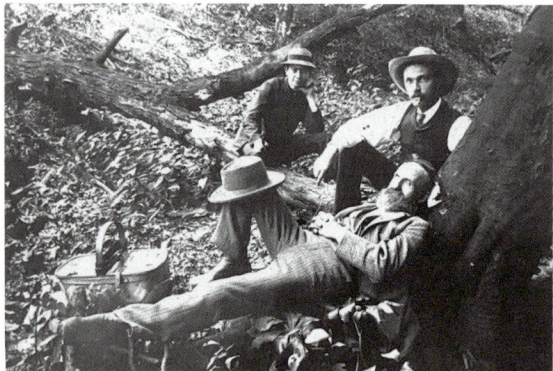

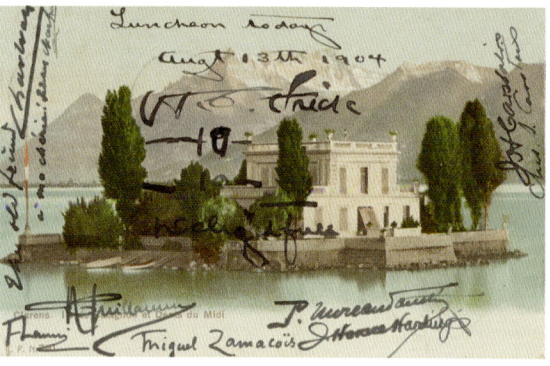

Europeans such as Anton Mauve and Jacob Maris, inviting them to show in the fair; others came to serve as jurors. In 1898, Frits Thaulow judged the submissions to the International and developed a following in Pittsburgh. Frick bought eight paintings by the Norwegian artist and gave several away as gifts, another instance of his promoting a favored painter (fig. 24).

Fairs in other cities also influenced Frick's taste. The most famous of all, the World's Columbian Exposition in Chicago of 1893, drew Frick for business reasons. He is said to have spent $60,000 on the Frick Coke Booth, trumpeting the quality of his factory's product. He must have stopped by the Art Pavilion, as well as the commercial booths. The Exposition famously introduced European art and culture to the millions who attended (fig. 25). Prior to 1893, Frick did not own any paintings by Théodore Rousseau or Corot, Jules Breton or Millet. Within a decade, he had bought more than a dozen works by these artists.

The Barbizon School was well known and avidly collected in Boston in these years, but it was the fair in Chicago that seems to have inspired Frick to pursue it. Other artists, such as Gérôme and Bouguereau, known for historical or allegorical subjects, were widely acclaimed at the fair. Frick succumbed to the trend and bought some of their works, though his interest in them waned quickly.

FIG. 22
George Hetzel (front) with John W. Beatty (directly behind him) and Walter Miller, n.d.

FIG. 23
Postcard from Henry Clay Frick to Helen Clay, commemorating a luncheon hosted by artist Théobald Chartran at his villa on Lake Geneva, August 13, 1904.

FIG. 24
Frits Thaulow, *Steel Mills Along the Monongahela River*, 1898.

FIG. 25
William Henry Jackson, *Details of Main Entrance to Art Palace* (World's Columbian Exposition, Chicago), 1893.

SEEKING ADVICE:
DEALERS AND FRICK'S EARLY COLLECTING

Pittsburgh's social and cultural life set the stage for Frick's interest in collecting. Paintings hanging on the walls of the city's collectors furnished examples to emulate; conversations with artists deepened his knowledge and trained his eye; art fairs displayed an abundance of choices and highlighted painters whose stars were rising. His travels exposed him to European culture and raised his ambitions to acquire what he had seen in palaces and museums. His most significant influence, however, came from the dealers who sold him the art. In many ways, they were the strongest and steadiest guides in developing his tastes.

Frick's first purchases from dealers, in 1881, reflect these varied influences and his divergent tastes. At the New York gallery of William Schaus—in the nascent art district centered on lower Broadway—Frick bought Luis Jiménez Aranda's *In the Louvre* (Frick Pittsburgh), which depicts fashionably dressed women distracted by a nude ancient Roman statue. In light of his later purchases, this humorous genre scene by a successful Salon artist was a surprising choice, one perhaps inspired by fond

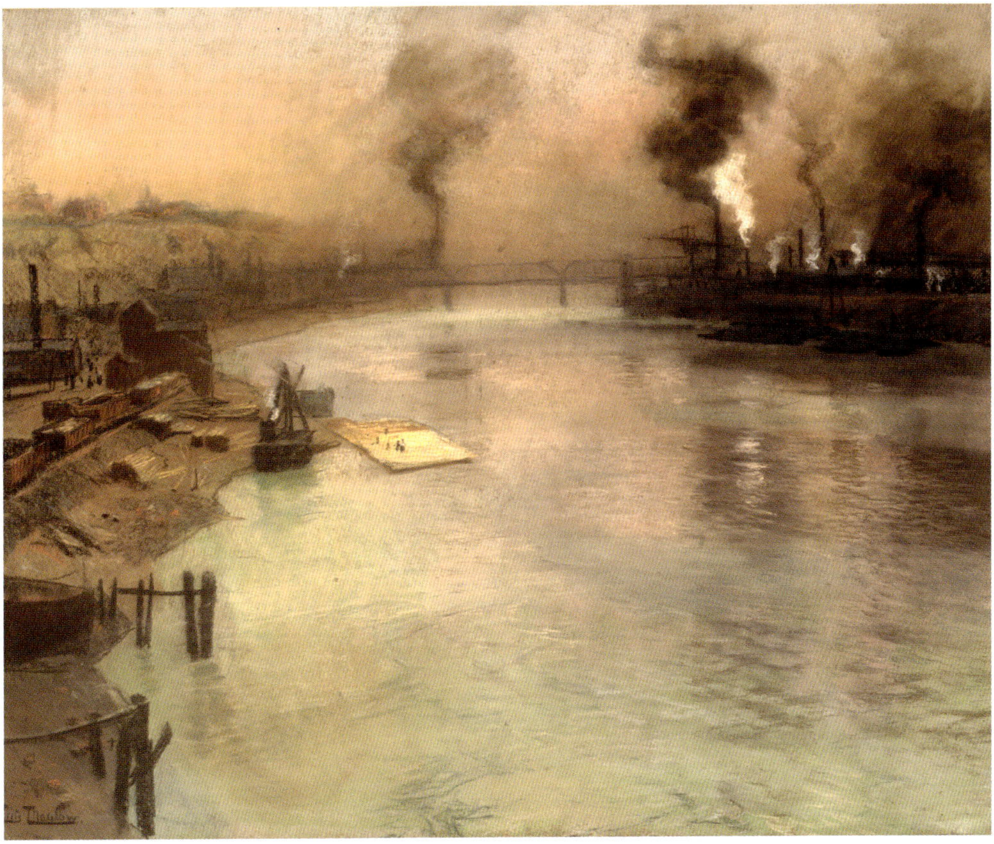

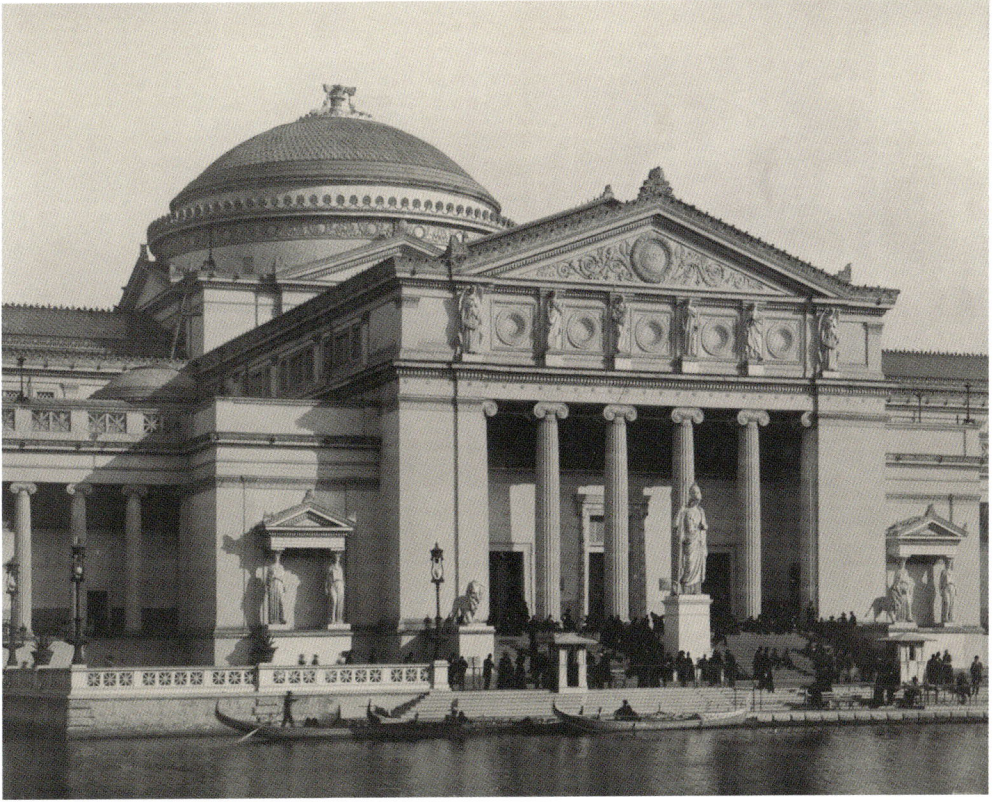

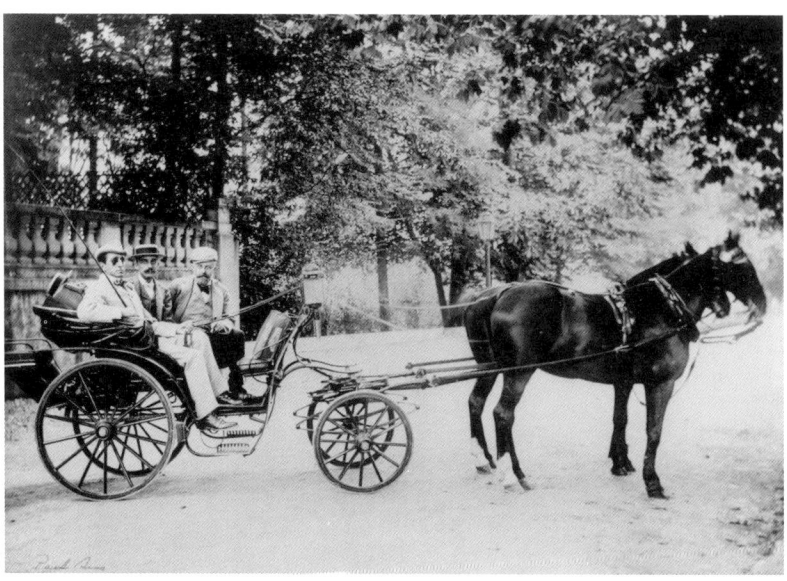

FIG. 26
Charles Knoedler, Andrew
W. Mellon, and Henry Clay
Frick in a carriage, 1898.

memories of his trip to Europe the year before. In Pittsburgh, he wrote a check on T. Mellon and Sons Bank to S. Boyd & Co. for the painting by Hetzel, his earliest documented art purchase. Charged to his room at Monongahela House, the canvas by a local artist joined the other works Frick hung on the walls of his living space.

The gallery that forged the most decisive relationship with Frick was M. Knoedler & Co. In 1846, when the French print-publishing house Goupil & Cie opened a branch in New York, it was first managed and later purchased by Michael Knoedler. Michael's son Roland and brother Charles, along with another gallery director, Charles Carstairs, were young men roughly Frick's age, well connected and affable (fig. 26). They encouraged Frick's interests, traveling with the family in America and Europe, arranging studio visits, and introducing him to artists and collectors. Late-night poker games and rounds of golf cemented their friendship and developed trust. When Frick contemplated building an art gallery in his home at Clayton, he consulted Roland. (He would later change his mind about the addition [fig. 27].)

In their company, Frick picked up tricks of the trade. He moved quickly through art galleries—"like a streak of lightning," recalled Helen Clay, though "he remembered more than the rest of us . . . his powers of observation were remarkable."[11] Frick also learned to study the art market. He tracked the prices of paintings by Turner, for example, long before he ever owned one. He also took advantage of his relationships with dealers by frequently trading back pictures he had bought in order to upgrade his collection. In the late 1890s, for example, as his interest in American art waned and he concentrated more on French art, he exchanged paintings by Inness for ones by Corot and Troyon. Similarly, he later returned Daniel Ridgway Knight's *Coming from the Garden* (private collection) that Carstairs sold him in 1894 for credit toward Daubigny's *Ferry Boat*. Representing another transformation in his taste, Frick bartered a Hetzel (the painter he had first spent his money on) and an Alfred

Bryan Wall for his very first Old Master painting: *Still Life with Fruit* by Jan van Os (1769). Carstairs later described Frick as "a born trader and close buyer and a d ----- smart man, much more in that way than Morgan."[12]

Frick was a major client. In 1895, he bought eighteen paintings from Knoedler for $67,250; from other galleries that year, he acquired seven for $9,313. His patronage was one reason the Knoedler firm established a branch in Pittsburgh in 1897. Frick's relationship with Knoedler worked both ways. As his collection rose in stature, it was an advertisement for the gallery, as the partners themselves recognized. Frick's promotion of Chartran, represented by the firm, significantly boosted the artist's profile in Pittsburgh. The art dealers made a lot of money off Frick, but the relationship the collector built with them led to favored-client status and gave him leeway to make good deals and to return works whenever he wished.

FIG. 27
Roland Knoedler and
Adelaide Frick in Palm
Beach, 1904.

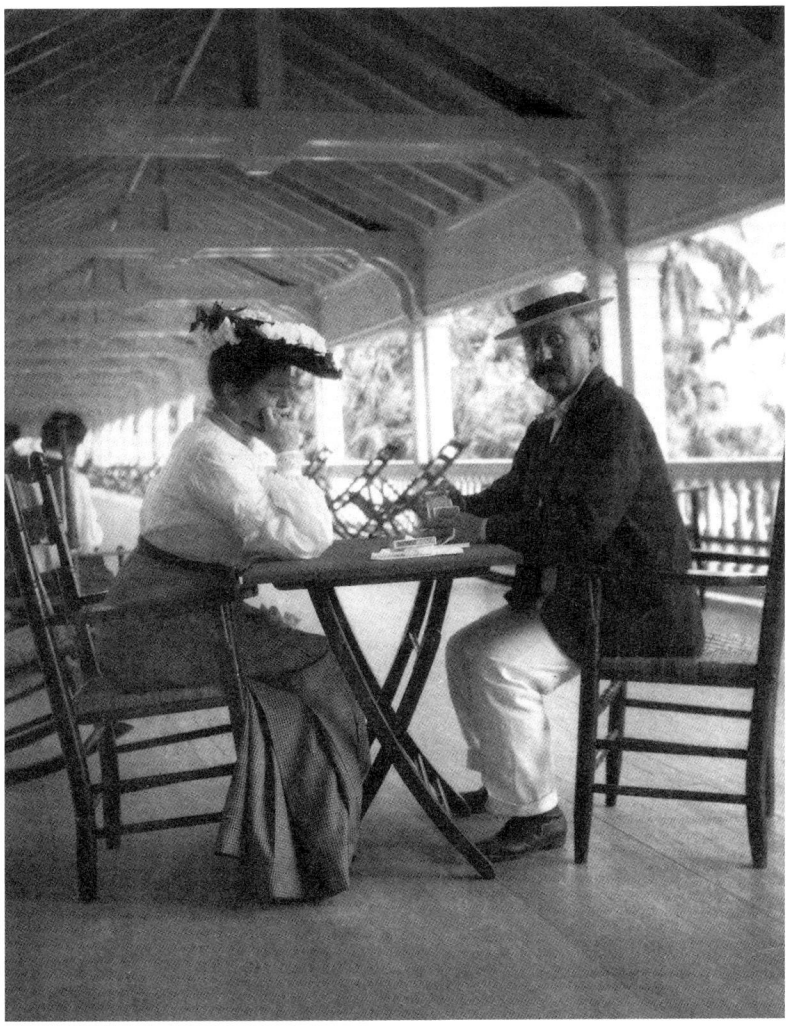

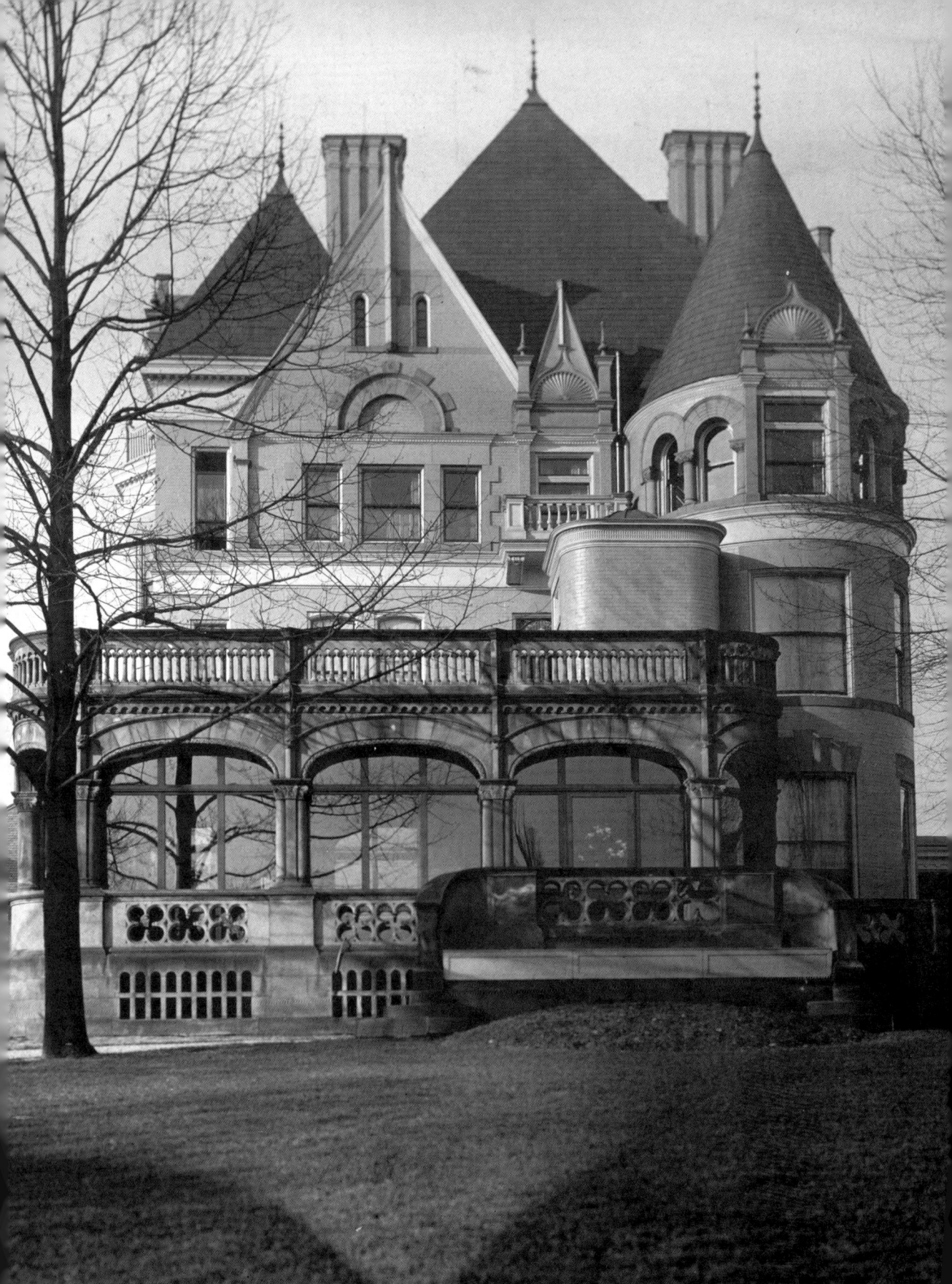

III

CLAYTON, THE FIRST HOME,
THE FIRST COLLECTION

Henry and Adelaide's marriage in 1882 prompted the purchase of their first home, an Italianate-style house built in the 1860s in fashionable Point Breeze, several miles from the center of Pittsburgh. They hired local architect Andrew J. Peebles to renovate the house, renamed Clayton, for $50,000, twice as much as was spent on the property itself (fig. 28).

Prior to Clayton, Henry's taste in furnishing is revealed in a garniture he purchased in 1881 to ornament his Monongahela House rooms. The ornate onyx and gilt bronze clock is flanked by matching candelabra (fig. 29) that were made in France by R. Lefebvre & Fils Inc. and retailed in the United States by Tiffany & Company. Frick took them from the hotel to Clayton, where, despite subsequent renovations, they continued to occupy a place of honor on the reception room mantel two decades on (fig. 30). Years later, he still favored intricate French furniture and decorations, though his tastes advanced to considerably more sophisticated eighteenth-century furniture by André-Charles Boulle and garnitures in Sèvres porcelain.

The Fricks followed popular tastes of the day, centered on the Aesthetic Movement, an eclectic combination of styles ranging from Gothic to Islamic and Chinese motifs. Upholstered and fringed parlor chairs and richly carved bedroom furniture followed the dictates of English architect Charles L. Eastlake's influential *Hints on Household Taste* (1868). Letters from Frick to New York furniture designer and manufacturers D. S. Hess & Company reveal how closely he supervised the work at Clayton, applying the exacting standards and obsessive bookkeeping that characterized his own business dealings. Hess & Company's mahogany and leather armchair, purchased in 1883, gives a sense of the decor the couple admired (fig. 31). Its basic lines are rectangular and functional, but it is enlivened by the tracery of a Gothic arch at the back and pierced arm rests in an elegant pattern. A carved tablet bearing Frick's monogram emblazons the chair back. Clayton's subsequent renovations make it difficult to reconstruct the original placement of art on its walls, but Frick's major investment in paintings came only in the last decade of the century, after he had been living in the house for some years.

FIG. 28
Clayton, ca. 1901.

39

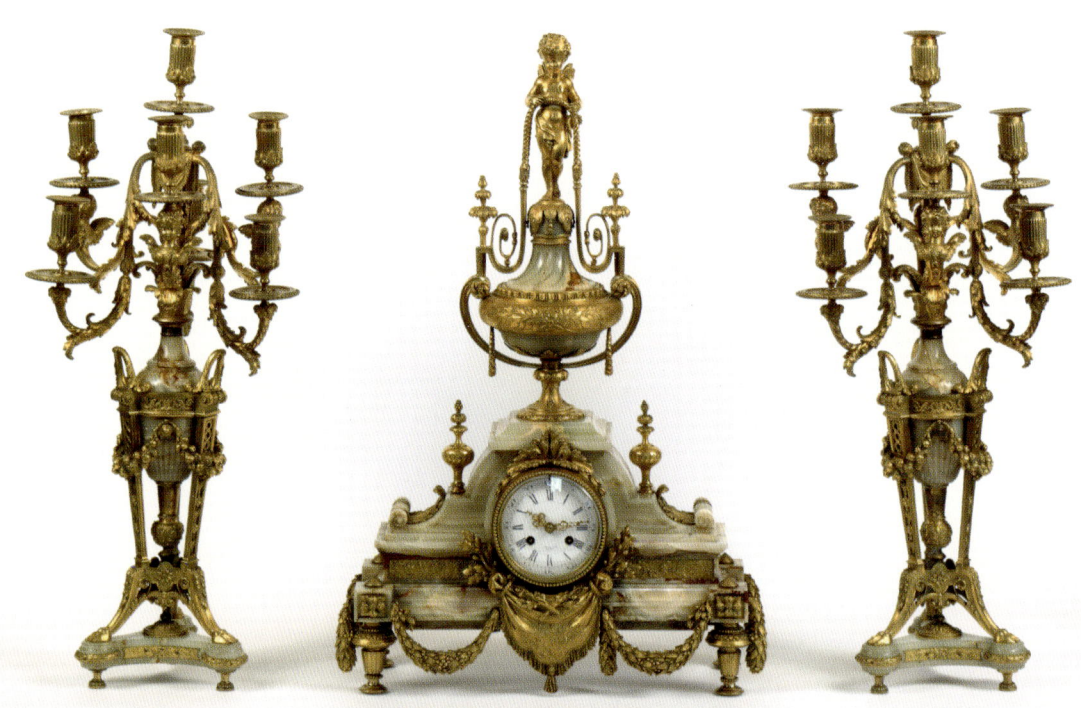

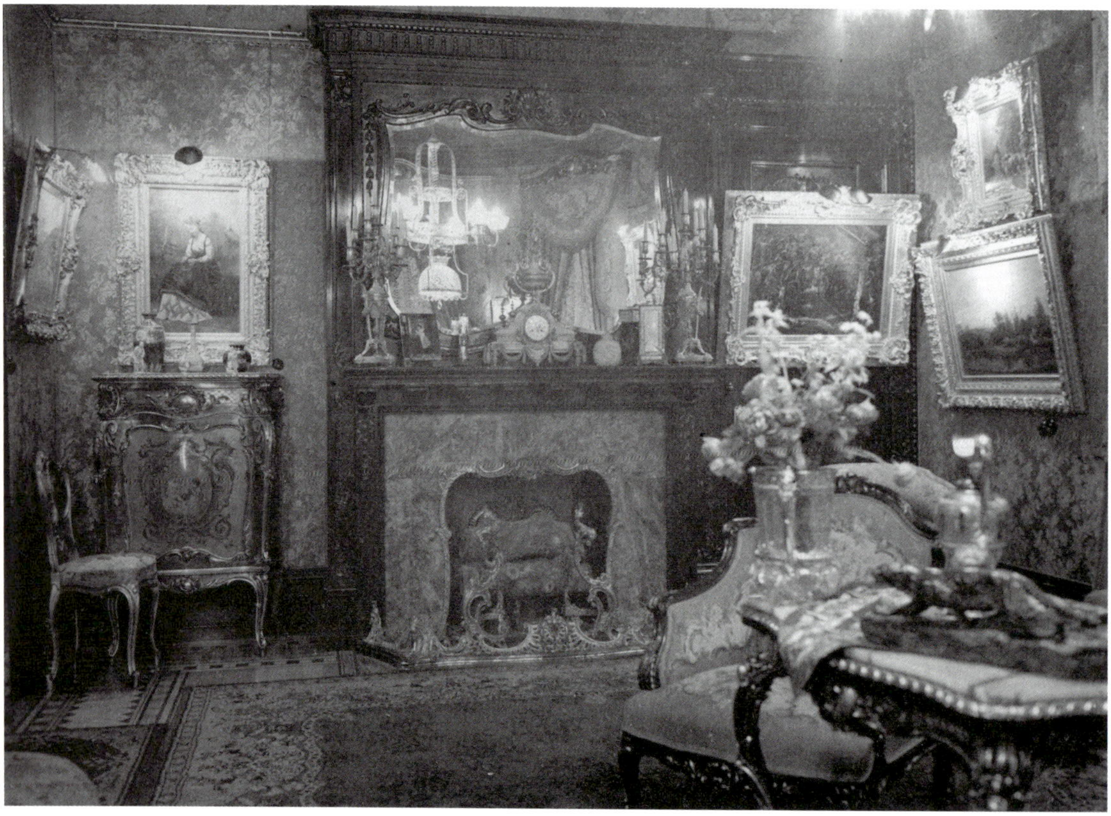

Nearly a decade later, changes in Frick's professional and personal lives led to a second renovation of Clayton. In 1889, he became chairman of Carnegie Steel Company, and his increased salary and stature required a grander domicile. For this second renovation, Frick hired Frederick J. Osterling, an architect who had made his name working on residences or workplaces of Pittsburgh's elite, such as Henry J. Heinz and George Westinghouse, whose famous companies were founded in the 1880s and '90s. Osterling's grandiose first proposal was rejected, but the finished house nonetheless contained many more rooms than before and its transformed exterior reflected the fashion for French Renaissance chateaux. What this designer brought to the revamped interior was greater unity of concept. The library's oak woodwork, for example, was carved with a consistent vocabulary of motifs—urns and classical trophies—that drew on Italian Renaissance sources. The most accomplished of these spaces is the dining room, which, after a recent refurbishment, has been restored to its 1890s luster. In a harmonious ensemble of revival styles popularized by *The Grammar of Ornament*, Owen Jones's 1856 bible of style, the decor joins furniture, stained-glass transoms, velvet curtains, and leather wall coverings in what the Germans term *Gesamtkunstwerk*, a unified artistic whole (fig. 32). Filling out the dining room were furnishings and tableware from the finest New York and London manufacturers. A. Kimbell & Co. provided eighteen dining chairs, more massive and baronial in feeling than Hess & Company's simpler and lighter predecessors (which were moved to the breakfast room). Porcelain plates and serving vessels for use on the table and display in the sideboards came from the British firms Minton, Copeland, Doulton, and Royal Worcester, through the New York purveyor Davis Collamore & Co. One of the first documented purchases for the renovated house is a set of W. T. Copeland & Sons plates centering birds in woodland scenes against cobalt blue and gilded surrounds. Some twenty years later, Frick's New York mansion would be ornamented with eighteenth-century Sèvres, similarly rich but more technically refined and then still a rarity in America. Echoing the Copeland service, one of the New York sets was a Sèvres tea service (1767)—decorated by Antoine-Joseph Chapuis, who specialized in paintings of birds—and an important potpourri vase that also featured birds (see fig. 83). Silver vessels and utensils from the American firms Gorham and Tiffany, alongside cut glass from England, Venice, and New York, completed the dining-room services.

Frick's rapidly growing art collection soon filled Clayton's sumptuous interiors. Around 1895, his enhanced status at the Carnegie Company and developing acumen as an art collector led to an explosion of painting purchases. Frick was truly becoming a collector, but the dining room's wood paneling and

FIG. 29
Lefebvre et Fils, supplied by Tiffany & Company, *Garniture Set*, ca. 1881.

FIG. 30
The reception room at Clayton, ca. 1901.

FIG. 31
D. S. Hess & Company, *Armchair*, 1883.

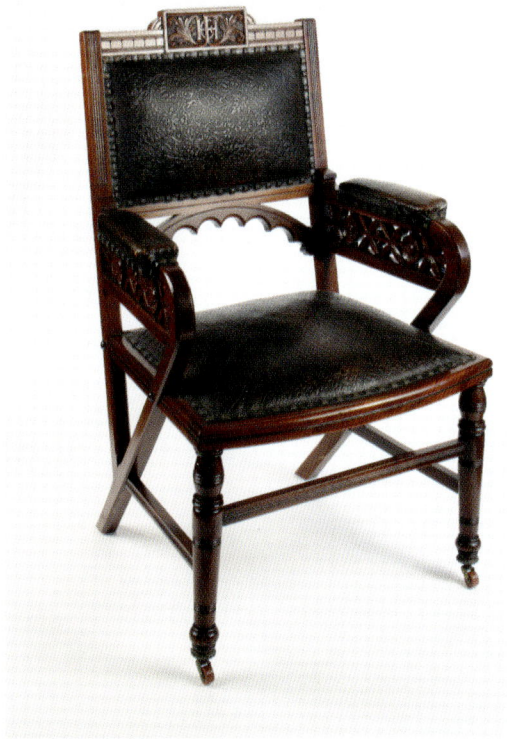

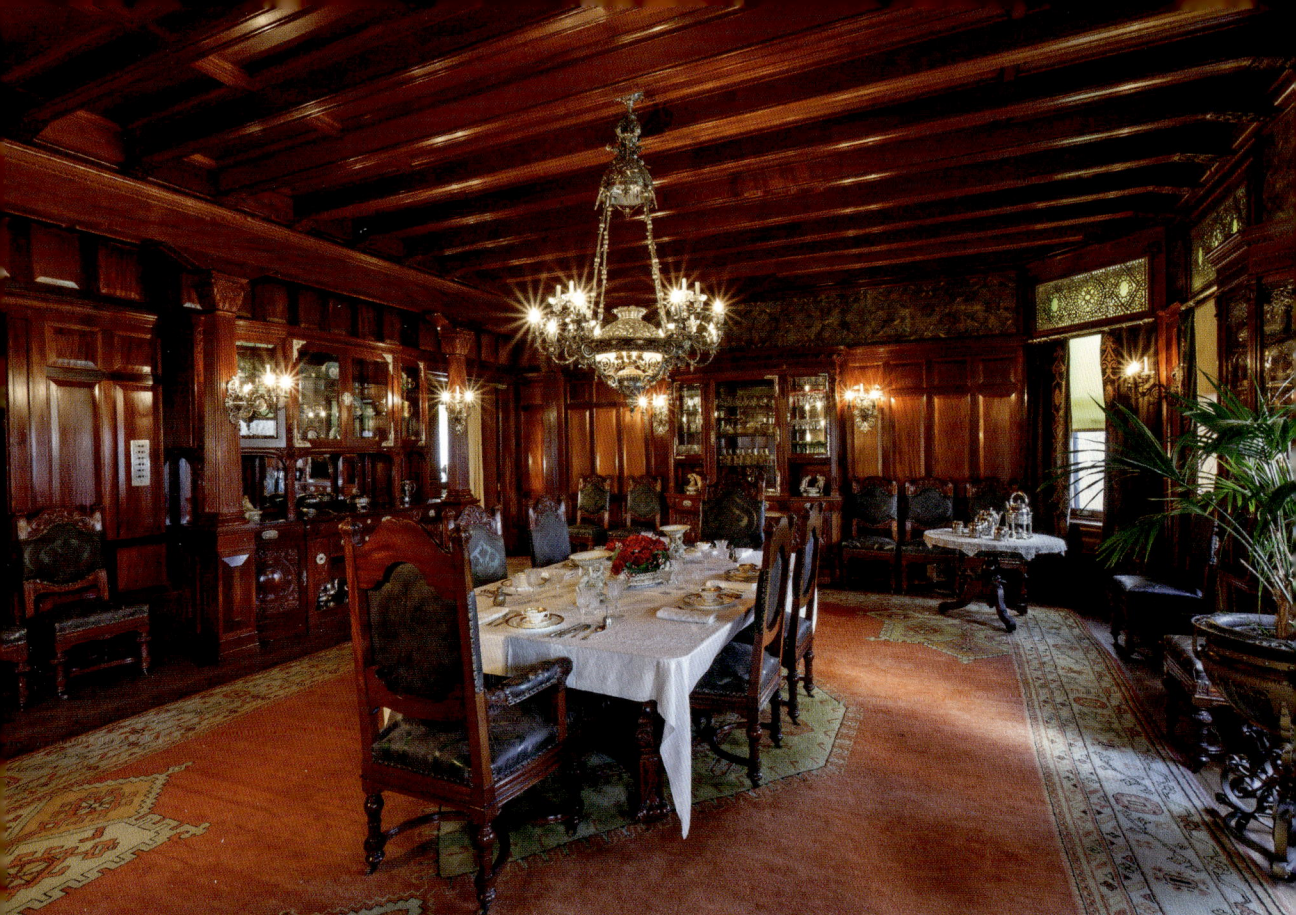

FIG. 32
The dining room at
Clayton, designed by
Frederick J. Osterling,
1892.

FIG. 33
The dining room at
Clayton, showing
Pascal-Adolphe-Jean
Dagnan-Bouveret's
Consolatrix Afflictorum,
1899.

built-in sideboard and glass cases left little wall space for hanging paintings. Early photographs reveal the profusion of framed works of art that filled the other rooms. By 1901, when the reception room was photographed, Frick's propensity for hanging paintings by Barbizon School artists had overtaken his American works; at this point, he had the largest collection of this French School in Pittsburgh. Narcisse-Virgile Diaz de la Peña's *Pond of Vipers* (Frick Pittsburgh) squeezes into the room, hanging over a door to the right of the fireplace. A Corot depiction of a peasant woman is to the left. The function of the room required comfortable seating, so Rococo-style upholstered chairs are provided. The French garniture brought from the Fricks' Monongahela House apartment, still in keeping with this historicizing decor, shares the mantelpiece with contemporary English porcelain and glass. Works of art are beginning to overwhelm the rooms; it is no wonder that Frick was considering adding an art gallery to the house. The next urban house he built, the Fifth Avenue mansion in New York, would leave ample space for—in fact, privilege—the works of art, which mainly dated from earlier centuries. Historical—that is to say, actual eighteenth-century—chairs and chests of drawers would replace historicizing imitations.

Interestingly, the character of some rooms largely survived the move to New York. For example, the breakfast room at Clayton, with silk damasks lining walls hung with Barbizon School landscapes, was replicated in New York. Perhaps the Fricks felt that the comfort of this intimate dining room could not be bettered. The principal difference between the Pittsburgh and New York houses is that the later one was specifically designed to accommodate works of art, while neither the 1882 nor 1891 renovations of Clayton anticipated the large growth of Frick's collection.

Tension between Frick's desire for stylish houses and taste for avant-garde art came to a head with his commission of the trendy French artist Pascal-Adolphe-Jean Dagnan-Bouveret for a painting of *Consolatrix Afflictorum* [Comforter of the Afflicted] (fig. 33), a religious subject Frick found emotionally appealing after the death of two of his children. Yet the painting proved too large for the dining room, and many people were mystified by its style and subject. "Frick buys a freak," blared the headline of a newspaper.[13] The experience seems to have taught him a lesson about the perils of commissioning art specifically for a house. He repeated this rarely—notably with the decorative ceiling painting on the second floor of the New York mansion.

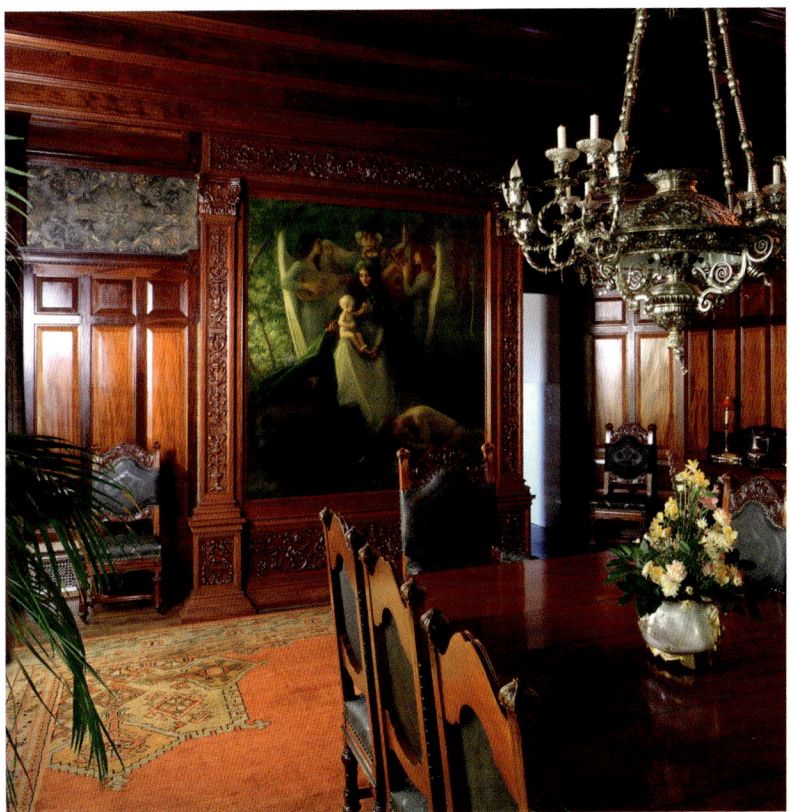

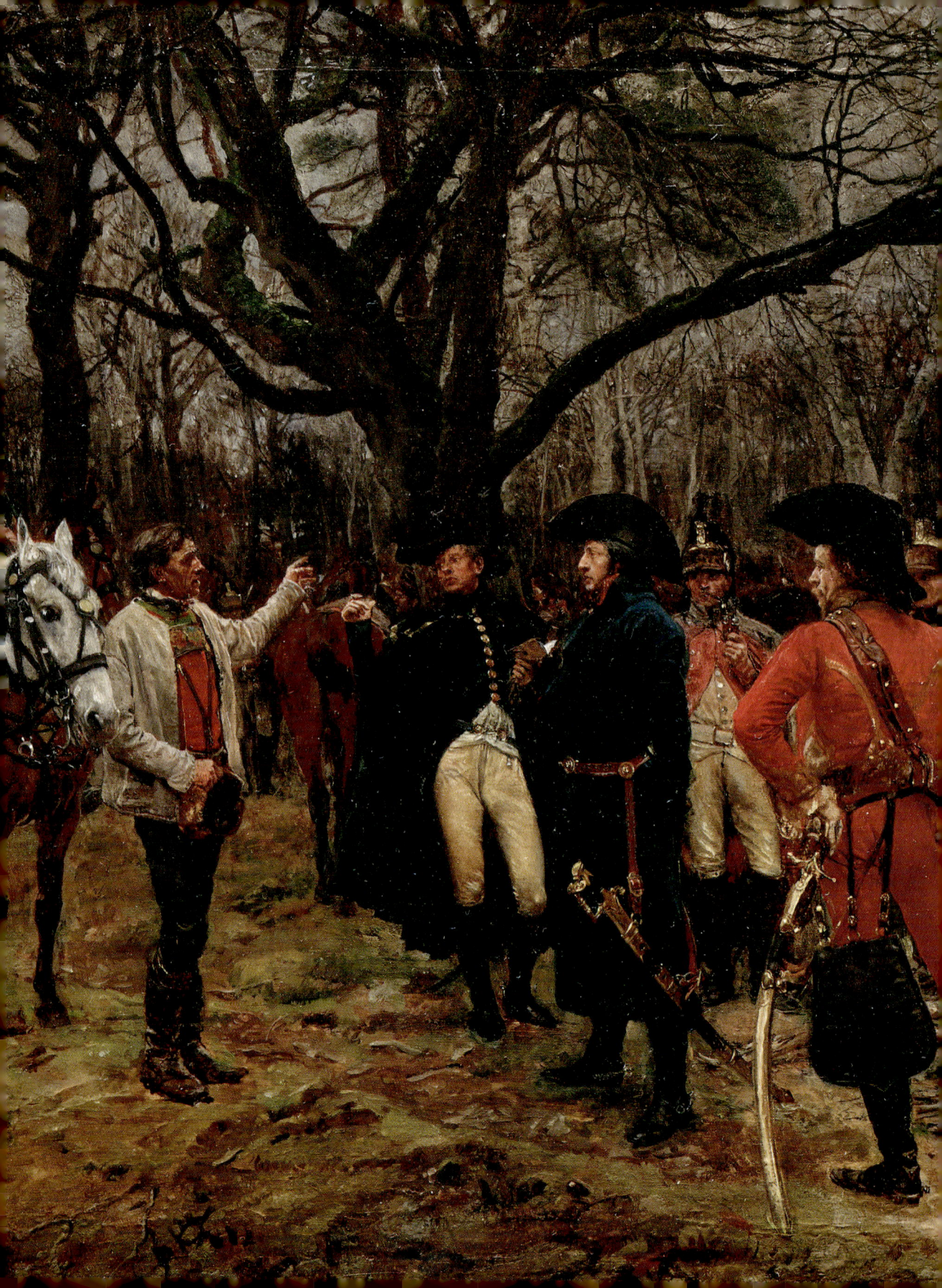

IV

THE VANDERBILT MANSION AND
ITS ART COLLECTION

In January 1905, when it became known that the Fricks were looking to settle in New York, the real estate firm of Robinson, Brown & Co. approached the couple to determine their interest in renting the William H. Vanderbilt House, at 640 Fifth Avenue, between 51st and 52nd streets (fig. 35). Built by Vanderbilt, this famous property (now demolished), known as the Triple Palace, was designed by the architects John B. Snook and Charles B. Atwood and completed in 1882. In addition to the mansion, which was William's residence, there were two adjoining houses occupied by his two daughters.

When William's father, Cornelius Vanderbilt, known as the richest man in America, died in 1877, William set out to acquire the trappings appropriate to his wealth. In addition to the mansion he built, William began amassing a huge art collection. While Cornelius favored American painting, William turned to costlier European art, his tastes running to those highlighted in the French academic salons. The subjects that appealed to him most were genre scenes, depictions of battles and military maneuvers, and renderings of North African locales. Artists specializing in such works included Gérôme, Alma-Tadema, Bouguereau, and Meissonier, of whom he had seven canvases, including the Napoleonic wartime scene *Information (General Desaix and the Peasant)*, 1867 (fig. 34). The list included Alfred Stevens, the Belgian painter of wistful women, and the animal painters Rosa Bonheur and Edwin Landseer. In time, Vanderbilt added works by the increasingly popular Barbizon School artists, including six by Millet, four by Troyon, two by Corot, six by Diaz, and seven by Rousseau. Some 207 oils and watercolors filled the house.

The Herter Brothers were hired to decorate the interiors of the William H. Vanderbilt house. Their approach introduced notable variety from room to room, for example, Louis XV style in one, Japanese in the next. The centerpiece of the mansion, quite literally, was the three-story art gallery (fig. 36). Every corner of this spacious room—28 by 36 feet and some 35 feet high—was lit in the daytime by skylights and at night by 169 gas jets. The Vanderbilts ensured that their art would be

FIG. 34
Detail of Ernest
Meissonier, *Information
(General Desaix and the
Peasant)*, 1867.

seen and admired. On the evening of December 21, 1883, some twenty-five hundred guests were invited to view the collection, refreshing themselves with champagne and lemonade supplied by Delmonico's restaurant.

Vanderbilt was keen to share his gallery with those beyond New York's elite and, for a time, opened his home (through a separate entrance) to the general public on Thursdays from eleven in the morning to four in the afternoon. But he felt the visitors behaved badly, so he discontinued the practice. Apparently, he considered building a museum across the street, but the land was unavailable. In any event, his will stipulated that the house and its collection would instead remain in the family.

Proud of what he had achieved at 640 Fifth Avenue, Vanderbilt promoted his collection through the privately published ten-volume book series *Mr. Vanderbilt's House and Collection*, written by the art historian Earl Shinn under the pen name Edward Strahan. Five of these volumes were devoted to the art collection, and in 1884 and 1885 Frick bought four of them. Frick also acquired a set of twenty satin photogravure reproductions of Vanderbilt's paintings, some of which he hung at Clayton. Jean-Louis Harmon's *Spring Flowers*, for instance, can be seen in a photograph of a guest room. Most of these prints, which he bought for $100, were of historicizing genre scenes, such as *A Musical Party* after Ferdinand Victor Léon Roybet, fancifully imagined in seventeenth-century costume (see fig. 7). Within a few years, Frick decisively turned away from this kind of art. It is also known that Frick and Mellon, as young bachelors, had seen the house under construction on their visit to New York in the summer of 1880.

After William Vanderbilt's death in 1885, the house remained with his widow, Maria Louisa Kissam Vanderbilt, descending to their son George after her passing. Obsessed with Biltmore, his vast North Carolina estate, George had little interest in maintaining the Fifth Avenue property, even lending a large number of the paintings

FIG. 35
The William H. Vanderbilt residence on Fifth Avenue, between 51st and 52nd streets, ca. 1908.

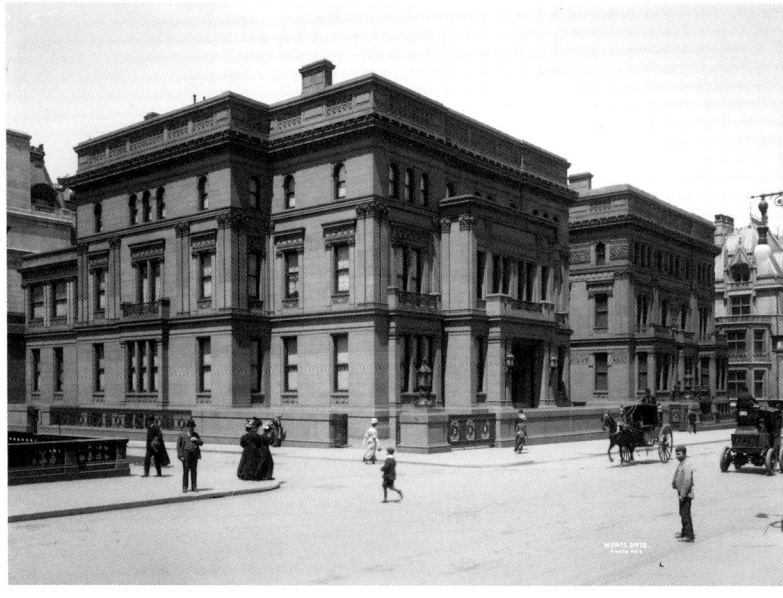

46

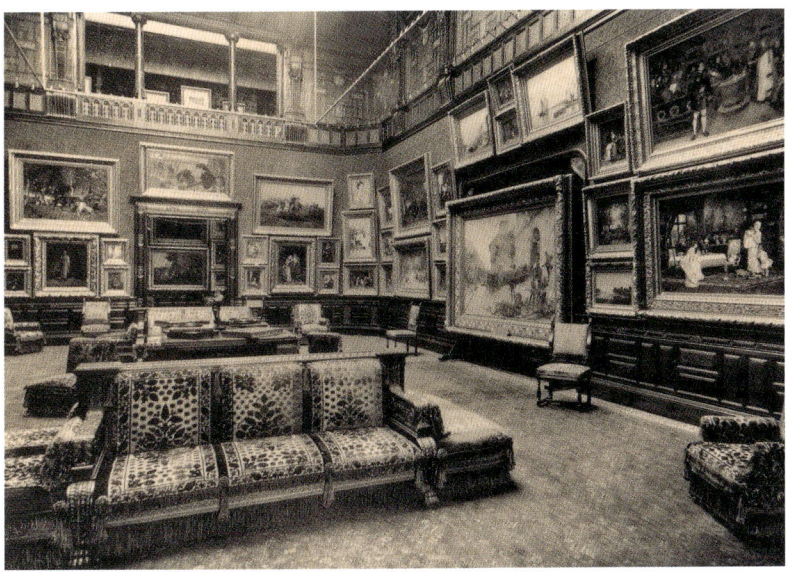

FIG. 36
The Picture Gallery at
the William H. Vanderbilt
residence, 1883.

to the Metropolitan Museum of Art. (Most of these were sold in 1945, and the house itself was demolished in 1947.) Thus, it came to pass that the house could be offered to Frick to rent in 1905, at the princely sum of $50,000 per year. Henry and Adelaide rented the house and made some improvements, such as adding electric lights. There is some evidence that Frick considered purchasing the house, but by 1907 he had acquired the land farther up Fifth Avenue on which he would eventually build his own mansion. Not everyone admired the Vanderbilt house. That arbiter of taste Edith Wharton called the Vanderbilts' decorations a "Thermopylae of bad taste," referencing a disastrous ancient battle.[14] Such criticism does not seem to have bothered the mansion's occupants, though the house Frick eventually built himself was less overbearing in scale and decor.

For Frick, the Vanderbilt house and collection represented aspiration. As a young man, the photogravures of works belonging to William Vanderbilt had captured his imagination, and many of his early purchases, such as those by Gérôme and Bouguereau and especially the Barbizon School paintings, reflect his desire to emulate what was then one of the most famous collections in America. As he sought to make his name in New York, renting the house he had seen under construction decades earlier appealed to his desire for social standing. However, by the time he moved into the Vanderbilt mansion, his tastes in art collecting had shifted to Old Masters. As his own paintings began to fill the art gallery alongside some furnishings and works of art the house's owner left behind, he was competing not so much with the Vanderbilts as with Morgan, Widener, and others for whom European works of earlier centuries now became the cynosure of their interests. In 1908, while still living in the Vanderbilt mansion, he issued a privately published catalogue of forty-nine paintings in his collection. Eight of the artists represented were active in the nineteenth century; the other twenty-four were Old Masters. Frick's transition to older art is clearly documented, and his ambition to set his own collection against those of others is marked.

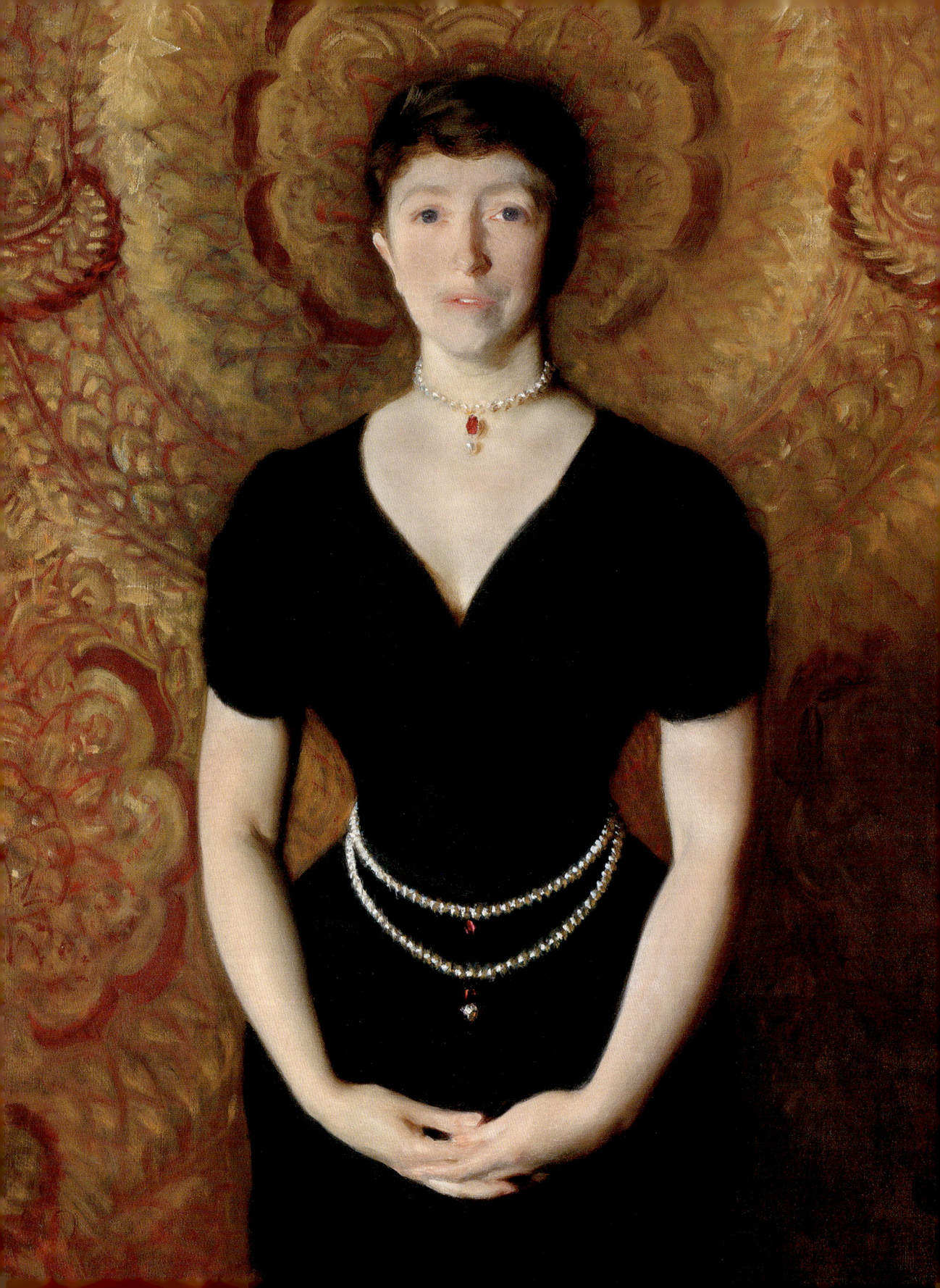

V

RIVAL COLLECTORS

Driving Frick's new focus on Old Master art was his admiration for collectors who pursued it avidly, among them Isabella Stewart Gardner, J. P. Morgan, Benjamin Altman, John G. Johnson, Peter Widener, Henry and Louisine Havemeyer, and Arabella Huntington. These were his rivals, and with his new wealth he was able to outbid them in the art market, sparking his competitive nature. Gardner's 1891 inheritance from her father, David Stewart, combined with the money of her husband, Jack, to put her in the highest tier of wealth. Still, she exclaimed, "Woe is me! Why am I not Morgan or Frick?"[15] What prompted her comment was the highly publicized rivalry between wealthy men over art prizes such as Rembrandts. In 1906, when the Earl of Ilchester's Rembrandt became available, Carstairs cabled Frick, "JUST CONCLUDED PURCHASE GREATEST REMBRANDT PORTRAIT OF HIMSELF EXISTING SEE ROLAND FOR PARTICULARS AND CABLE DECISION."[16] With considerable backroom drama, a battle ensued in which the Metropolitan Museum of Art, Morgan, and Frick were all vying for the picture. In the end, Frick prevailed. When the *Self-Portrait* was the cover image of the museum's bulletin and was called "supreme" by William Valentiner, the Metropolitan's organizer of the first major Dutch painting exhibition in America, Frick could now join the ranks of the greatest collectors.

Even though she could not match Frick's wealth, Gardner had already set the bar high for collecting before he came to challenge her (fig. 37). By 1903, when she opened her Venetian palazzo–style museum in Boston's Back Bay, she could fill it with some of the finest Old Master pictures in the country (fig. 38). In 1892, Gardner was the first American to buy a Vermeer when, despite the attempts of the National Gallery in London and the Louvre to own it, she purchased *The Concert*. Not until a decade later did Frick buy the first of his three paintings by the Delft master. Advised by the art historian Bernard Berenson (now controversial because of his financial arrangements with dealers), Gardner acquired such portraits as Raphael's *Tommaso Inghirami* and Rubens's *Thomas Howard, Earl of Arundel*, two of the greatest paintings by those artists to have arrived in the country by that date. (Frick never bought a

FIG. 37
John Singer Sargent,
Isabella Stewart Gardner,
1888.

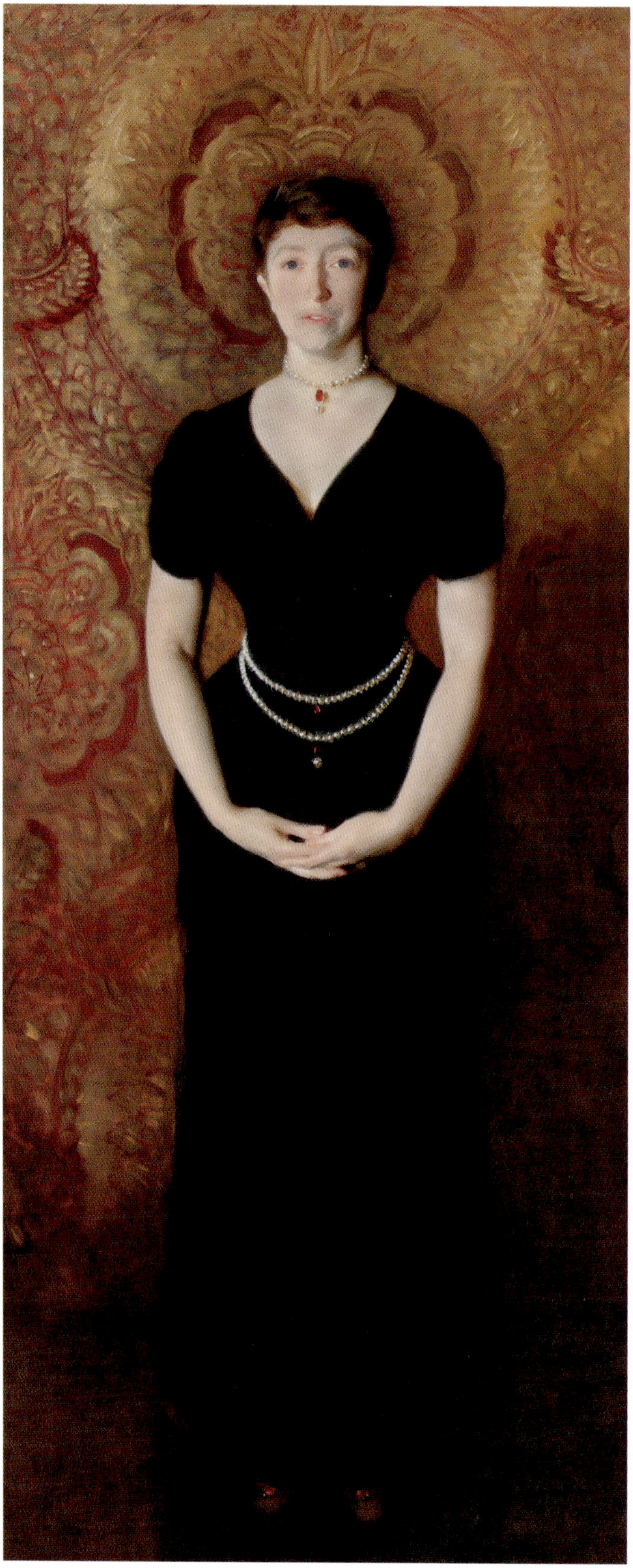

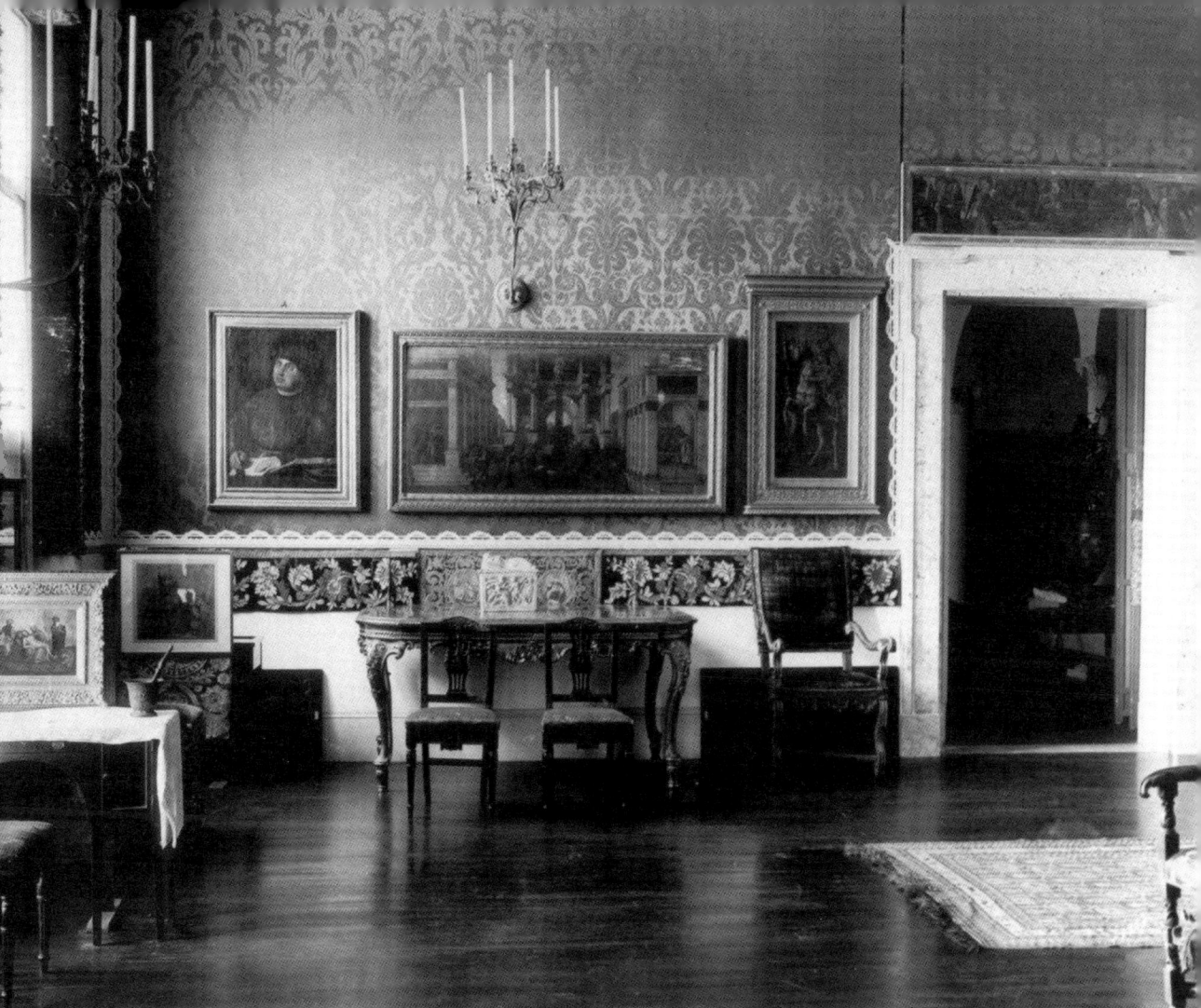

FIG. 38
The Raphael Room at the
Isabella Stewart Gardner
Museum, 1903.

Raphael, and his Rubens turned out to be by a follower rather than the master himself.) Titian's *Rape of Europa* arrived in Gardner's collection in 1896, raising concerns in Britain that the country was in danger of losing some of its finest works to America. Frick's and Morgan's purchases, in addition to Gardner's, led to a growing movement in European countries to enact patrimony laws protecting cultural assets.

Gardner was a trailblazer in art collecting, and her conversion of her private obsession into a public museum must have been a catalyst for Frick. In an exchange of letters to Frick in 1910, she thanks him for the roses he sent after visiting her and which she placed before a marble statue of a warrior—"weeping tears of red blood for his death."[17] She also sends him a photograph of John Singer Sargent's portrait of her, letting him know that the same photographer had completed a set of images of her collection; evidently, he was impressed by her art, as well as its documentation. A voracious acquisitor, Gardner amassed objects in a different way from Frick—like a magpie picking up swatches of fabric or objects of modest quality that appealed to her, alongside outright masterpieces. Her goal was to create an atmosphere that reflected

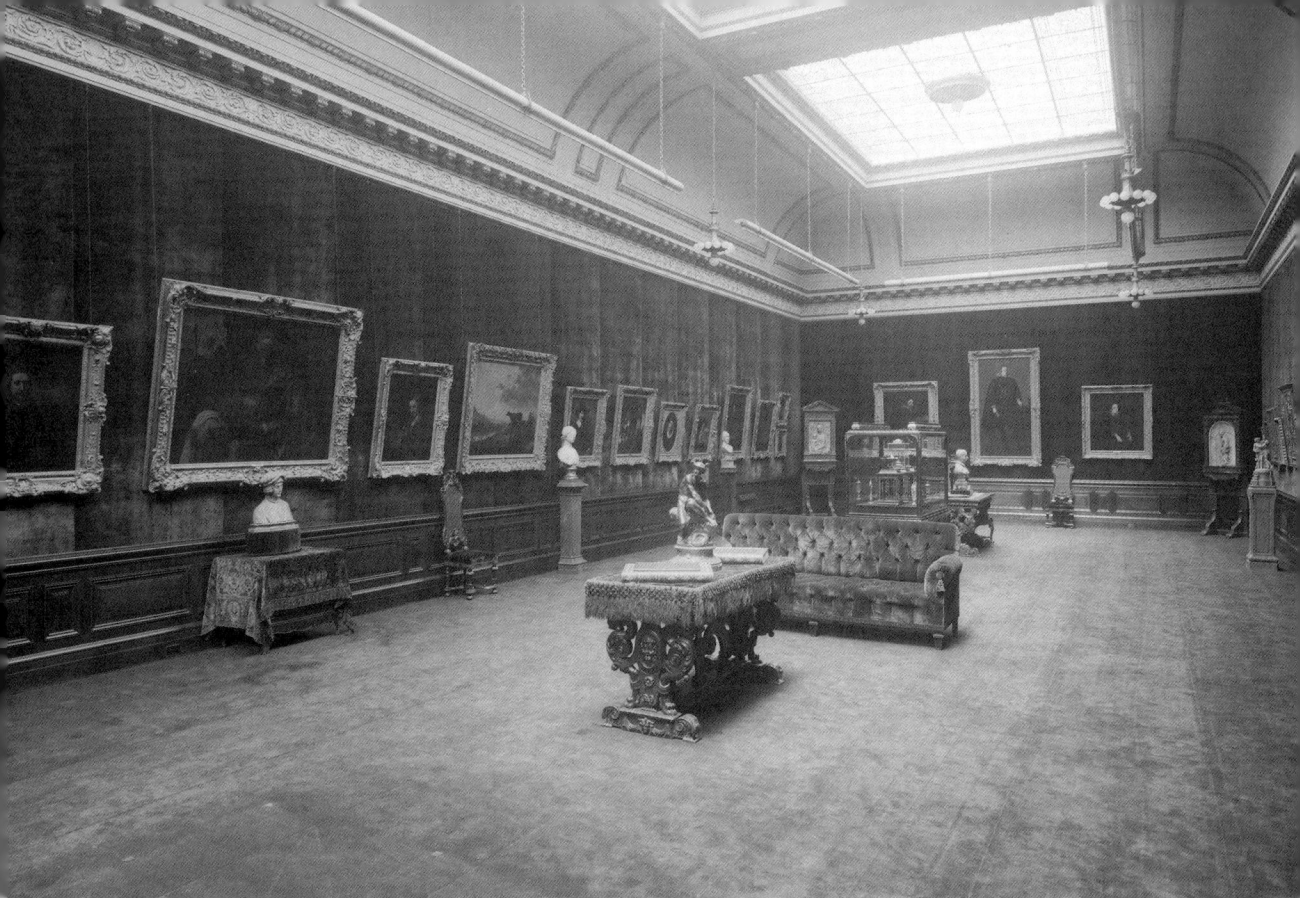

FIG. 39

Benjamin Altman's Picture
Gallery at 626 Fifth Avenue,
ca. 1910.

her tastes and interests, and she succeeded brilliantly. Hers was not the single-mindedness of Frick to acquire only works of the highest level of quality, but a selection of her very best alongside Frick's would put them on an equal footing.

Benjamin Altman turned a small dry-goods shop into one of the most successful department stores in New York. By the time of his death in 1913, he had assembled one of the foremost collections, and his bequest to the Metropolitan Museum of Art was one of its foundational donations of art. Like Frick, Altman began by collecting American and Barbizon paintings in the 1890s. By the turn of the century, he was attracted above all to seventeenth-century Dutch art. His purchases in 1905 of paintings by Rembrandt and Frans Hals established him as a collector. Further acquisitions from the famed Rodolphe Kann Collection of Paris in 1907 included three more Rembrandts, a Pieter de Hooch, and a Vermeer. The prickliness of Frick's rivalry with Altman can be seen in the latter's complaints when a dealer showed Frick a painting before he saw it. On the other hand, Frick was envious of Altman's ninety-foot Picture Gallery in the house one block south at 626 Fifth Avenue (fig. 39). He asked the dealer Roland Knoedler for its dimensions, and Knoedler later noted that the collector was "more anxious than ever to add to his present holdings something exceptional, fine."[18] When Frick's gallery was finished in 1914, at 96 feet long and 33½ feet wide it was the largest private art gallery in New York.

An important collector whom Frick knew well professionally was John G. Johnson, the Philadelphia corporate lawyer who successfully defended him in his lawsuit against Carnegie. Like Frick, Johnson began collecting contemporary art in the late 1870s and '80s, including more progressive artists such as Edouard Manet and Gustave Courbet; by 1892, he switched his focus to Old Masters. He later wrote that "private collectors, in the end, find it necessary to discard the paintings which, in early years, filled them with satisfaction."[19] As Johnson began to devote himself to Old Masters, he favored early Italian Renaissance, as well as Flemish and Dutch. His large *Crucifixion with the Virgin and Saint John the Evangelist* (ca. 1460) by Rogier van der Weyden (now in the Philadelphia Museum of Art) is one of the greatest Flemish paintings in America. Other northern European paintings by artists such as Pieter Brueghel the Younger and Jan van Eyck are distinguished. Italian works by artists such as Titian and French paintings by masters such as Nicolas Poussin added to the nearly thirteen hundred works that this voracious collector bequeathed to the Philadelphia Museum (fig. 40). Johnson was hitting his stride as a major collector in 1900, when he took Frick's side in the courtroom against Carnegie; his example must have inspired his fellow Pennsylvanian.

Like Altman and Johnson, Henry Havemeyer, who died in 1907, and his wife, Louisine, who outlived her husband by two decades, also bequeathed collections that provided a foundation for a museum in its early stages of growth. In the case of the Havemeyers, it was the Metropolitan Museum that benefited; it is particularly for French avant-garde art of the late nineteenth century that they are remembered. The artist Mary Cassatt counseled them to purchase works by Courbet, Manet, and Edgar Degas. The couple fared less well in the area of Old Master art, as many of these works, such as the eight Rembrandts they thought they had acquired, were later reattributed to lesser artists (though, in the long run, they acquired excellent earlier Dutch paintings). They found more success in the area of Spanish art of the sixteenth through eighteenth centuries, purchasing paintings by El Greco and Francisco Goya well before

FIG. 40
The John G. Johnson Collection at 506 South Broad Street, Philadelphia, ca. 1884.

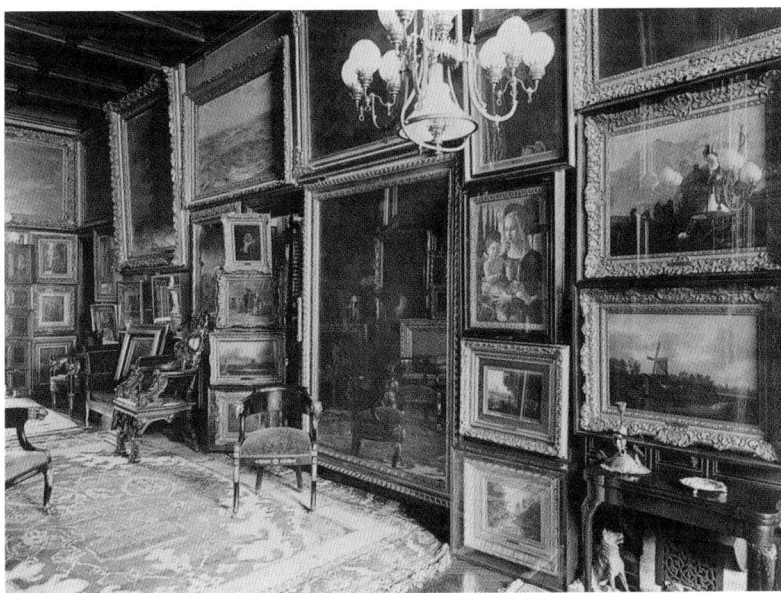

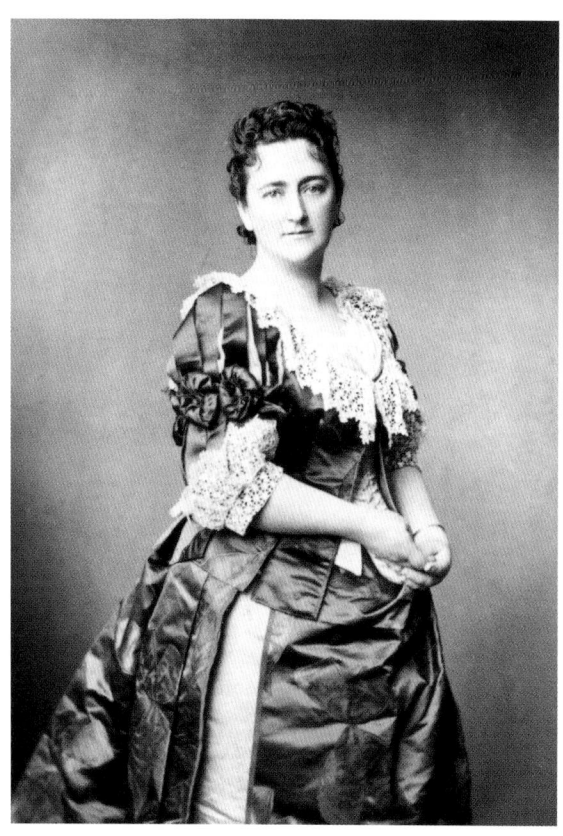

FIG. 41
Louisine Waldron Elder
Havemeyer in a Worth of
Paris dress, ca. 1889.

this taste spread to others in the United States. It may be that the Havemeyers inspired Frick, as El Greco and Goya were to become two of his favorite artists. Louisine recalls, "He [Frick] enjoyed coming to see my pictures and we would spend many a pleasant hour together in the library or the gallery" (fig. 41).[20]

Another formidable Philadelphia collector and fierce competitor of Frick's was Peter Widener, who made his fortune in transportation systems, such as cable and trolley cars, in a number of American cities. A friendship with Johnson inspired Widener to collect, and his willingness to pay large sums of money for major works of art got Frick's attention. In 1907, when Frick hesitated to acquire some Van Dyck portraits from the artist's Genoese period, Widener stepped in and bought them. Frick later interrogated the dealer about the terms of the purchase. Then, in 1911, Widener paid a record £100,000 for Rembrandt's *Mill* (ca. 1645–48, National Gallery of Art, Washington), a painting Frick and Altman had both coveted. Two years later, he paid the top price in the world ($565,000) for a painting by Raphael known as *The Small Cowper Madonna* (ca. 1505, National Gallery of Art, Washington). This period in which world-record prices rapidly succeeded one another— Morgan started the spree by spending $400,000 for Raphael's *Virgin and Child with Saints* (also known as the Colonna Altarpiece) (ca. 1507–8, Metropolitan Museum of Art)— encouraged Frick to match his competitors. When Frick paid a personal high of $475,000 in 1911 for the great Velázquez portrait of King Philip IV, he was comforted that the burgeoning market would support his price. Frick and the Widener family could easily communicate since Frick's mansion was built immediately adjacent to the 1909 house of the collector's son, George Widener, at 5 East 70th Street.

Another rival, Arabella Huntington, then the world's richest woman, lived at Fifth Avenue and East 57th Street, a few blocks north of Frick's rented Vanderbilt house. Her purchase in 1907 of Rembrandt's *Aristotle with a Bust of Homer* (1653)— famously acquired by the Metropolitan in 1961—gave notice to the world that she was a serious buyer of Old Masters. Ultimately, the eighteenth-century English portraits gathered in Pasadena, California, became the best-known feature of the Huntington Library, Art Museum, and Botanical Gardens. The most famous of all, Gainsborough's *Blue Boy* (1770), spent the night at the Frick mansion (after Frick's death), en route from London to the West Coast to be sold to Arabella's second husband, Collis (fig. 42). Five of the Gainsborough paintings Frick bought remain at 1 East 70th Street; he shared this taste with the Huntingtons and indeed with most of the top collectors of the time.

Collecting rivalry spurred Frick to buy the best and to increase his spending, satisfying his competitive spirit and validating the sums he expended. Between 1909 and 1912, the high bids made at auction by Duveen and record prices paid by Altman, Frick, Widener, and others became a regular feature on the front page of the *New York Times* and other newspapers. All this attention must have appealed to Frick's ego. He also enjoyed visiting fellow collectors and discussing his latest acquisitions with those knowledgeable about art and its market. They may have been rivals, but they were also the ones who best understood Frick's pursuit.

FIG. 42
Thomas Gainsborough,
The Blue Boy, 1770.

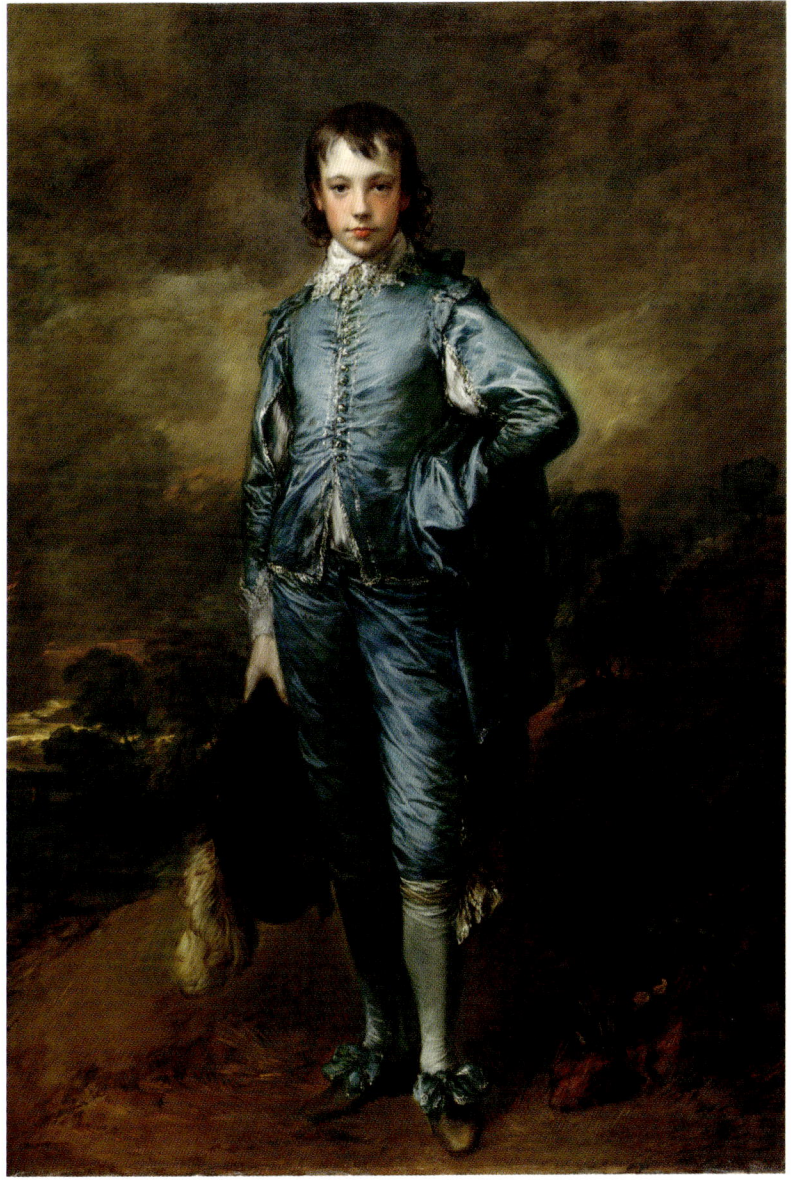

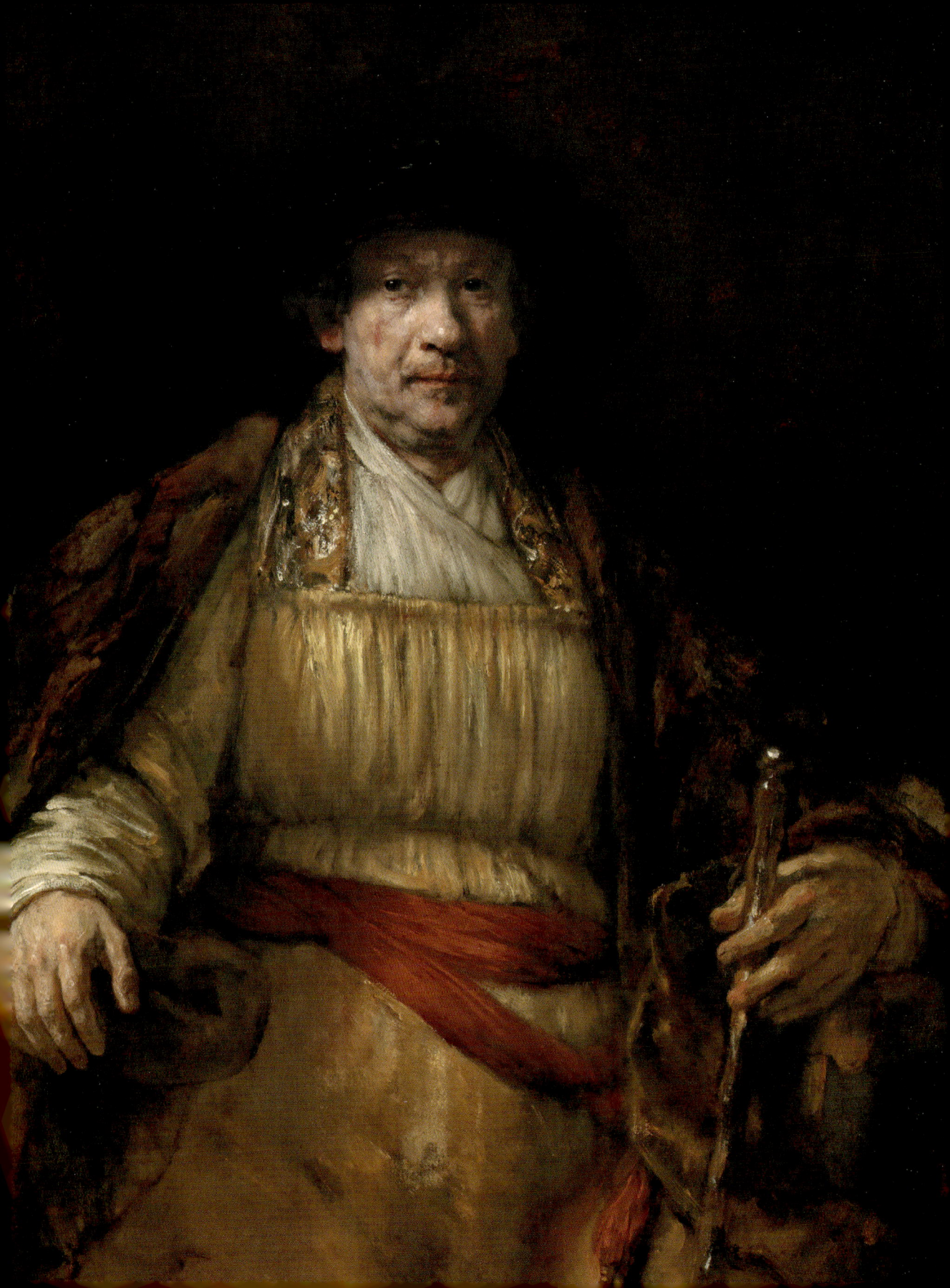

VI

CHARLES CARSTAIRS AND
M. KNOEDLER & CO.

Frick patronized several dealers in Pittsburgh, but by 1897, the year Knoedler established a branch in the city, he turned to that firm above all others. The late 1890s were critical in his development as a collector. With increased wealth, he was able to buy work by many of his favorite Barbizon School artists. As his collection grew, he began to refine it by returning a number of works to dealers for credit. This was also the moment his gradual transition in taste from contemporary to older art began. As mentioned above, in 1896, he traded two recently painted canvases, a Hetzel and an A. B. Wall, for Van Os's *Still Life*. It is not a distinguished work, and he did not take it to New York, but its purchase edged him toward earlier art. While he had bought some still lifes, such as a William Michael Harnett from 1890 (Frick Pittsburgh), it was not a genre that continued to appeal to him; no still lifes bought by Frick are in The Frick Collection today. In 1898, he made his first beginner's mistake: on the advice of respected scholars, he purchased a *Portrait of a Young Artist* that was attributed to Rembrandt but later thought, by the consensus of experts, to be by someone in the artist's circle (fig. 45).

The dealer Charles Carstairs helped guide Frick away from such mistakes and toward better acquisitions (fig. 44). Born in Philadelphia in 1865, Carstairs joined Knoedler in 1894 before transferring to Pittsburgh to establish its branch there. It was Carstairs who led the firm's shift in prioritization from contemporary Parisian painters to Old Master artists. With Roland Knoedler, he controlled the New York venue and was so successful that he was tapped to lead its London headquarters in 1908. Under his leadership, the firm dominated sales of British painting in America during the early years of the twentieth century.

Carstairs and Frick became close, personally and professionally. They enjoyed each other's company on the links, around the poker table, and traveling abroad. Frick relied on Carstairs's advice, and, more than anyone, the dealer influenced the collector's taste. In 1908, Frick wrote, "There is no-one whose judgment of the beautiful I have more confidence in than yours."[21]

FIG. 43
Rembrandt Harmensz.
van Rijn, *Self-Portrait*, 1658.

57

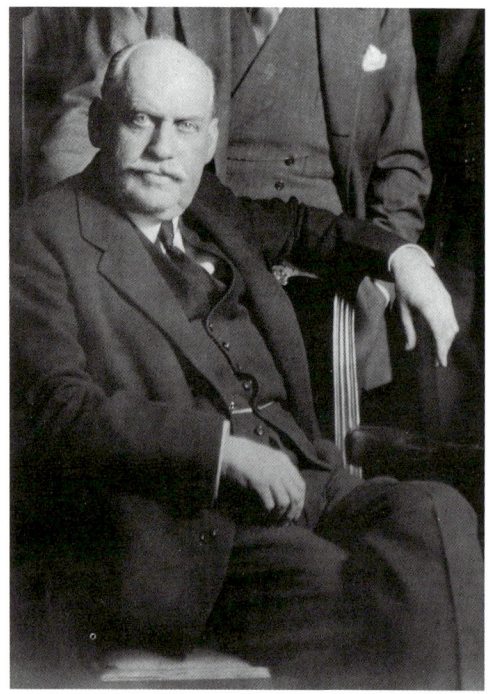

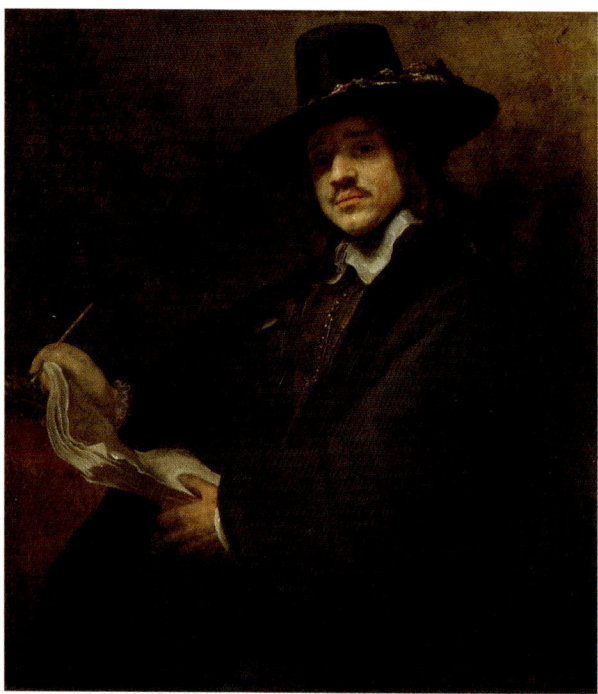

FIG. 44
Charles Carstairs of
Knoedler Partners, 1928.

FIG. 45
Follower of Rembrandt
Harmensz. van Rijn.
Portrait of a Young Artist,
1650s.

Carstairs steered Frick toward Old Masters and, over time, to better and better ones. Between 1900 and 1919, Frick returned more than a dozen Barbizon and Impressionist works for credit, eventually purchasing Dutch works by Vermeer, Salomon van Ruysdael, and Meindert Hobbema, as well as English paintings by Gainsborough and Joshua Reynolds. Information and trust were essential to their relationship. In a letter of October 29, 1895, that Frick wrote to the New York collector Thomas B. Clarke, he made clear how important research on works of art was to him: "I like to know all I can about the picture I purchase."[22] Carstairs took care to supply Frick with the art historical details his client required, as well as the records of the marketplace that satisfied his need to understand—and master—any financial transaction.

Nothing illustrates the complexity of this relationship better than the purchase of Rembrandt's *Self-Portrait*, one of the greatest paintings in The Frick Collection (fig. 43). When, in 1906, the Earl of Ilchester confronted steep death duties on accession to his title, he was forced to put this famous painting up for sale. The acting curator of European paintings at the Metropolitan Museum of Art, Roger Fry, tried to engage J. P. Morgan to bid on it. When Morgan hesitated, Carstairs saw an opening and contacted Frick: while holding off other interested parties and negotiating the price among his partners and Frick, Carstairs wrote his client a critical letter:

> I regret having been unsuccessful in arranging the purchase of the Rembrandt for you at $200,000. [It was now $225,000.] I worked hard but my persuasive powers were unavailing. I must however tell you that

it was not because I was satisfied with the profit, but simply my great desire that you should possess this matchless masterpiece . . . I have pictured it in your gallery since first beginning negotiations for it over four months ago.[23]

Carstairs goes on to justify the price, citing lesser examples compared to the Rembrandt painted when the artist was "at the zenith of his powers [in] 1658," writing, "It is most powerful, grand, monumental." He quotes the opinion of the expert Wilhelm von Bode and compares its price and size to other works cited in publications Frick could access. He relates the financial involvement at the gallery and raises the threat of a potential competitor. Finally, he gives Frick a deadline and concludes, "If you could only see the picture over your mantel dominating the entire gallery just as you dominate those you come into contact with, you wouldn't let it pass for $500,000. I can't imagine a more suitable picture for you."[24] Carstairs used every argument he could think of to persuade Frick, backing them up with facts, figures, expertise, and as much flattery as he could get away with; in the end, he succeeded. Frick bought the painting, but he insisted on trading in *The Last Gleanings* (Huntington Art Museum, San Marino) by Breton for a credit of $25,000, which brought the Rembrandt price down to what he wanted to pay. Frick's approach of gathering information and expertise, as well as negotiation on price, for a work of art was very much like the acquisition of a railroad company, the current focus of his business endeavors. Frick and Carstairs were evenly matched, each getting what he wanted out of the deal, a transaction made possible by affection and trust. In 1970, the Knoedler gallery moved to 19 East 70th Street, on the same block as The Frick Collection, and remained there for forty-one years; by this point, the relationship of the collection and the gallery was historic rather than active, but the location had symbolic import.

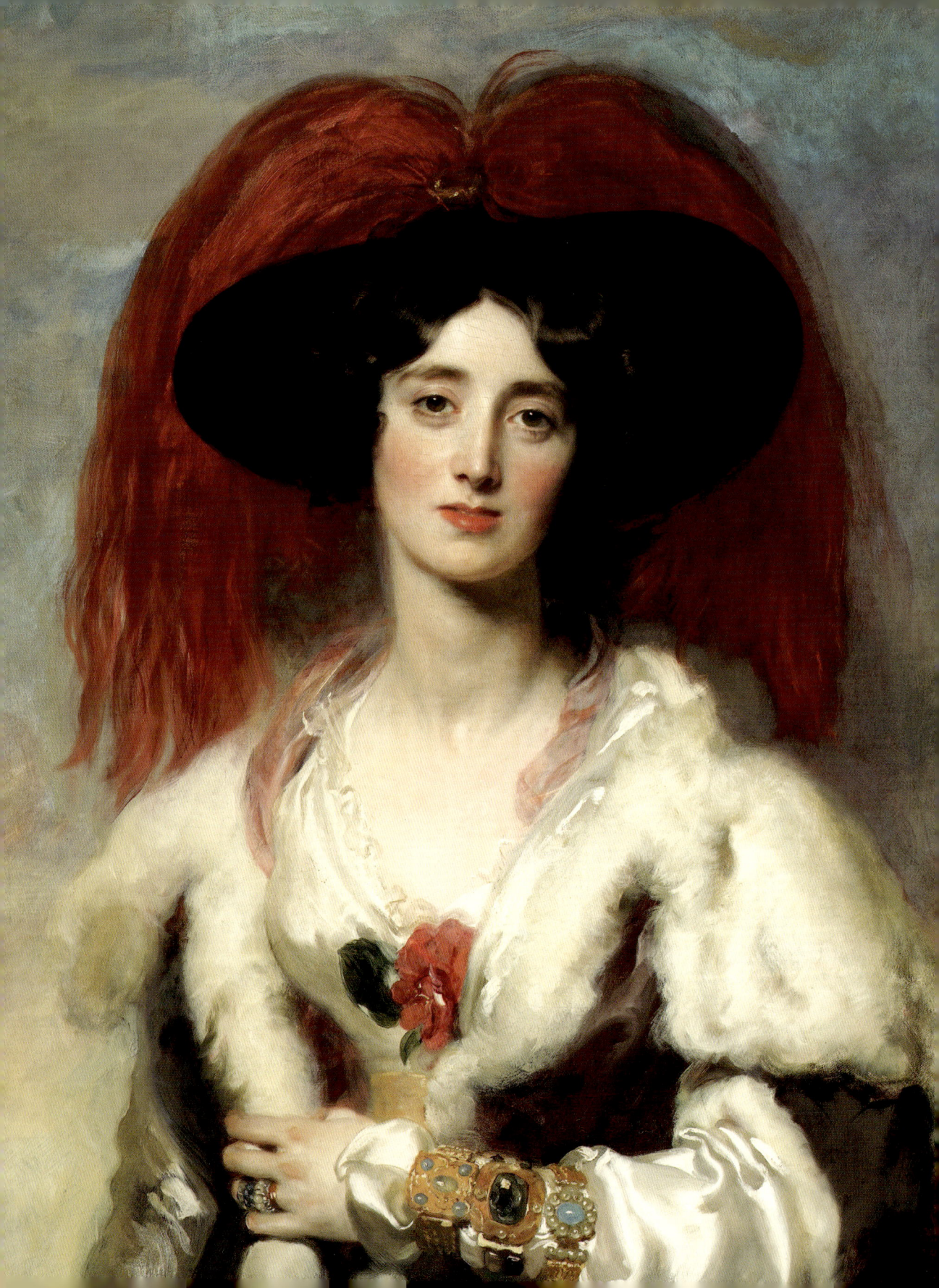

VII

COLLECTING PAINTINGS,
1900–1911

Frick's focus on Old Master paintings began conventionally. He bought subjects he liked, rarely straying from accepted norms of taste. The Aelbert Cuyp *Cows and a Herdsman by a River* (after 1650) he acquired in 1902—depicting a cow standing above a herd seated in an expansive landscape—was virtually identical to the composition of *Pasture in Normandy* (1850s) by Troyon that he bought three years before, but the Cuyp dated to two centuries earlier. Other landscapes by more esteemed artists, such as Hobbema and Ruysdael, entered his collection over the next several years. While his focus shifted to the art of earlier periods, he did not completely abandon the contemporary field. In 1904, he acquired Daubigny's *Dieppe* (1877) and in 1906 Corot's *Lake* (fig. 47). Not surprisingly, the subjects of these Barbizon School artists were landscapes, Frick's long-standing favorite.

Where Frick showed zeal was in his selection of portraits. Carstairs knew his client's fondness for images of attractive women; at the same time, the dealer was maneuvering his customers toward eighteenth- and early nineteenth-century British art. Satisfying both the client's and dealer's wishes was a picture by George Romney that depicted the notorious beauty Emma Hart, later Lady Hamilton, the wife of Sir William Hamilton and mistress of Lord Horatio Nelson, as an allegory of nature (fig. 48). Of the portraits of Hart in the guise of characters from history and myth or in various "attitudes" (aesthetic poses), Frick chose an especially fresh rendering. It was the first of some sixty paintings Romney made of Hart as his muse. The same year, 1904, Frick acquired Thomas Lawrence's *Julia, Lady Peel*, a spirited portrait of the flamboyantly dressed wife of British prime minister Sir Robert Peel (fig. 46). Both famous women have been well served by their portraitists; Frick clearly admired the brilliant colors that animate the subjects, as well as the beauty of the sitters.

Over the course of the next year, between 1905 and 1906, Frick turned to male portraits of a soberer nature. The portrait by the great Venetian painter Titian of his equally famous literary counterpart Pietro Aretino is a somber study in brown and gold (fig. 49). Controversy around this man of letters did not prevent the awarding

FIG. 46
Thomas Lawrence, *Julia, Lady Peel*, 1827.

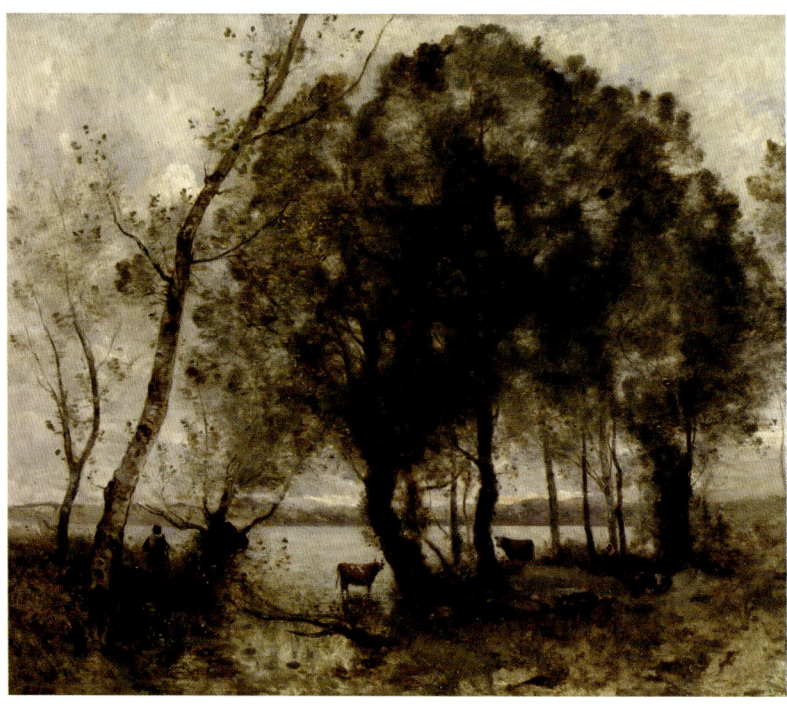

FIG. 47
Jean-Baptiste-Camille
Corot, *The Lake*, 1861.

FIG. 48
George Romney, *Emma
Hart, Later Lady Hamilton,
as "Nature,"* 1782.

of many honors, such as the gold chain he wears. Among those bestowing chains on the writer were King Francis I of France and Cardinal Ippolito de' Medici. The chain in the portrait—possibly from Empress Isabella of Portugal, which he received in 1537, around the time he sat for this portrait—may be the most significant one. Titian captures Aretino's strength of character, which perhaps is what appealed to Frick. In proposing that this would fill out the display, Carstairs took advantage of the empty space in the Vanderbilt mansion. Frick had just occupied the house in October 1905, and the dealer sent the portrait there directly from London. Frick paid $90,000.

In the case of another portrait bought that year, Frick encountered one of the pitfalls of collecting internationally. He was offered a work by the painter known as El Greco, who was born in Crete, trained in Italy, and flourished and found fame in Spain. The canvas, which had languished in Spain in the sacristy of Valladolid Cathedral and bore the title *Cardinal Quiroga*, was thought to be the likeness of a contemporary of the artist rather than the image of the stern church father St. Jerome, as was later correctly recognized. Translator of the Bible into Latin, Jerome presses down on the volume with his fingertips as he eyes us admonishingly. The artist's typically elongated forms, intense expression, and sensual colors combine to make this the finest of several versions (fig. 50).

The El Greco painting became famous when Spanish newspapers denounced its sale for depriving the country of a great work of art. In response to the perceived loss to the nation, patrimony laws were subsequently passed to protect the country's artistic heritage from being transported unchallenged to foreign buyers. Carstairs gave the painting a place of honor in the Vanderbilt mansion that Frick was poised

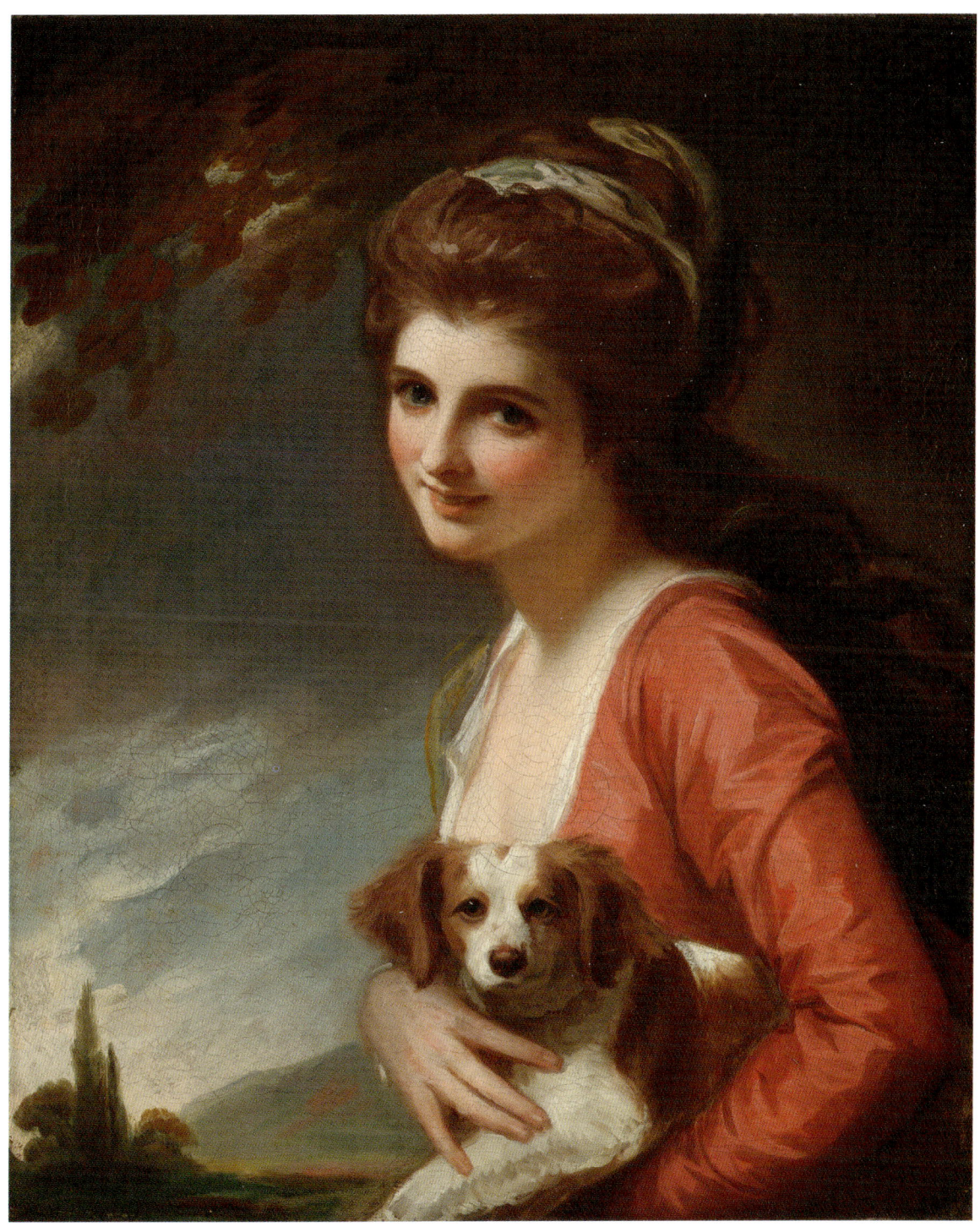

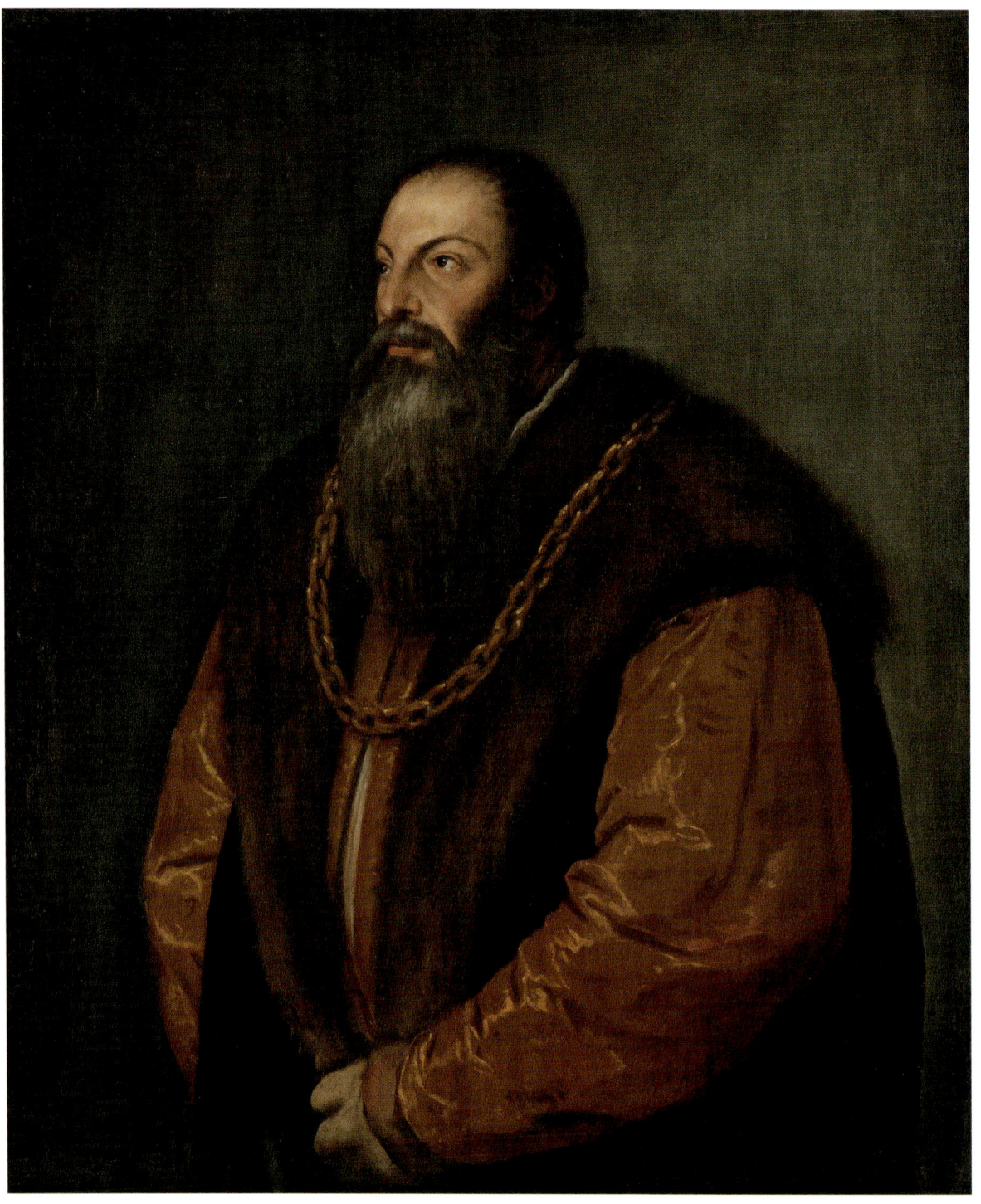

to occupy. One of Knoedler's men reported to Carstairs: "The Grecho [*sic*] was hung over the mantelpiece instead of the Rembrandt [*Portrait of a Young Artist*, now attributed to a follower of the artist]."[25] Since 1914, the *St. Jerome* has hung prominently over the fireplace in the Living Hall at 1 East 70th Street, a reminder of Frick's coup in acquiring it.

The purchase of Rembrandt's *Self-Portrait* in 1906—on which Carstairs had written so persuasively to Frick—signaled that Frick was moving up to the highest level of quality. The Van Dyck portraits he acquired in 1909 confirmed this new stature. His portraits of Frans Snyders and Margareta de Vos are two of the earliest and finest works by the artist who became the most sought-after portraitist in seventeenth-century Europe (figs. 51, 52). Majestic columns and sweeping landscapes give the impression of an aristocratic setting, though the couple were part of Van Dyck's artistic circle in Antwerp. The artist captures his friends' lively expressions, painting their costumes with flair. Van Dyck would become one of Frick's favorites. The acquisition of the two portraits also represents another interest

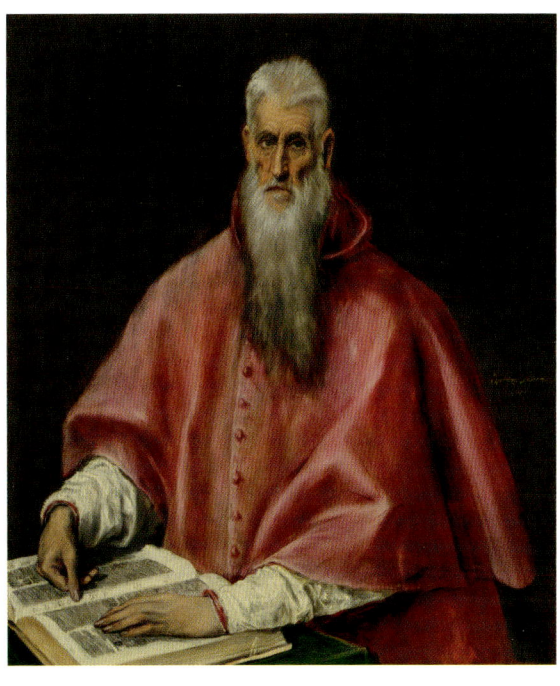

of Frick's: reuniting couples. After the paintings were auctioned from the famous Orléans collection in Paris in 1793, they parted ways, going into two different English noble collections, those of the Earl of Carlisle and the Earl of Warwick. Through Knoedler, Frick brought the pair together again, an exercise he repeated with two portraits by Hals (though as it turned out, they were unrelated). Frick went on to acquire six more Van Dyck portraits over the next decade, representing later phases of the painter's career, when he moved to Genoa and then to London.

One of the greatest, if most enigmatic, pictures Frick bought arrived without help from Knoedler, as the collector began to source his works in other ways. The English art critic Roger Fry, no longer employed by the Metropolitan Museum of Art, became aware that Rembrandt's *Polish Rider* could be available for sale (fig. 53). In a haunting landscape, a Polish cavalryman, identified by characteristic costume and weapons, rides at twilight into unknown territory. Owned by Count Zdzisław Tarnowski in Poland, the canvas had been seen by few until a major Rembrandt exhibition in Amsterdam in 1898 brought it out of hiding. Frick put his faith in Fry's estimation of its quality and condition and, sight unseen, paid $308,651.25, including a commission to Fry—more than he had ever previously spent on a work of art. Fortunately for all concerned, his telegrammed response to the art expert was the single word: "Enchanted." (Fry later lost Frick's confidence when he recommended a painting that the collector recognized as of lesser quality. After that, he rarely relied on art historians for advice.)

The Polish Rider generated enormous interest and front-page newspaper headlines when Frick purchased it. The *New York Times* announced on July 3: "The magnificent Rembrandt 'The Polish Rider,' which Henry C Frick has purchased . . .

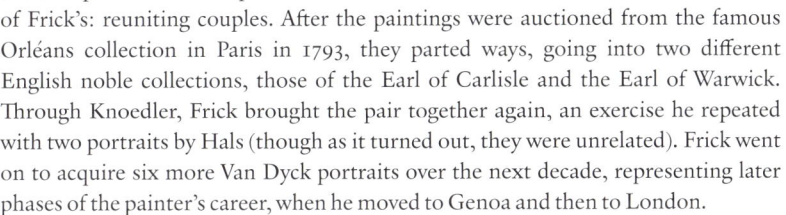

FIG. 49
Titian (Tiziano Vecellio),
Pietro Aretino, ca. 1537.

FIG. 50
El Greco (Doménikos Theotokópoulos),
St. Jerome, ca. 1590–1600.

FOLLOWING PAGES
FIG. 51
Anthony van Dyck,
Frans Snyders, ca. 1620.

FIG. 52
Anthony van Dyck,
Margareta de Vos, ca. 1620.

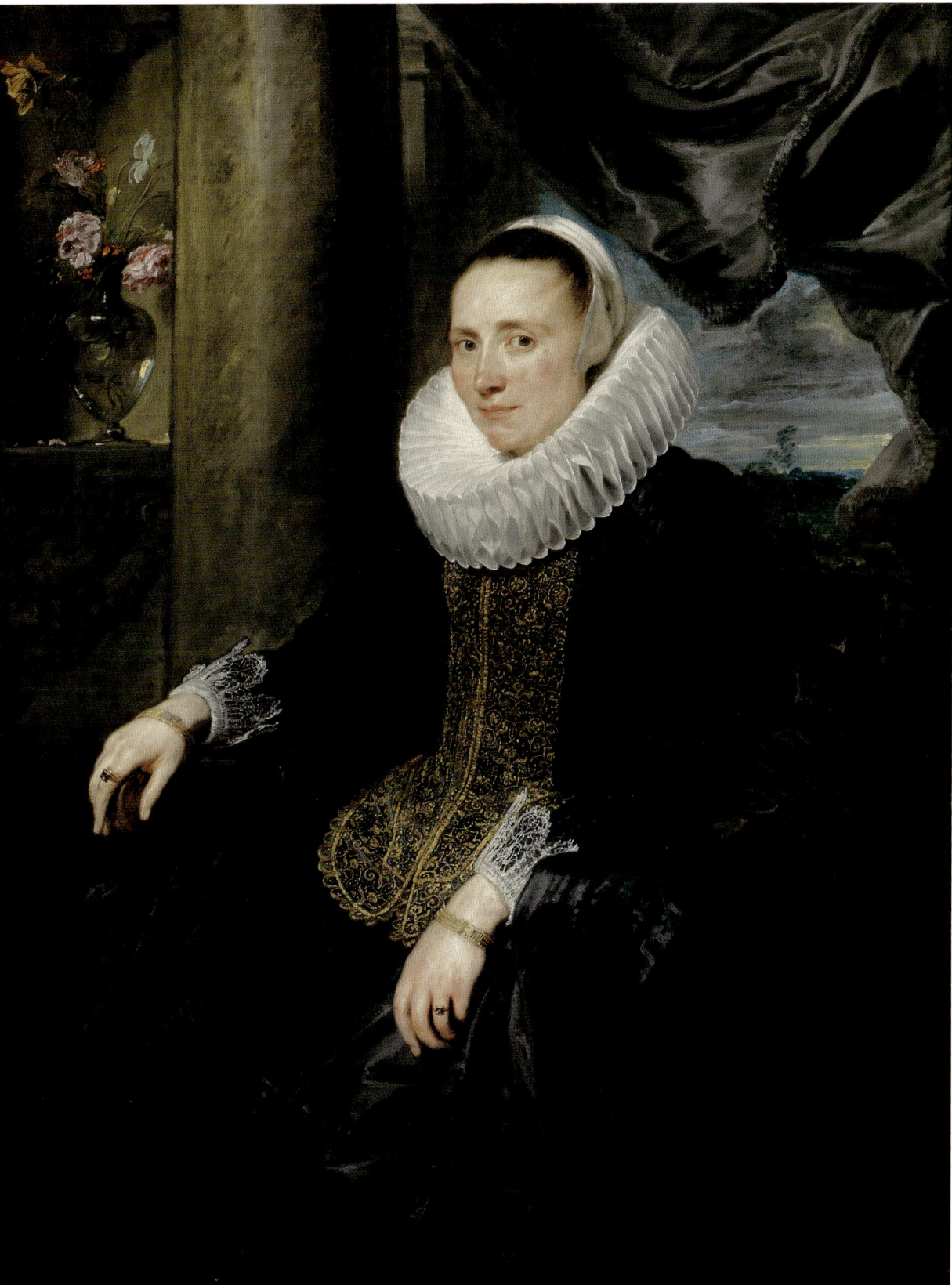

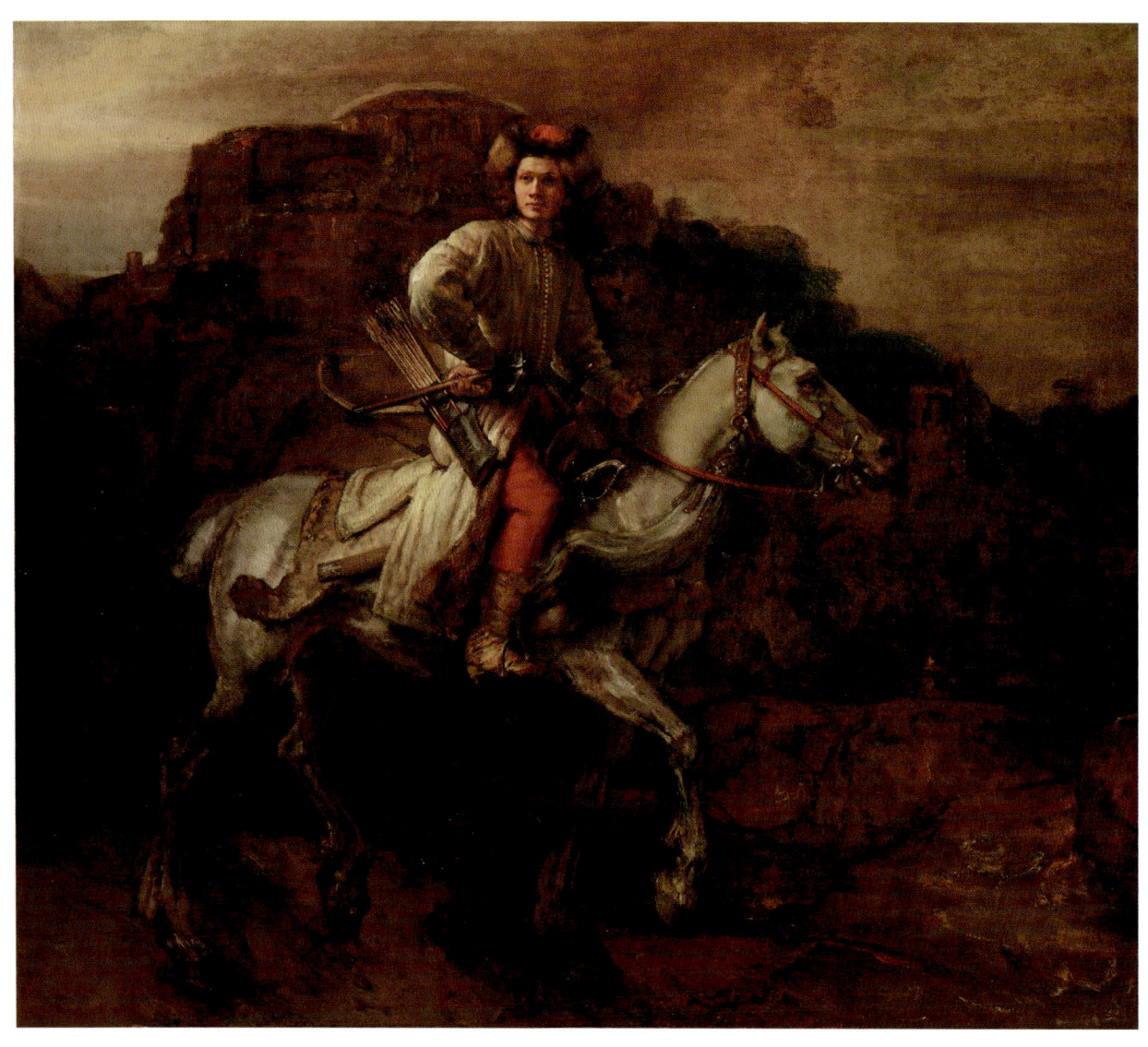

FIG. 53
Rembrandt Harmensz.
van Rijn, *The Polish Rider*,
ca. 1655.

will probably soon be in New York, and Londoners have been having a last opportunity to look at it at the Carfax gallery."[26] He was gratified that it became the centerpiece of an exhibition of his collection at the Boston Museum of Fine Arts in 1910. Although it is unquestionably one of the great paintings of the seventeenth century, its attribution has been doubted by some. One member of the Rembrandt Research Project, a group of Dutch scholars and conservators who sought to clarify what was by the master and what was not, rejected it as Rembrandt's in an article of 1984. In 2014, the Research group unequivocally affirmed it as by the master. Beyond its artistic importance, its historic significance is such that in 2022–23 the Frick lent it back to the Łazienki Palace in Warsaw, where it had hung in the eighteenth century, when it belonged to Stanisław August Poniatowski, the last king of Poland.

Like many Americans, notably Henry Huntington, Frick fancied grand British portraiture, possibly because it could remedy the lack of ancestral portraits in a young country. In the previous decade, he had bought smaller paintings by Reynolds, Romney, and Gainsborough. In 1911, he purchased the eight-foot-high canvas of the Hon. Frances Duncombe, the first of several full-length portraits to enter his home (fig. 55). Posed out of doors in an ideal, classicizing landscape, the woman is luxuriously clothed in rich satins that recall the style of an earlier portraitist, Van Dyck. These characteristics were a winning combination for Frick, who, as mentioned above, eventually owned eight Van Dycks and seven Gainsboroughs. Ironically, the Bouverie family—with whom the orphaned Frances Duncombe lived until her marriage—being of mercantile background and only recently ennobled, acquired Van Dyck portraits of other families to give an appearance of long standing, much as the nouveau riche, such as Frick, who sought an instant pedigree through portraits from an earlier era.

FIG. 54
Diego Rodriguez de Silva y Velázquez, *King Philip IV of Spain*, 1644.

The same year, 1911, Frick bought two of his greatest paintings. The Spaniard Diego Rodríquez de Silva y Velázquez's masterful technique earned him the reputation of a "painter's painter." As *pintor del rey* (king's painter), Velázquez was constrained to a consistent rendering of the famous Habsburg jaw and facial features in all his images of Philip IV (fig. 54). Yet, the circumstances of the commission of *King Philip IV of Spain* (1644) gave the artist unusual freedom in his representation of the royal garb. In a makeshift studio at Fraga, near the battle the king had just won against the French at Lérida, Velázquez began this portrait of the king dressed in the rose and silver-embroidered costume worn in the military skirmish. Remarkable facility with brushwork, suggesting light flickering over the metallic threads, was a signature of his artistic brilliance; such effects entranced Impressionist painters two centuries later and inspired their free application of color. As described above, this was one of Frick's costlier

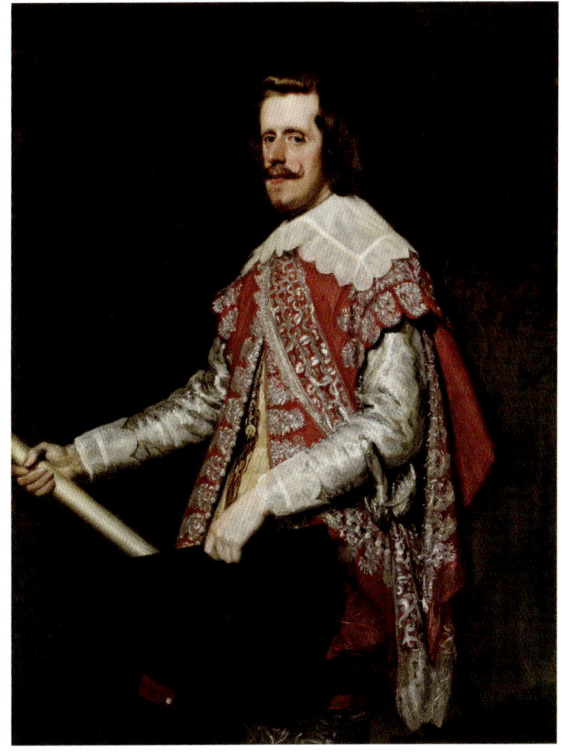

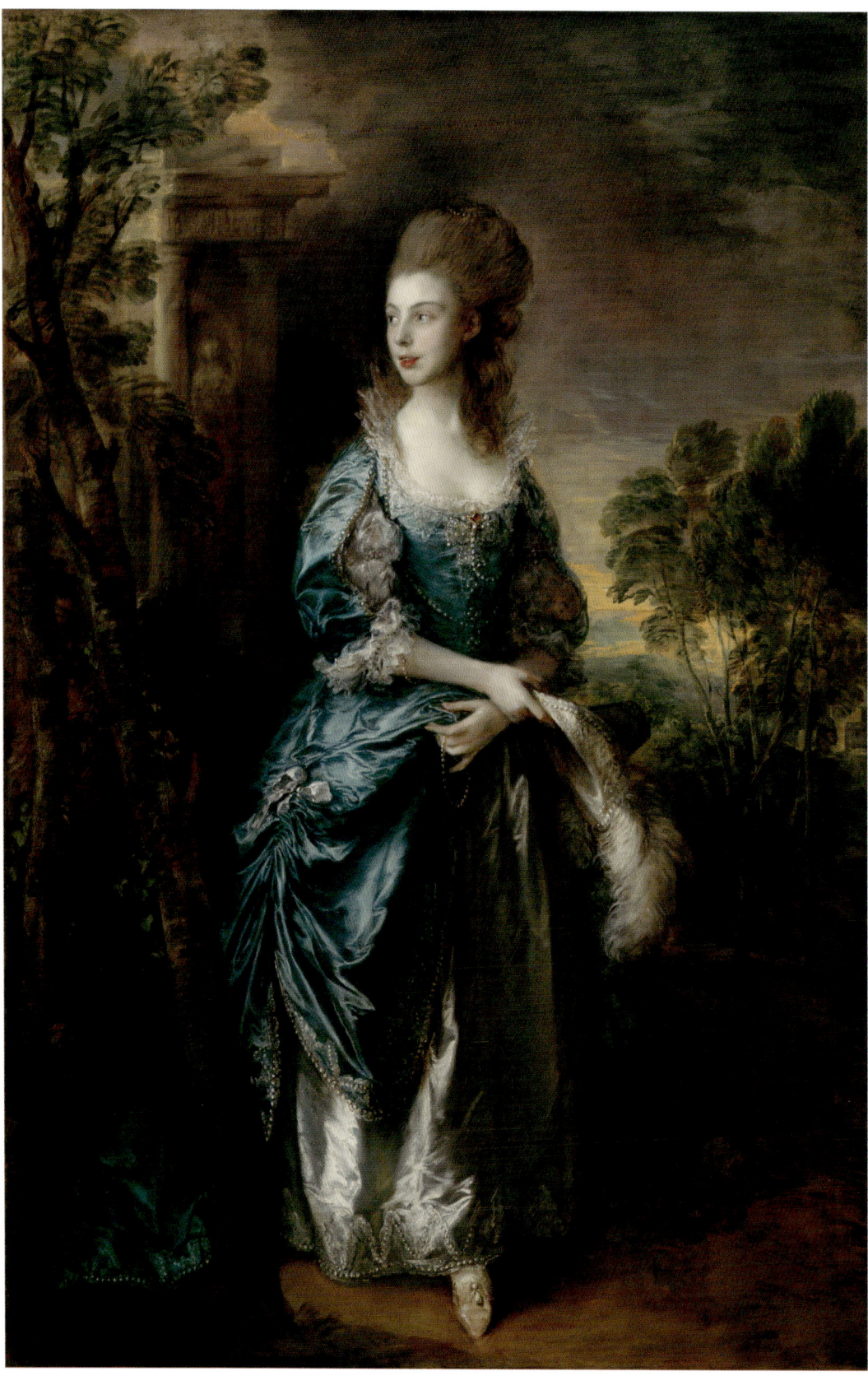

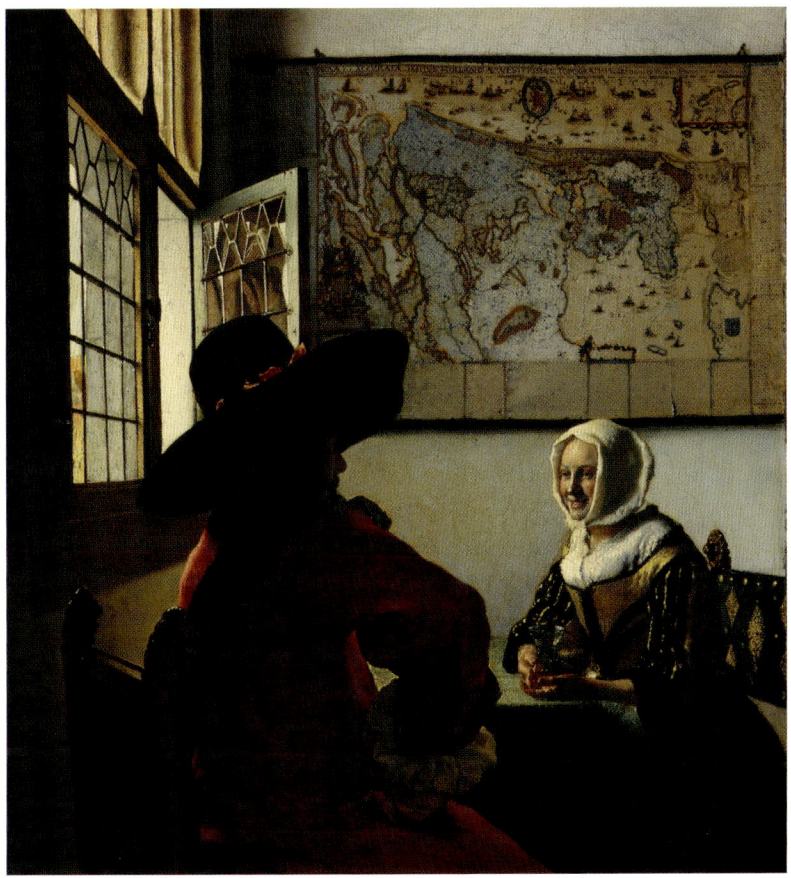

single acquisitions, but he was determined to acquire the finest works he could afford; his choices have stood the test of time, and they continue to be acknowledged as constituting one of the best collections of its kind ever assembled.

The other great painting Frick bought that year was Vermeer's *Officer and Laughing Girl* (fig. 56). It was not his first by this master, of whom only around thirty-five extant paintings are thought to be actually from his hand. Ten years earlier, Frick had purchased *Girl Interrupted at Her Music* (ca. 1658–59) for roughly one-tenth the asking price of this acquisition, $225,000. Ever since the seventeenth-century Dutch master had been rediscovered in the late nineteenth century, prices for his scarce pictures had risen rapidly. Frick must have recognized that the quality of *Officer and Laughing Girl* exceeded that of his other one. Indeed, the 2023–24 retrospective at the Rijksmuseum in Amsterdam, where the three Frick Vermeers were publicly shown outside of their New York home for the first time in a century, confirmed its importance as one of the first works of his mature style. Vermeer's use of light to depict the surfaces of windowpane, cloth, and parchment and the intriguing ambiguity of the couple's interaction make his interior scenes a world of their own. Frick's eye appreciated the brilliance of what he saw, and his mind registered the significance of the work of art.

FIG. 55
Thomas Gainsborough,
The Hon. Frances Duncombe,
ca. 1777.

FIG. 56
Johannes Vermeer, *Officer
and Laughing Girl*, ca. 1657.

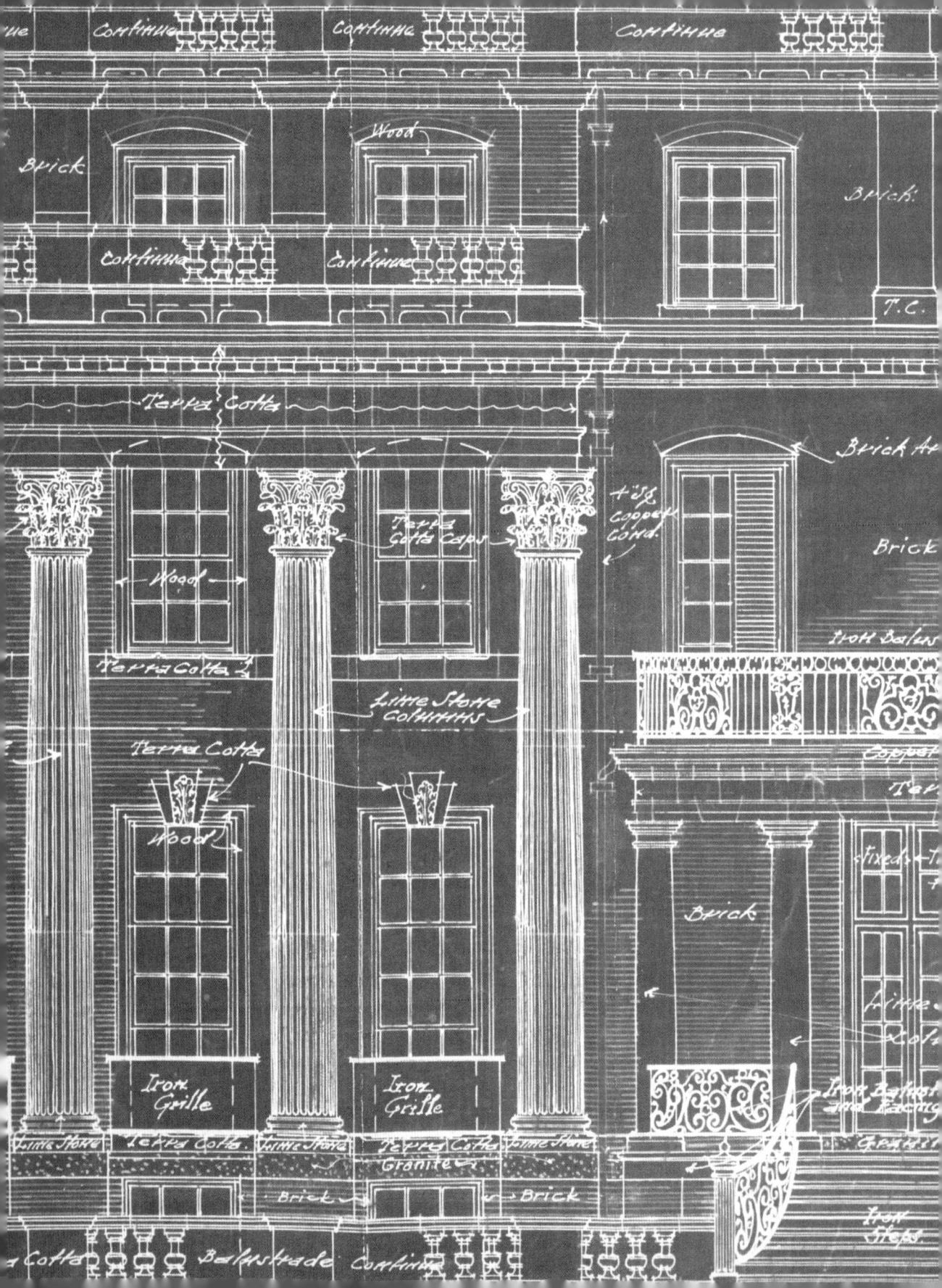

VIII

EAST COAST HOUSES

EAGLE ROCK,
THE FRICKS' SUMMER HOME

While Henry and Adelaide Frick were living in rented space in New York, first in a hotel and then in the Vanderbilt house, they enjoyed spending part of their summers on Boston's North Shore, an area introduced to them by the artist Joseph Woodwell and his wife. Here, too, the Fricks began by renting a place for several years, in this case in the town of Pride's Crossing. They took to the beautiful coastline and, in 1902, acquired land overlooking the sea. In 1906, the Little & Browne Architects finished a 104-room house, which the couple named Eagle Rock (fig. 57). To decorate their Georgian-style summerhouse, they engaged the firm Cottier & Co. Frick insisted that the interiors "be made of the best materials." "We want it severely plain," he said.[27] In October 1906, however, Frick turned to Duveen for furnishings, buying decorative objects and furniture, most of modest value, as well as some of higher quality, such as important groups of Chinese porcelain. Frick continued to contract with Duveen to fill his house with furniture, spending $138,000 in 1913. In 1916, a large group of furniture he bought was split, with the more important pieces going to New York and the lesser to Pride's Crossing.

This pattern of saving the best furniture for New York and sending that of lesser quality to the Massachusetts home held true for paintings, too. Yet, until the New York house was finished, Frick often had paintings brought for him to live with at Eagle Rock (fig. 58). When Carstairs showed him Vermeer's *Officer and Laughing Girl* in May 1911, Frick had it shipped to his country house. After he bought the painting, however, it found a permanent spot in the New York residence. While most of his paintings accumulated in the Vanderbilt mansion until 1914, in the summertime, Frick's private railroad car, the Westmoreland, transported many of them to Eagle Rock for the family to enjoy (fig. 59).

A number of eighteenth-century English paintings found their way to this Georgian-style house. Some good portraits by Reynolds and Gainsborough, for

FIG. 57
Little & Browne Architects, detail of elevation of garden front, Eagle Rock, Pride's Crossing, Massachusetts, 1904.

example, were purchased, the best of them eventually finding a home in New York, with the second tier remaining in Massachusetts. After Helen Clay inherited them, she moved many to Clayton. Gainsborough's portrait of Sir Richard Brinsley Sheridan (ca. 1785) was one of the last Frick bought by the artist, in 1919, and it stayed at Eagle Rock until Helen Clay brought it to Pittsburgh. Hogarth's *Portrait of Honorable Captain John Hamilton* (ca. 1740) followed the same pattern; Helen Clay took it to Pittsburgh in 1952. In 1914, Frick bought a much better Hogarth, *Miss Mary Edwards* (1742), a portrait of the richest woman in England and the artist's principal patron. It stayed in New York. In the case of Arthur Devis's large group portrait *Sir Joshua Vanneck and His Family* (1752), a fine work by this specialist in "conversation pieces"—informal group portraits—perhaps it stayed at Eagle Rock because it fit so well over a chimneypiece and its outdoor country setting suited Eagle Rock better than a city location. (It, too, is now in Pittsburgh.)

Though of ample quality to be shown in New York, a pair of Francis Cotes's best portrait paintings—of Sir Griffith Boynton (1768) and Lady Boynton (1769)—stayed with the family. Helen Clay lent them to the Frick for its public opening in 1935. A photograph of an interior at Eagle Rock (fig. 60) shows one of the Cotes portraits and the Devis conversation piece, alongside porcelains purchased from the Morgan collections and furniture of various periods, including an excellent writing table (ca. 1780) by Martin Carlin that is now in Pittsburgh. Another exception was Murillo's *Self-Portrait* (fig. 61). This was Frick's first Spanish Old Master picture, and he bought it at a moment when works from this country were rarely collected in the United States. A handsome and significant work, the Murillo stayed in the summer home. Perhaps Frick simply liked the way it looked at Eagle Rock. Gifted

FIG. 58
Garden facade at Eagle Rock, ca. 1910.

FIG. 59
Gathering of friends on the observation deck of the Westmoreland railcar, ca. 1915.

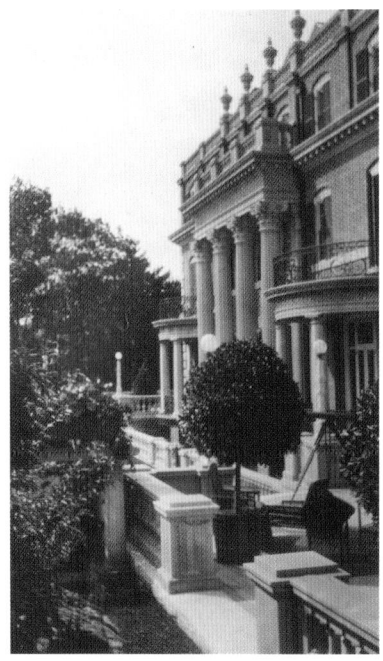

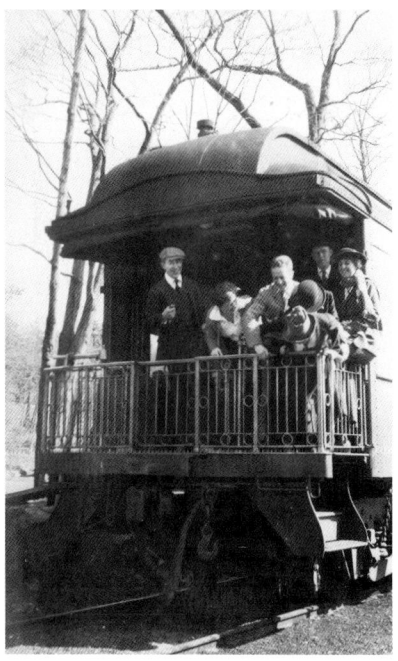

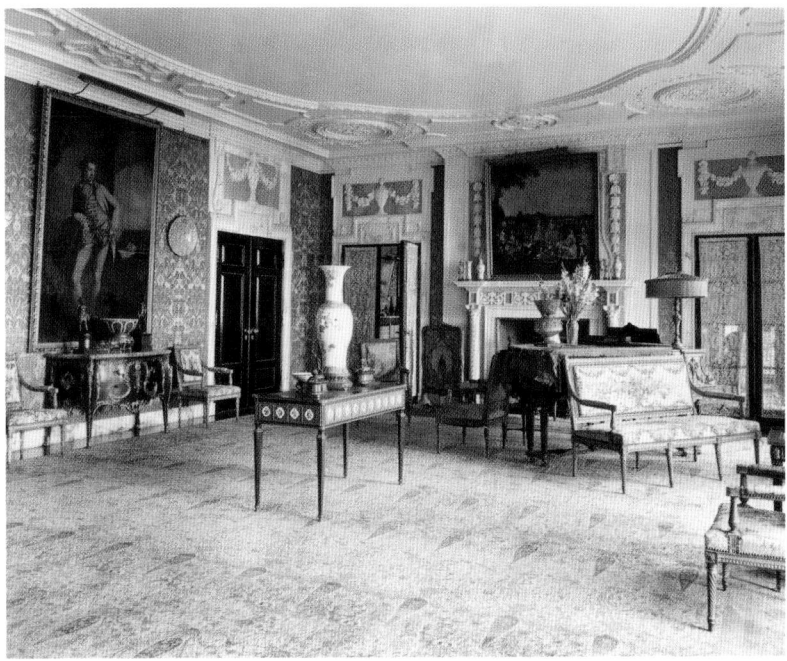

FIG. 60
The drawing room at Eagle
Rock, before 1938, show-
ing, on the left, Francis
Cotes's *Sir Griffith Boynton*
(1768) and, above the
mantelpiece, Arthur Devis's
*Sir Joshua Vanneck and His
Family* (1752).

to the Frick by Dr. and Mrs. Henry Clay Frick II in 2014, it is one of only two self-portraits by the artist.

1 EAST 70TH STREET, THE FRICK MANSION

In 1907, after searching for a site in Manhattan on which to build a house, Frick settled on a parcel of land on Fifth Avenue between East 70th and East 71st Streets. During this decade, men of new wealth, like him, were moving to the northern section of this fabled avenue. Carnegie built his house on East 90th Street, so far north that it was described as "only one remove from goatville."[28] The attraction of the lot for Frick was its size, stretching from one street to the next and well into the block. Yet it came with a caveat: it already had a substantial building on it, the Lenox Library. The original owner, James Lenox, had amassed one of the foremost book and art collections in the city before he died in 1880, and his heirs decided to transfer the collection to the New York Public Library, then in formation. Thus, before he could build, Frick had to wait until construction of the public library was complete and the Lenox books moved. Once he took title to the house, he offered to move the empty Lenox building, at his expense, to Central Park to serve as the Department of Parks administration facility. When citizens objected to the proposed incursion on public land, Frick had the building demolished. At Carstairs's urging, Frick hired Thomas Hastings of Carrère & Hastings, the architectural firm that had just finished the new public library at Fifth Avenue and East 42nd Street.

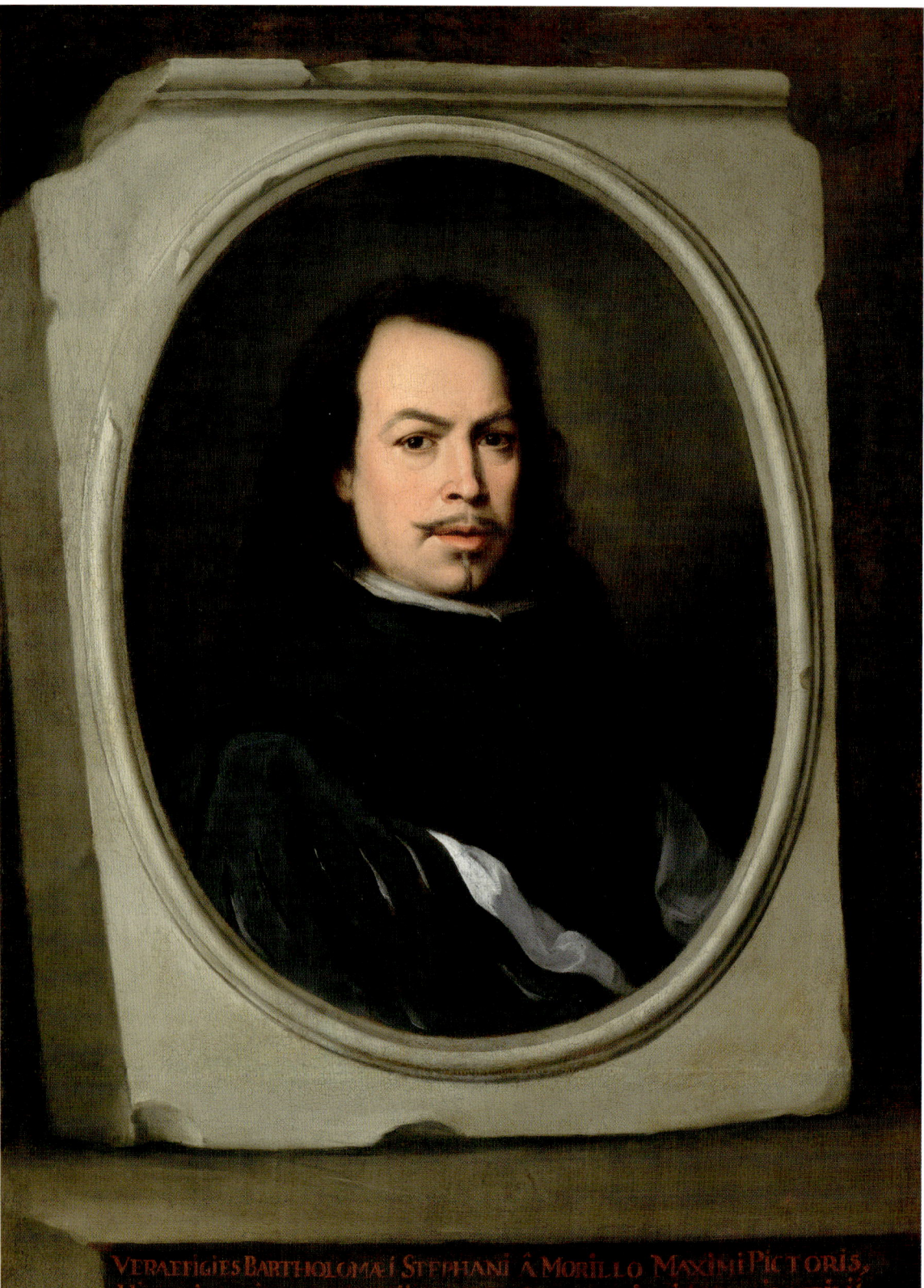

VERAEFIGIES BARTHOLOMAEI STEPHANI â MORILLO MAXIMI PICTORIS,
HISPALI NATI ANNO 1618 OBIIT ANNO 1682 TERTIA DIE MENSIS APRILIS

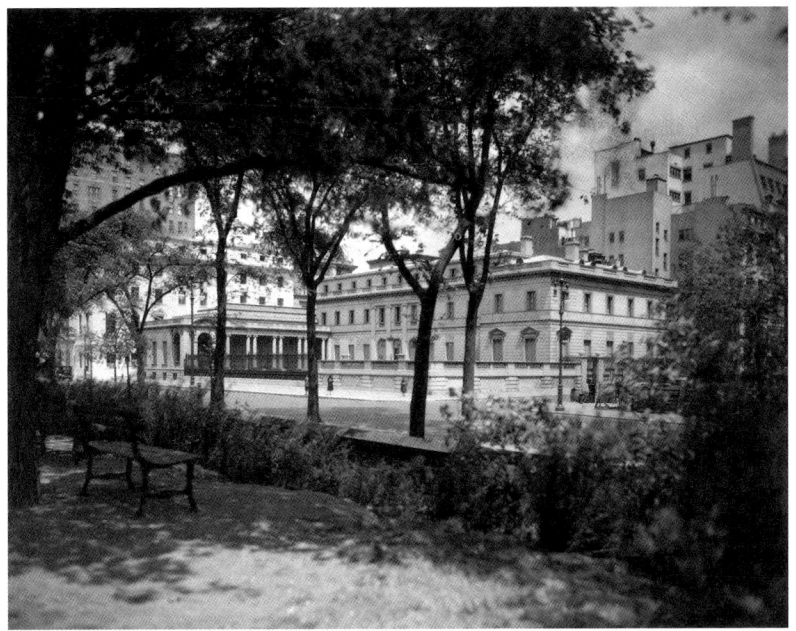

What Frick wanted was "a comfortable, well-arranged house, simple, in good taste, not ostentatious" with ample space around it so it did not crowd the side-walks.[29] Hastings delivered a low-lying building, seventy-five feet back from the avenue (fig. 62). In contrast to many of the Beaux Arts houses built nearby, notably the lavishly decorated William A. Clark house six blocks north, finished in 1911, Frick's was restrained. Its limestone facades were flat and perfectly smooth. Only fluted columns and pierced balustrades at the roofline interrupted these surfaces, with sculptural decoration reserved for curved pediments at the corners of the loggia or the porte cochère.

The limestone continued on the walls of the entrance lobby and halls. Richly colored marbles patterned the floors of these spaces, and carved decorations sur-mounted the doors and ornamented some of the smaller ceilings. The ground floor presented a series of grand rooms suitable for entertaining. Along the west side, a Dining Room led to a Drawing Room, followed by a Living Hall and a Library; this sequence culminated in the enormous gallery—at the time, the largest private space for art in New York (fig. 63). From every one of these rooms except the Art Gallery, lit by skylights, large windows or French doors opened onto the garden, offering views across Fifth Avenue to Central Park.

When the Fricks moved in, these imposing rooms intended for socializing were hung with their most impressive paintings and filled with their best furnish-ings, generally original pieces from the sixteenth through eighteenth centuries. The decorators and dealers guided Frick in these selections more than the architect. Originally, Frick's private study was situated at the western end of the Art Gallery, but we know little of its appearance as a new office was created in 1916. The acquisition of Morgan's Limoges enamels prompted Frick to vacate this private study to make room

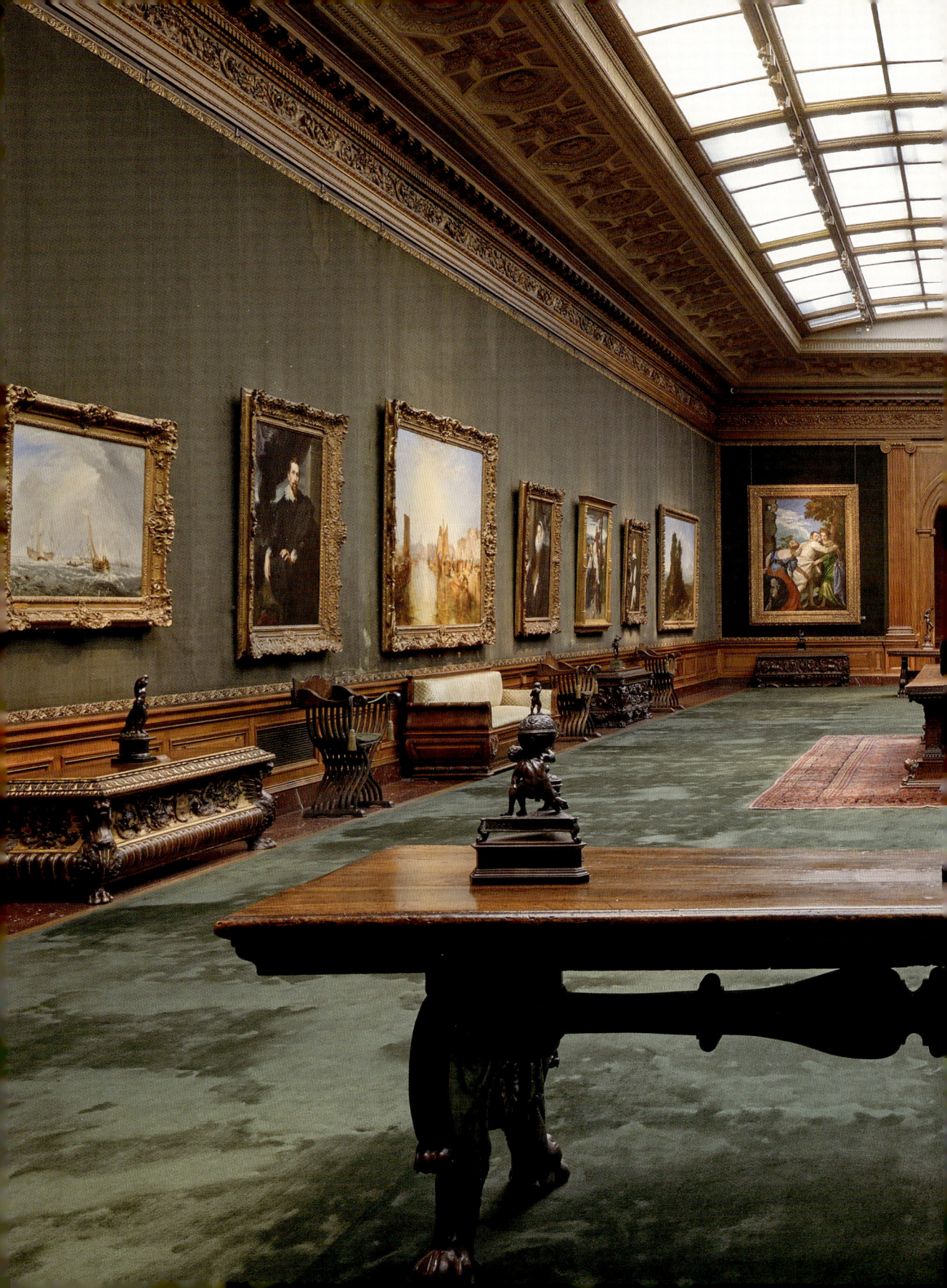

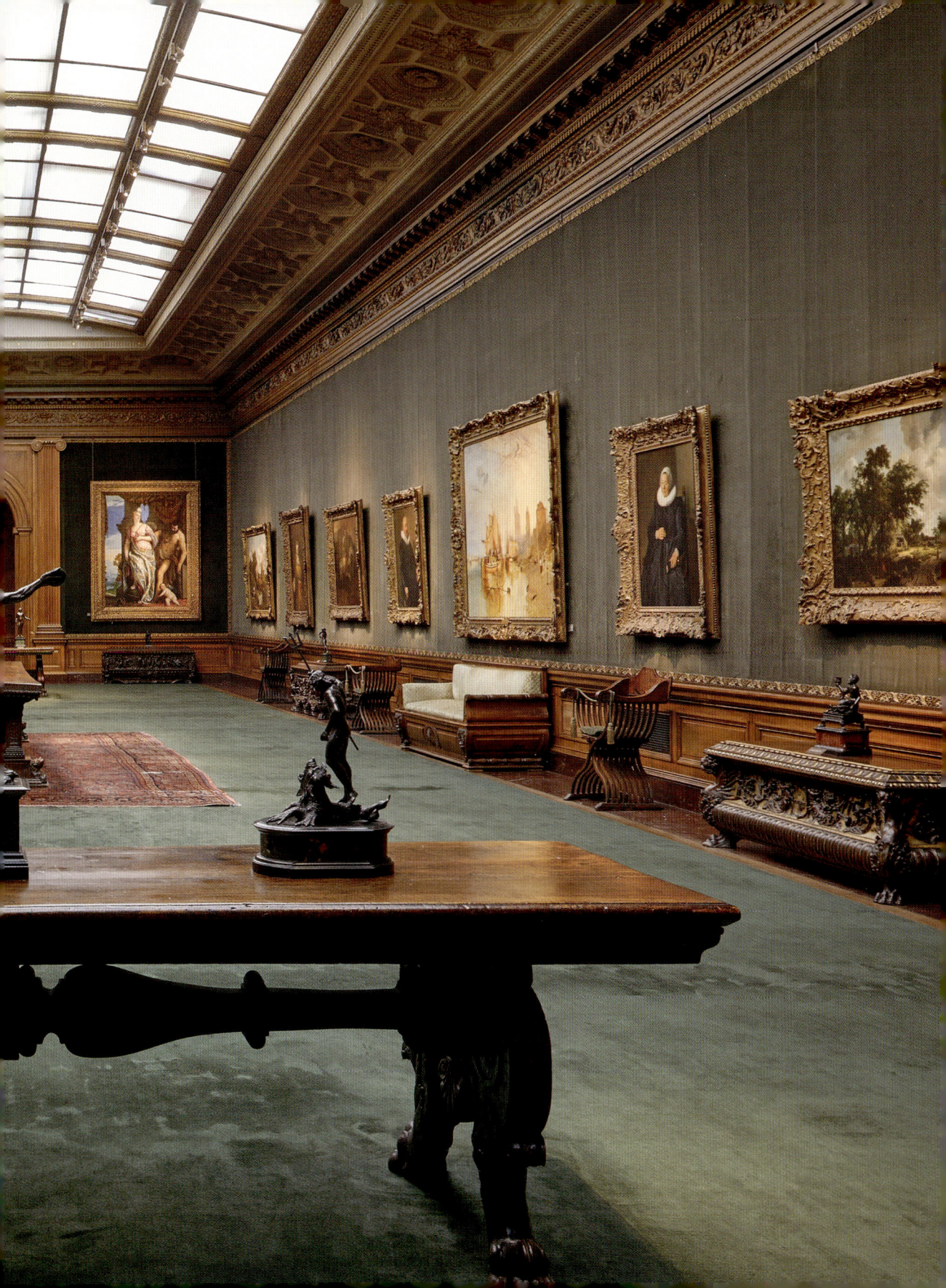

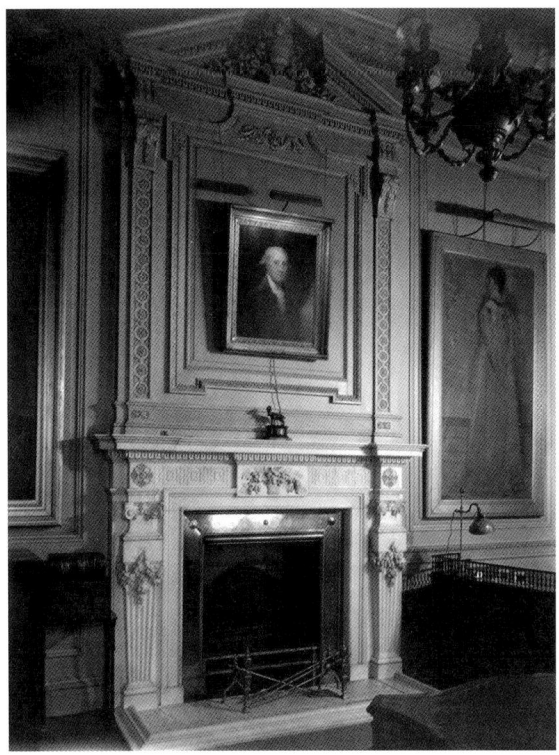

FIG. 64
Henry Clay Frick's office,
1927.

FIG. 65
The Grand Staircase from
the South Hall, 2010.

for display cases for the enamels; Frick's new office, at the eastern end of the Art Gallery, featured a large white marble fireplace facing his desk. Above the chimneypiece hung one of the only American paintings in the house, Gilbert Stuart's portrait of George Washington (1795), the earliest surviving painting of this well-known image of the president (fig. 64). By way of explaining Frick's decision to hang this famous painting in his office, a dozen years later the dealer Albert Rosenthal wrote: "The growing estimation of Washington has reached a point that seems to make it necessary for every man of large means to have a Stuart Washington as a household decoration. We might visualize eventually an exclusive social caste based solely on the ownership of a Stuart Washington portrait."[30] The other paintings in this new office were also by an American, though an expatriate, James McNeill Whistler; his large paintings of Lady Meux, Mrs. Frances Leyland, and Rosa Corder fit so well into the wall paneling that they seem tailored to the space.

Walking up the Grand Staircase, one passed the organ console toward the carved and gilded screen of the organ pipes. This sumptuous decoration set the verticals of the fictive pipes (the actual ones were hidden by the screen) behind scenes of music-making boys loosely modeled after Luca della Robbia's reliefs for the Cantoria in the Florence Cathedral (fig. 65). At the top of the stairs, the size of the rooms scaled back for the more intimate family quarters. Off the landing of the staircase are two elevators and, beyond them, the Breakfast Room. The bedrooms and sitting rooms of Adelaide, Helen Clay, and Henry were located on the west side of the building. A corridor clad in marble and enlivened by ceiling paintings by John Alden Twachtman separated the family's rooms from guest rooms on the eastern side.

While the magnificent rooms of the first floor showed off the Fricks' most important art, what the family chose to look at in the upstairs private rooms was generally more modest. Henry's walnut-paneled bedroom, for example, held few paintings. Most notable was Romney's portrait of Lady Hamilton, set within carved garlands over the fireplace. Adelaide's bedroom, too, was decorated with images of eighteenth-century women; these were mezzotints after paintings by Gainsborough, Reynolds, and others, placed symmetrically around the room (see fig. 75). Another example of the fashion for decorating with prints after eighteenth-century English paintings could be seen in Ogden Codman's interiors for Kykuit, an estate in Pocantico Hills, New York, completed in 1913 for John D. Rockefeller. Their sitting rooms were more expressive of the couple's individual tastes in art. Featured over the chimneypiece in Henry's private sitting room was El Greco's *Purification of the Temple*, a brilliant small painting of contorted figures in vibrant colors that would have baffled many American collectors when he bought it in 1909. To its left was Eugène Carrière's

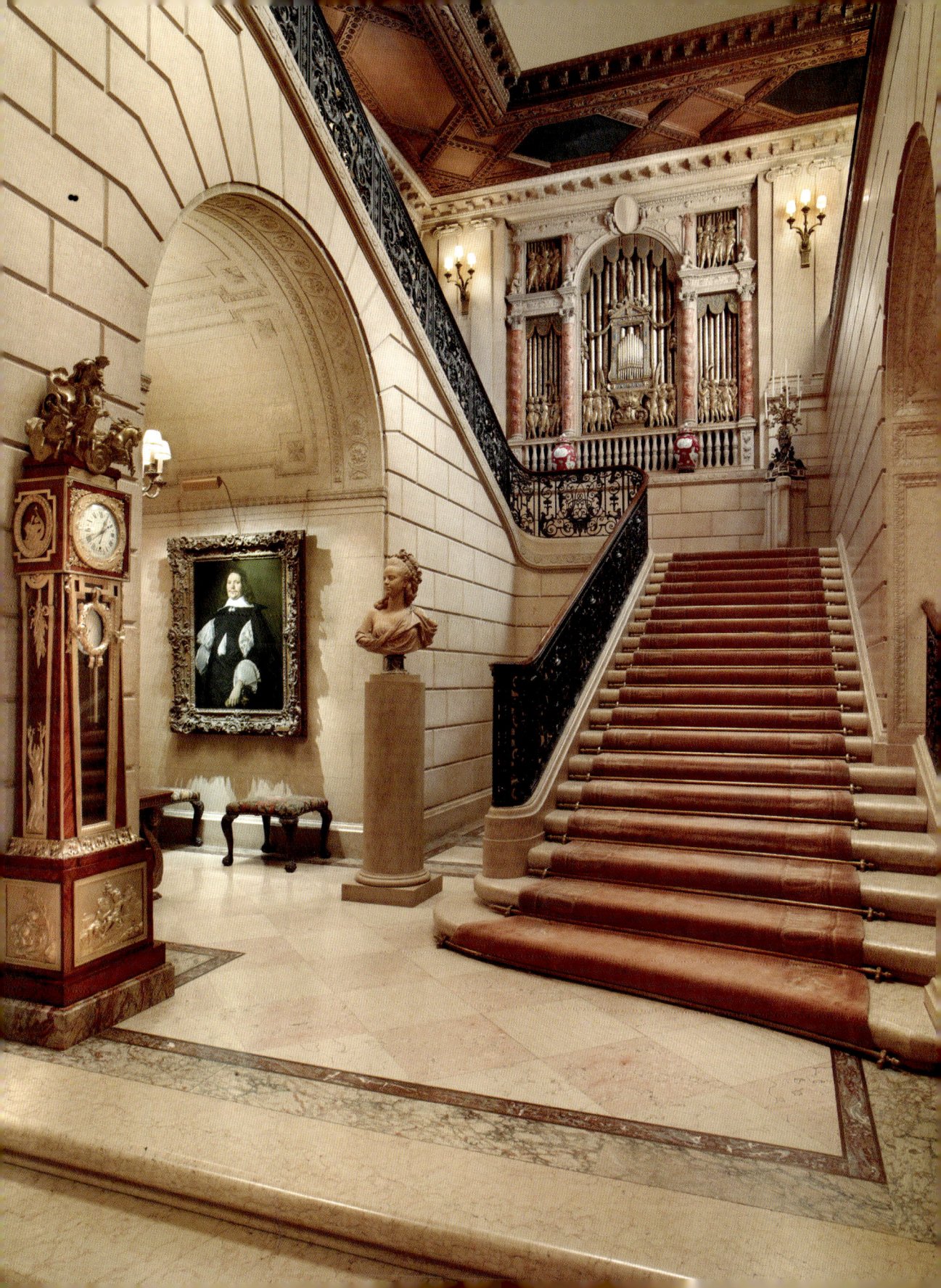

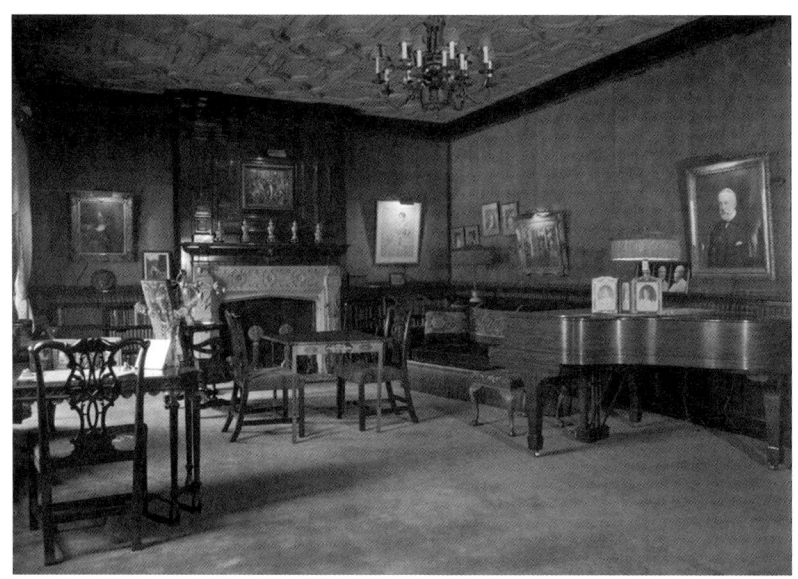

FIG. 66
Henry Clay Frick's sitting
room, 1927.

Motherhood, a grisaille painting of the 1880s, in soft, swirling forms that were progressive in style for its date. A piano, tables, and chairs—all in English style, mostly of recent fabrication—have a stolid rigor and suggest that this room was based on practicality. Rich, red damask, woven abroad, covers the walls, and the furniture is dark. Photographs taken eight years after the owner's death are the best evidence we have of the appearance of the house during and shortly after Henry's death, although there may well have been changes to this room by that time (fig. 66).

Adelaide's boudoir is, by contrast, feminine, light, and richly orchestrated (fig. 67). Cream-colored walls encase the paintings of children enacting the professions of the arts and sciences by the workshop of François Boucher. In this room, the furnishings are all eighteenth-century French originals: tables with gleaming gilt-bronze mounts and upholstered chairs. There is no place for additional canvases with the room's built-in painted panels, so the decorative arts prevail, especially the Sèvres porcelains gracing the mantelpiece and built-in cabinet.

Interestingly, the Breakfast Room was hung with Barbizon paintings, holdovers, as has been discussed, from earlier collecting (fig. 68). As the Fricks sipped their morning beverages, they were surrounded by bucolic images recalling stays in the countryside, away from the bustle of the city: Troyon's *Pasture in Normandy*, Daubigny's *Washerwomen*, Dupré's *River*, and three landscapes by Corot were among the paintings that adorned the walls.

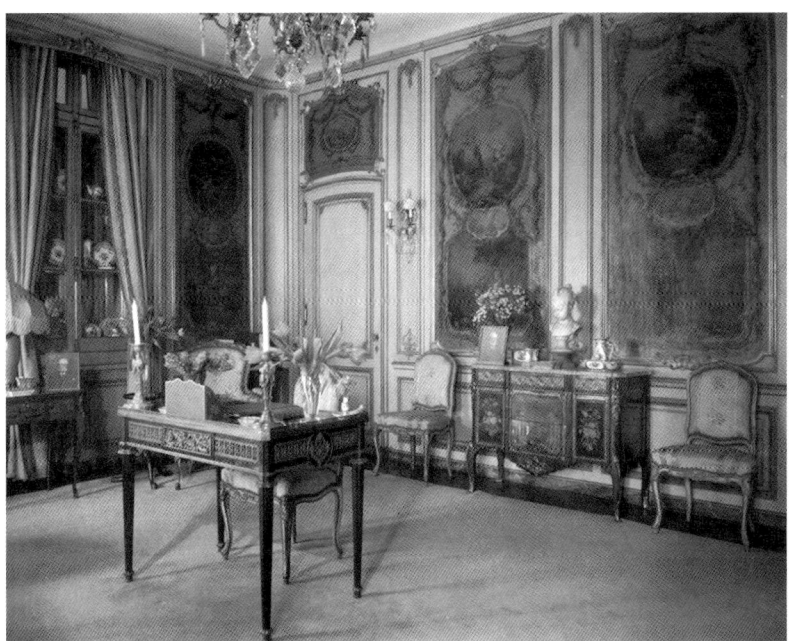

FIG. 67
Adelaide Frick's boudoir,
1927.

FIG. 68
The Breakfast Room, 1927.

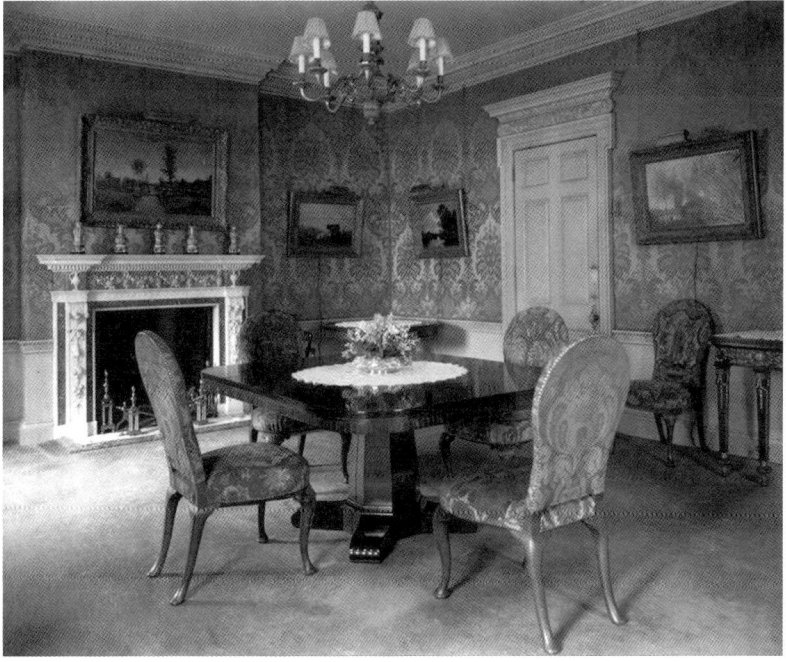

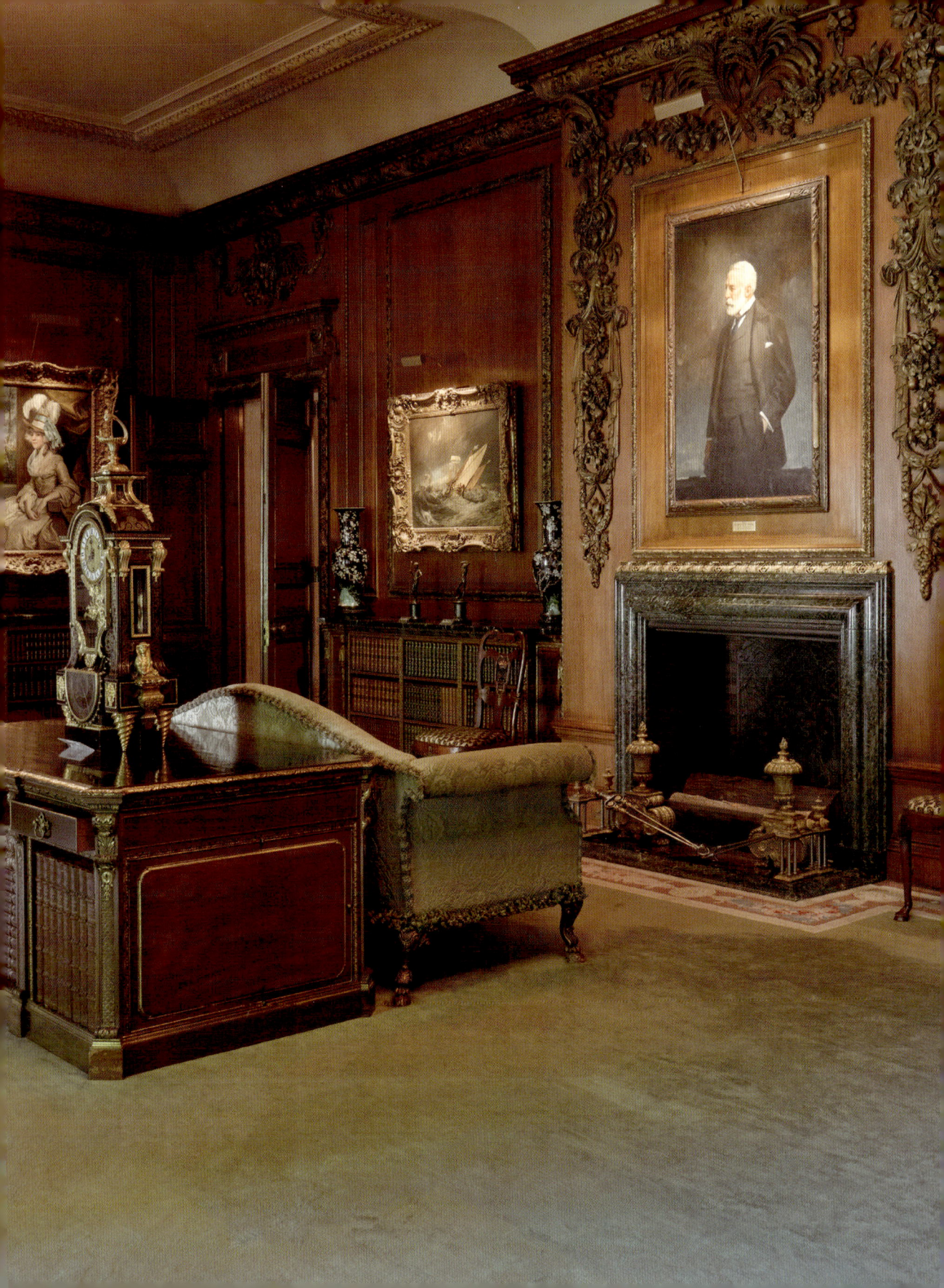

IX

THE DECORATORS:
WHITE, ALLOM & CO. AND
ELSIE DE WOLFE

While Thomas Hastings established the architectural context for Frick's art collection, two decorating firms—White, Allom & Co. and Elsie de Wolfe—set the tone for the interiors to display it. The principals of these firms influenced the choice of many furnishings the owner acquired and formed the backdrop for his paintings. In a number of cases, White Allom built antiques, such as chimneypieces, into the decor, and De Wolfe recommended specific pieces of furniture to complement her designs. As was commonplace, decorators often collaborated with dealers in creating spaces suitable for works of art that could be purchased on the market to the profit of the trade—and the decorators.

Hastings hoped that his designs for the interiors would continue beyond the marble floors and limestone walls he chose for lobbies and hallways. For example, he proposed an ornamental plaster ceiling for the Living Hall modeled on an historic English one. But Frick rejected the architect's "Specification for the Special Finish of Principal Rooms" of March 1913. As with some of the proposals for the exterior, Frick found Hastings's approach overly ornamental. He insisted on simplicity.

Instead, Frick turned to one of the most renowned decorators of the day, White, Allom & Co. Founded in 1893, the firm revolved around its principal, Sir Charles Carrick Allom (fig. 70). In 1907, Allom restored and redecorated rooms in Buckingham Palace for Edward VII, and in 1912 he redesigned the palace Centre Room for George V. In recognition of his service to the Crown, Allom was knighted in 1913. With this royal pedigree, he found favor with many of the American collectors Frick knew well, such as Henry Huntington, John D. Rockefeller, and Peter Widener. What Allom brought to the first floor of Frick's mansion, where his influence predominates, is an eighteenth-century English flavor, rich yet restrained. In a signal of Frick's transition from architect to decorator for the design of the interiors, Frick cabled Allom, "Please see that ceilings almost plain; Hastings favored too much carving. Please impress on him my earnest desire to avoid anything elaborate."[31]

FIG. 69
View of the Library, 2020.

Allom thought out the character of each room, referencing a specific English period while avoiding pedantic copying of details. The Library, he said, should be "a strong steady oak room of William and Mary character."[32] Allom designed low bookcases to leave ample room for paintings to hang on the wood panels above them (fig. 69), as had been the case at Clayton. The Dining Room was Georgian in design, with ornamental decoration over chimneypieces and doorways—presumably not ornate enough to annoy Frick—alongside large, simple wall panels to accommodate Frick's tall Gainsborough paintings (fig. 72).

Like other large European decorating firms, White, Allom & Co. assembled original architectural fragments from the sixteenth through nineteenth centuries to inspire clients and to serve as models for craftsmen. While the firm generally drew fresh designs along the lines of historic precedent, these three-dimensional examples provided the wood carvers with templates so their work would feel authentic to the period being followed. White Allom later donated its collection of "models" to the Victoria & Albert Museum. These architectural fragments influenced American taste. They could be inserted into interiors, served as examples of historical furniture bought to enhance the spaces, and appealed to collectors as well. In 1911, for instance, J. P. Morgan bought several thousand fragments and complete works from the firm of Parisian decorator Georges Hoentschel. Morgan's donation of this large assemblage to the Metropolitan Museum of Art, including many medieval objects, created the core collection of what is now the Department of European Sculpture and Decorative Arts (fig. 71). The line between original works of art and copies, and between modern re-creations of older periods and actual examples of older work set into the walls, blurred in a period when the clients could afford either and chose what was convenient or simply looked best. White Allom designed the lighting fixtures and many of the tables and chairs used by the Fricks; placed alongside these were outstanding examples of furnishings from the Renaissance to the Rococo periods.

An instance of architect and decorator agreeing on design is the wrought-iron balustrade of the Grand Staircase, a reimagining of the early eighteenth-century Dean's Staircase in St. Paul's Cathedral. Here, however, Allom featured the Renaissance-style organ console and organ case (see fig. 65), echoed by the cassoni (wooden marriage chests that were significant furnishings of Italian Renaissance residences) Frick acquired in the same years for the Art Gallery.

The decorators also provided the finishing touches to the Art Gallery. Its distinctive green-velvet wall hanging was commissioned from Prelle, the Lyon manufacturer in operation since 1752. The rich textile created a striking background for Frick's greatest paintings. Still in Prelle's archive, the loom

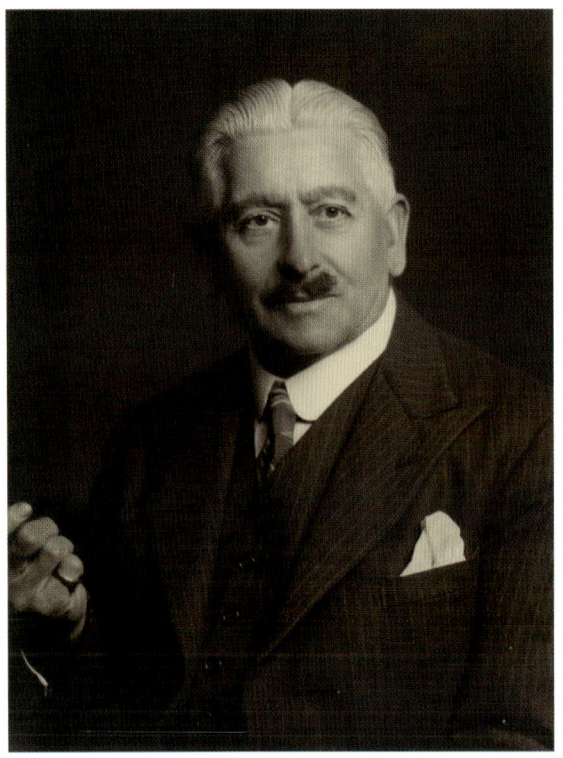

Fig. 70
Sir Charles Carrick Allom,
January 1940.

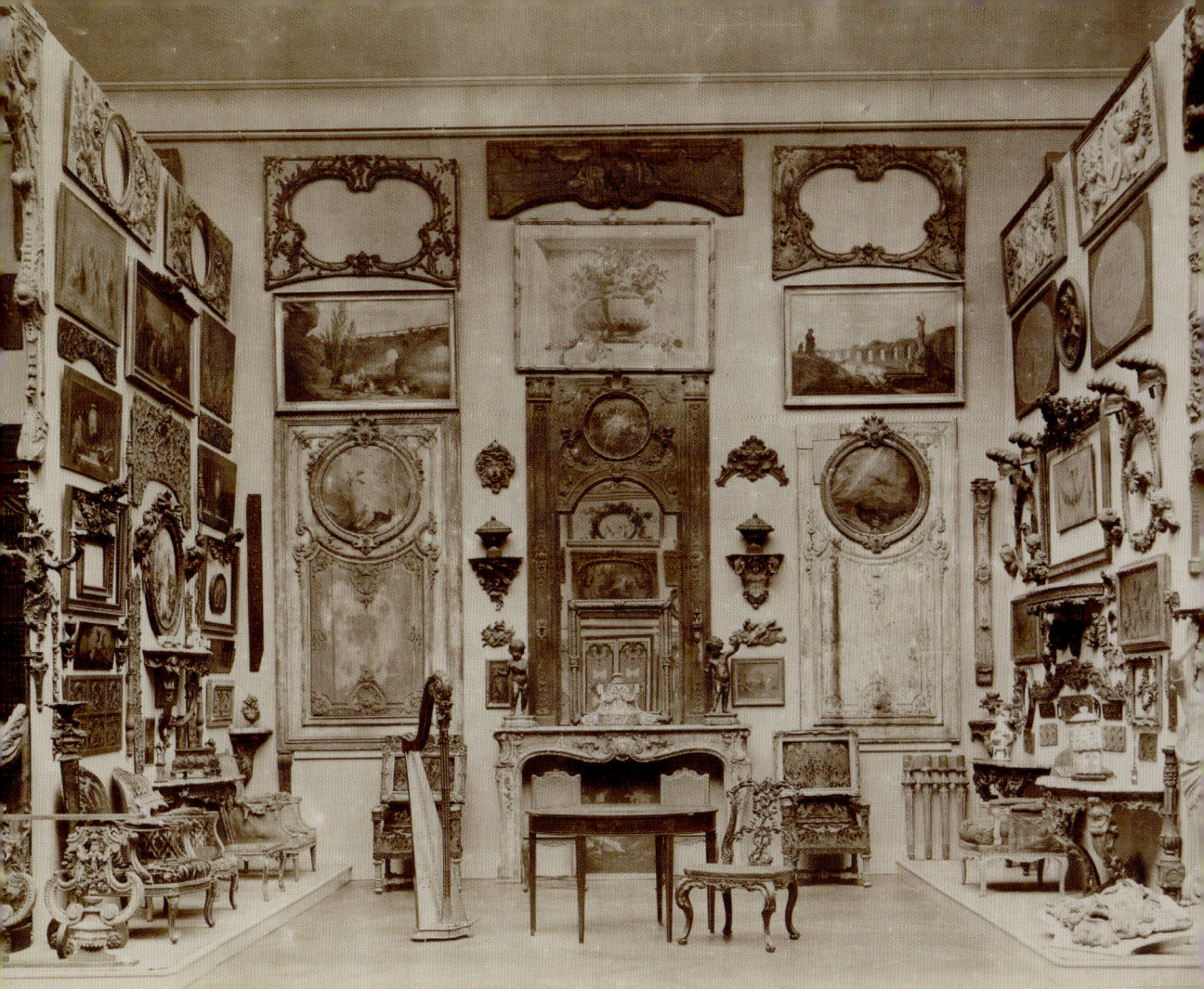

pattern and original silk threads for the commission served as the basis to reweave the fabric for the Frick's 2020–25 renovations. Many damasks for other rooms, dating from 1914 or the new building campaign of the 1930s, were rewoven and installed during the 2020–25 refurbishment.

While it is problematic to ascribe gender to decor, there is a case to be made for characterizing the Frick's first floor as masculine and its second floor as feminine. On January 27, 1914, De Wolfe wrote to Henry, "Please don't forget me!! . . . I am specially good at detail and the fitting up and the comfort of women's rooms, the intimate little tricks that no mere man, no matter how clever he may be, can ever know."[33] After a successful career as an actress, De Wolfe had left the stage in 1905 to establish her own business in the expanding occupation of interior decorator (fig. 73). She became a celebrity in her new profession, consolidating her fame with a book, *The House in Good Taste* (1913). She began modestly, operating out of her own home at 122 East 17th Street, but by 1914 she managed numerous assistants and was a financial success. In high-profile projects such as the Colony Club in New York, she created

FIG. 71
View of Georges Hoentschel's seventeenth- and eighteenth-century collection installed on the main floor of 58, boulevard Flandrin, Paris, ca. 1904–6.

FOLLOWING PAGES
FIG. 72
The Dining Room, 2009.

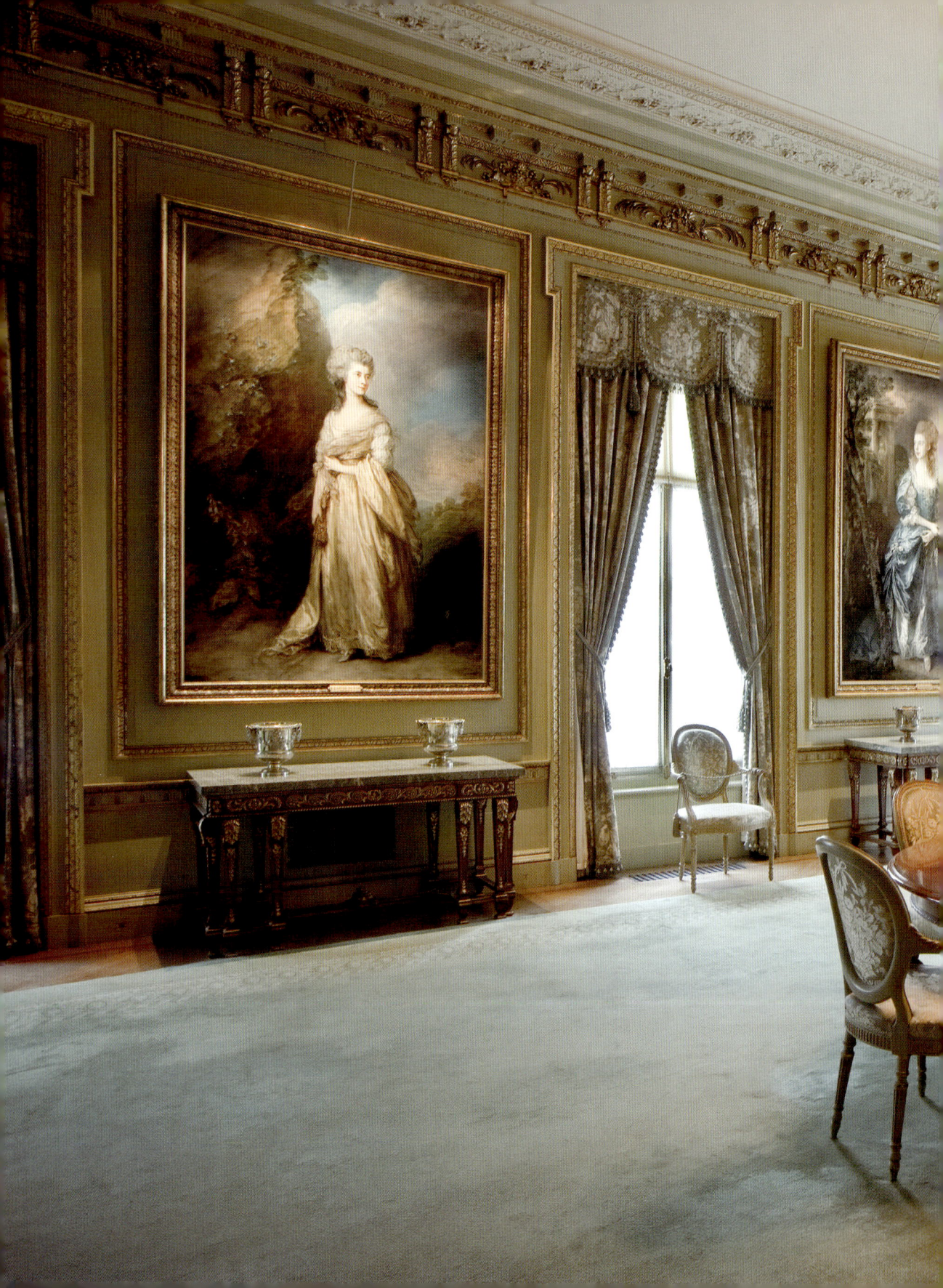

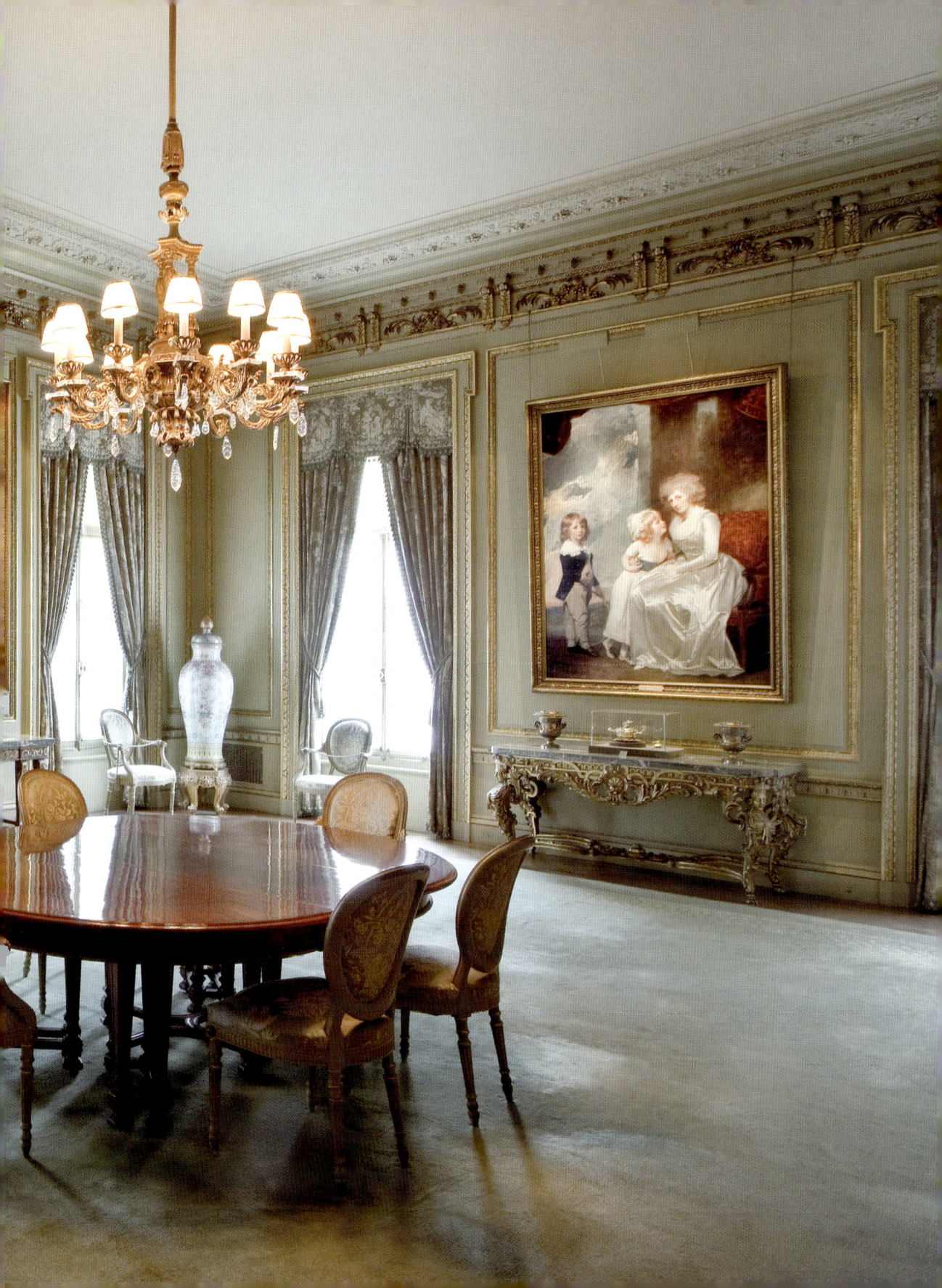

a sophisticated style, blending luxurious materials with sumptuous colors and striking patterns. An eclectic nature stirred her to mix furniture of different periods with contemporary design.

For the second floor of the Frick mansion, De Wolfe likely commissioned the Twachtman ceiling painting (mentioned above) along two corridors leading to the bedrooms. Above walls sheathed in marble and illuminated by concealed cove lighting—an innovation at the time—the curved cerulean sky and the suggested landscape along the edges teems with monkeys clad in Chinese costume and performing human activities. Most whimsical of all is one lighting the candles of gossamer-like lanterns that drift upward, a scene just before the entrance to Adelaide's bedroom suite (fig. 74). Freely adapting from singeries and chinoiseries—French Rococo decorative depictions of creatures and lands considered exotic—De Wolfe unveils a surprise amid the otherwise serious Frick rooms.

These pastel colors and whimsical ornaments carried over into Adelaide's bedroom, where the ceiling was painted with medallions, setting off a luxuriously curtained canopy bed resting on a richly patterned Chinese carpet (fig. 75). All this was coordinated in blue damask, silks, and velvet. It was in the furnishing of such rooms that De Wolfe influenced the Fricks' collecting, in the process making herself rich. By 1906, she described her business as supplying both "interiors" and "objets d'art." Her contract with Frick called for her to receive a 10 percent commission on all the antiques she acquired to fill the rooms. While the Fricks did not accept all her suggestions, they took many. A secretaire and console table by Jean-Henri Riesener were the luxurious furnishings that filled out De Wolfe's vision for Adelaide's bedroom; a corner cupboard attributed to Martin Carlin of Chinese scenes in black lacquer continued themes from the corridor; eighteenth-century, Turkish-inspired French console tables added an extravagant touch.

Allom and De Wolfe competed for some of the second-floor rooms. The English firm wrested away the design of the Breakfast Room and Frick's sitting room, both of which were clad in silk damask. The Breakfast Room (see fig. 68) was hung with some of Frick's earlier acquisitions—Barbizon School—while his latest, Impressionist canvases were in his sitting room. In the spaces designed by De Wolfe, the couple preferred prints after eighteenth-century English paintings.

FIG. 73
Elsie de Wolfe with one
of her Pekingeses, ca. 1920.

FIG. 74
Detail of John Alden
Twachtman ceiling

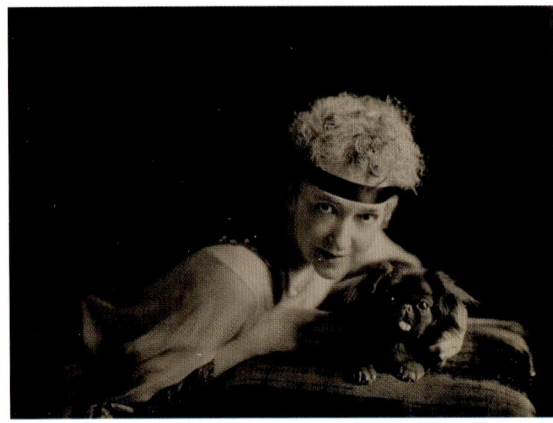

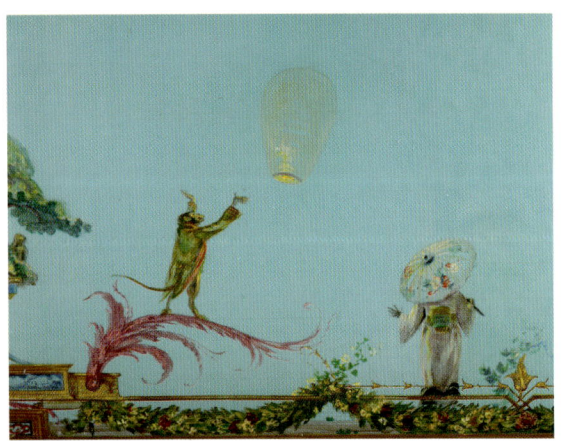

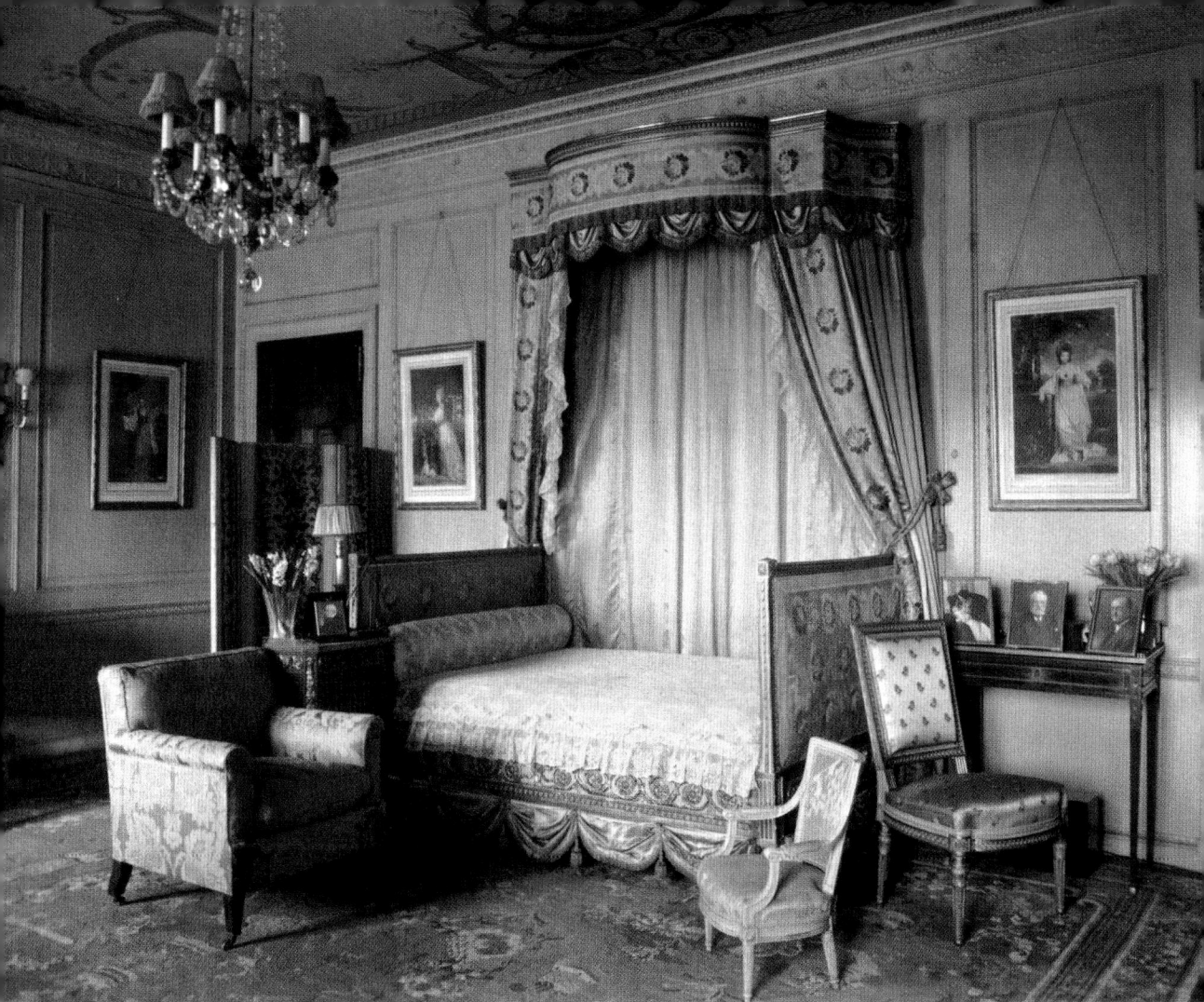

FIG. 75
Adelaide Frick's bedroom, 1927.

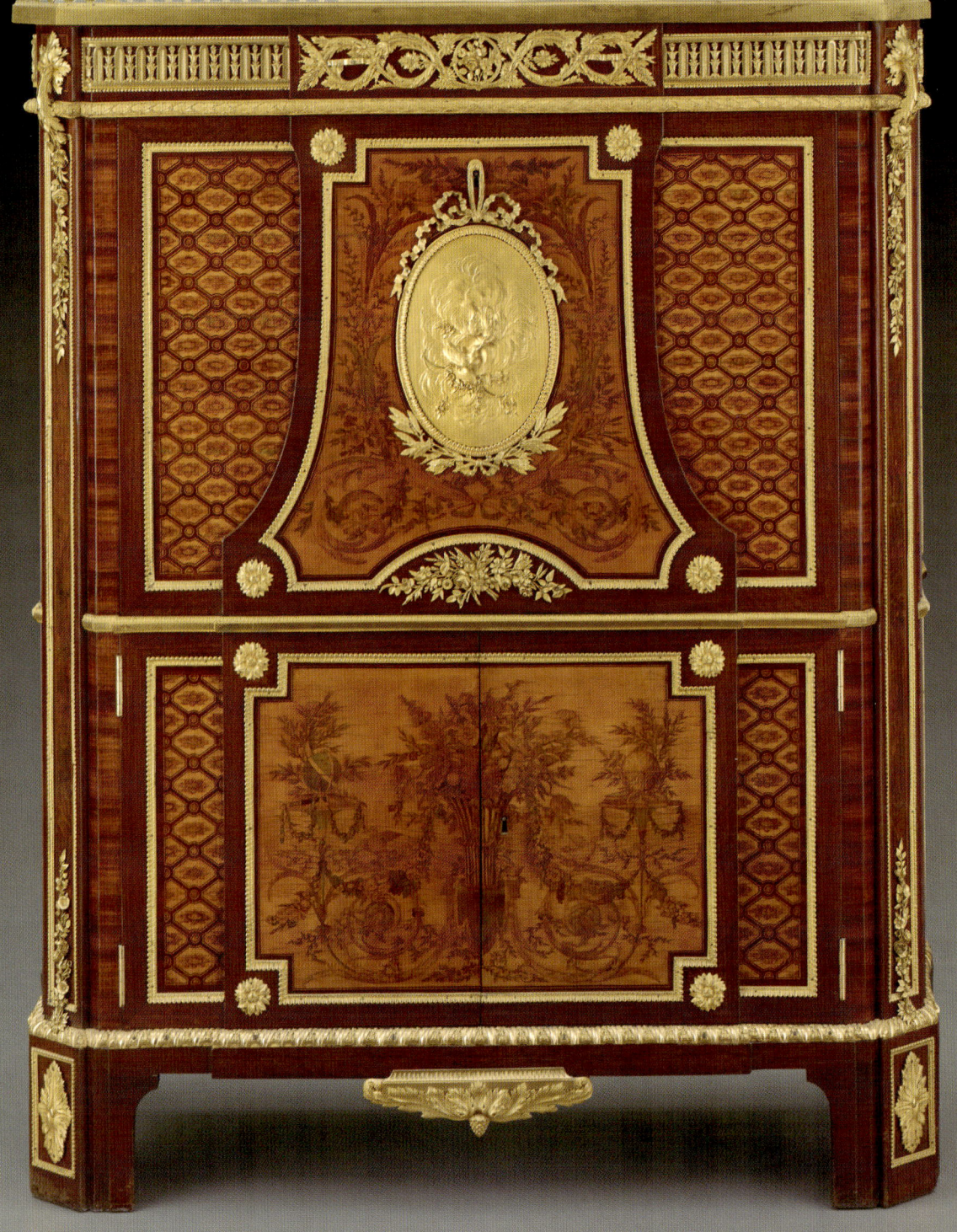

X

COLLECTING
FINE FURNITURE

Paintings drew Frick's attention in Pittsburgh and in the early New York years, but as he began to build permanent residences on the East Coast—first the Eagle Rock summerhouse and then the New York residence at Fifth Avenue and East 70th Street—he concentrated more often on furnishings. To fill the vast house in Pride's Crossing, he relied on decorators and dealers, much as he had during the remodeling of Clayton. To match Eagle Rock's Georgian style, many of its furnishings were English; their quality was respectable, suitable for a large summer home. For New York, where the furniture would be beneath or beside his finest paintings, he recognized the need to buy works of the highest quality.

As construction of 1 East 70th Street neared completion, travel to London and Paris in the spring of 1914 guided many of Frick's selections. After meeting Victor Cavendish, 9th Duke of Devonshire, at Lansdowne House in London and at Chatsworth, his country house in Derbyshire, Frick bought from him a suite of tapestry furniture thought to be eighteenth-century Gobelins. He was likely also impressed by the Wallace Collection. Formerly the residence of the marquesses of Hertford and Sir Richard Wallace, it opened to the public as a museum in 1900. Frick admired not only the paintings but also the French furniture, particularly that by André-Charles Boulle and his followers. Distinctive for their tortoiseshell-and-brass veneers, these sumptuous, sometimes flamboyant furnishings produced at the end of the seventeenth and into the eighteenth centuries are notable features of the Wallace. Through Duveen, Frick bought several major pieces of Boulle furniture, such as two octagonal pedestals (after 1686–1715) and a kneehole desk (fig. 77), as well as nineteenth-century copies, such as a spectacular pair of commodes with tendril marquetry. He moved quickly and acquired the best of what he could afford, settling for some high-quality reproductions alongside the finest originals he could find.

With De Wolfe as intermediary, Frick also purchased French furniture from the collection of Sir John Murray Scott (inherited from Lady Wallace, the widow

FIG. 76
Jean-Henri Riesener,
Secretaire, ca. 1780 and 1791.

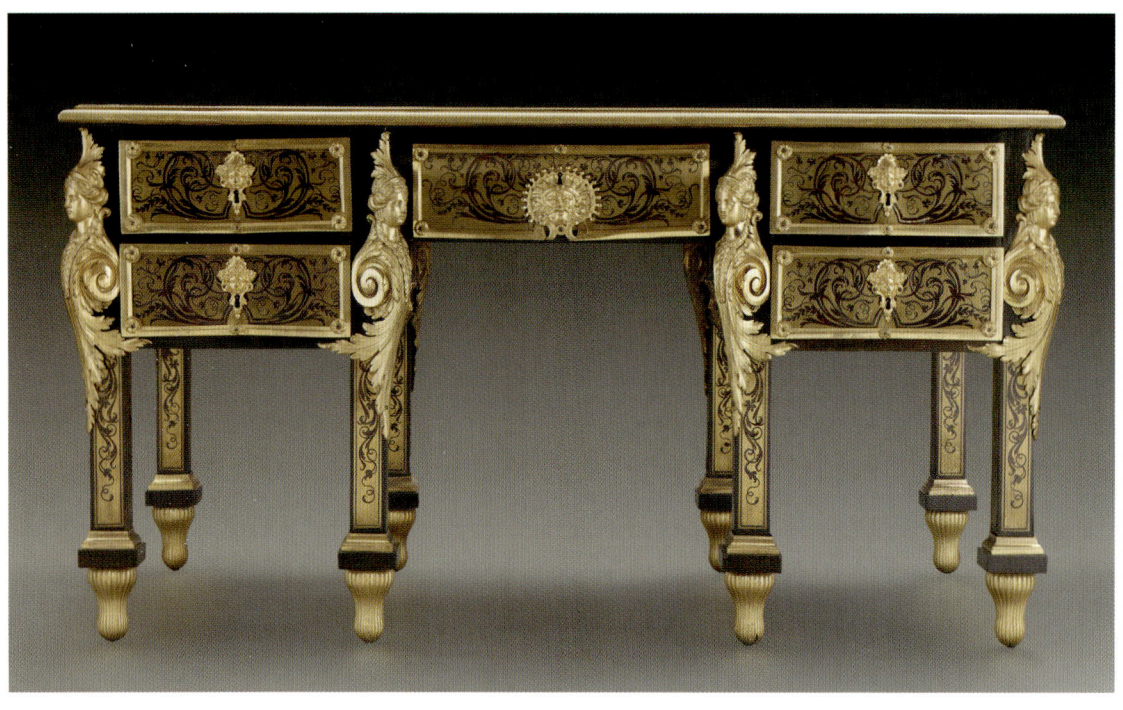

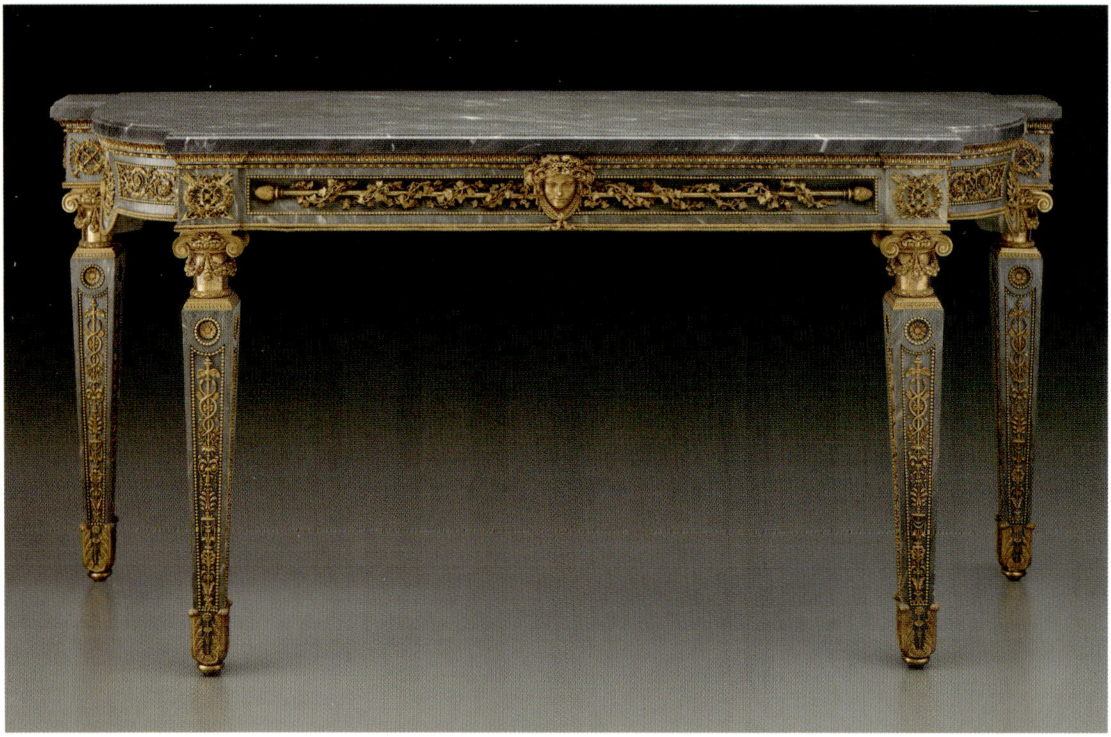

of Sir Richard Wallace, the founder of the Wallace Collection). In a single month, Frick spent more than $400,000, the most he had ever laid out on decorative arts. Provenance—recording the previous ownership of works of art—mattered to Frick, and experiencing the furnishings of the aristocracy in their fine houses spurred his purchases.

Following this initial foray, the next year, Frick refined his choices to the highest possible level of French furniture. Four pieces, all of which came through Duveen, serve to illustrate his acumen. First are a secretaire (fig. 76) and commode made by Jean-Henri Riesener for Marie Antoinette. The tall writing desk and matching chest of drawers, likely intended for the queen's chateau at Saint-Cloud, interweave marquetry of precious, colored woods with elegant gilt-bronze mounts. Marie Antoinette was so attached to these pieces that she asked Riesener to adapt them to her rooms in the Tuileries Palace when she was imprisoned there during the French Revolution. Another masterpiece of French furniture of the same years is a side table (fig. 78) designed for the Duchess of Mazarin by Jean-François-Thérèse Chalgrin and executed by François-Joseph Bélanger. En suite with other furniture (including the prototype for the chimneypiece now in the Fragonard Room), the side table was destined for a now-destroyed town house in Paris. Glorious gilt-bronze mounts by the master chaser and gilder Pierre Gouthière, the greatest practitioner of this decorative form, are the highlights of the bleu Turquin marble table; his matte and reflective surfaces make the twirling grape leaves flicker against crisp architectural details and arrow shafts. The table, along with its ornamentation, is one of the greatest surviving works by Gouthière.

The Clayton entrance hall featured an elaborately carved tall-case clock with grotesque features borrowed from the Renaissance; Frick may have had a similar role in mind for the longcase regulator clock. Combining the skills of three distinct

FIG. 77
Workshop of André-Charles Boulle, *Kneehole Desk*, ca. 1692–95, with later alterations ca. 1770 (before 1777).

FIG. 78
Pierre Gouthière, after a design by Jean-François-Thérèse Chalgrin, executed by François-Joseph Bélanger, *Side Table*, 1781.

FIG. 79
Italian (Rome), *Chest or Cassone (One of a Pair)*, third quarter of the 16th century with 19th-century alterations, additions, and restorations.

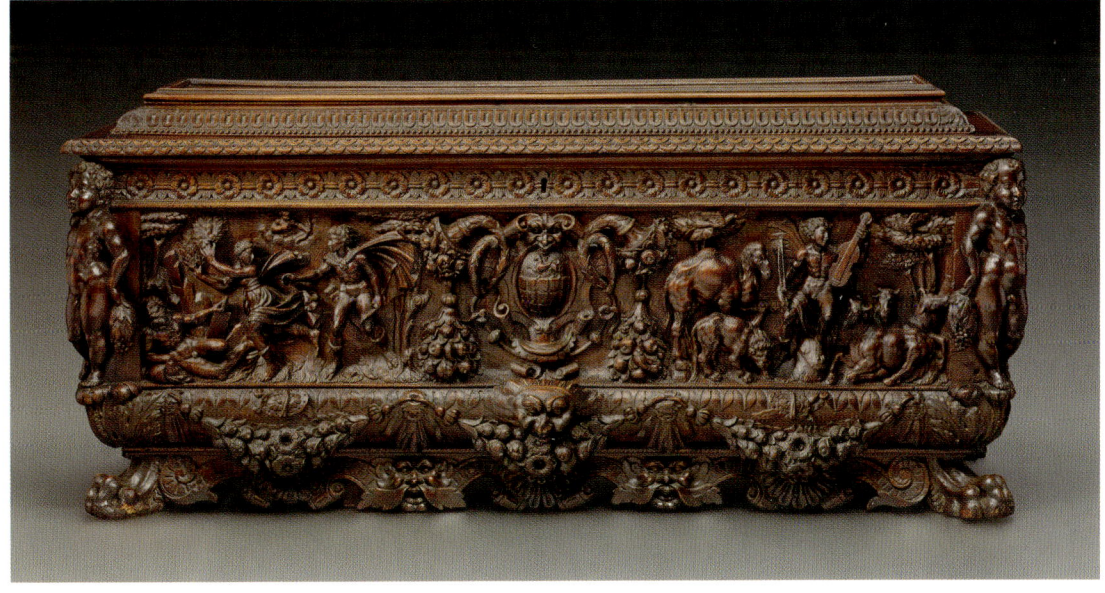

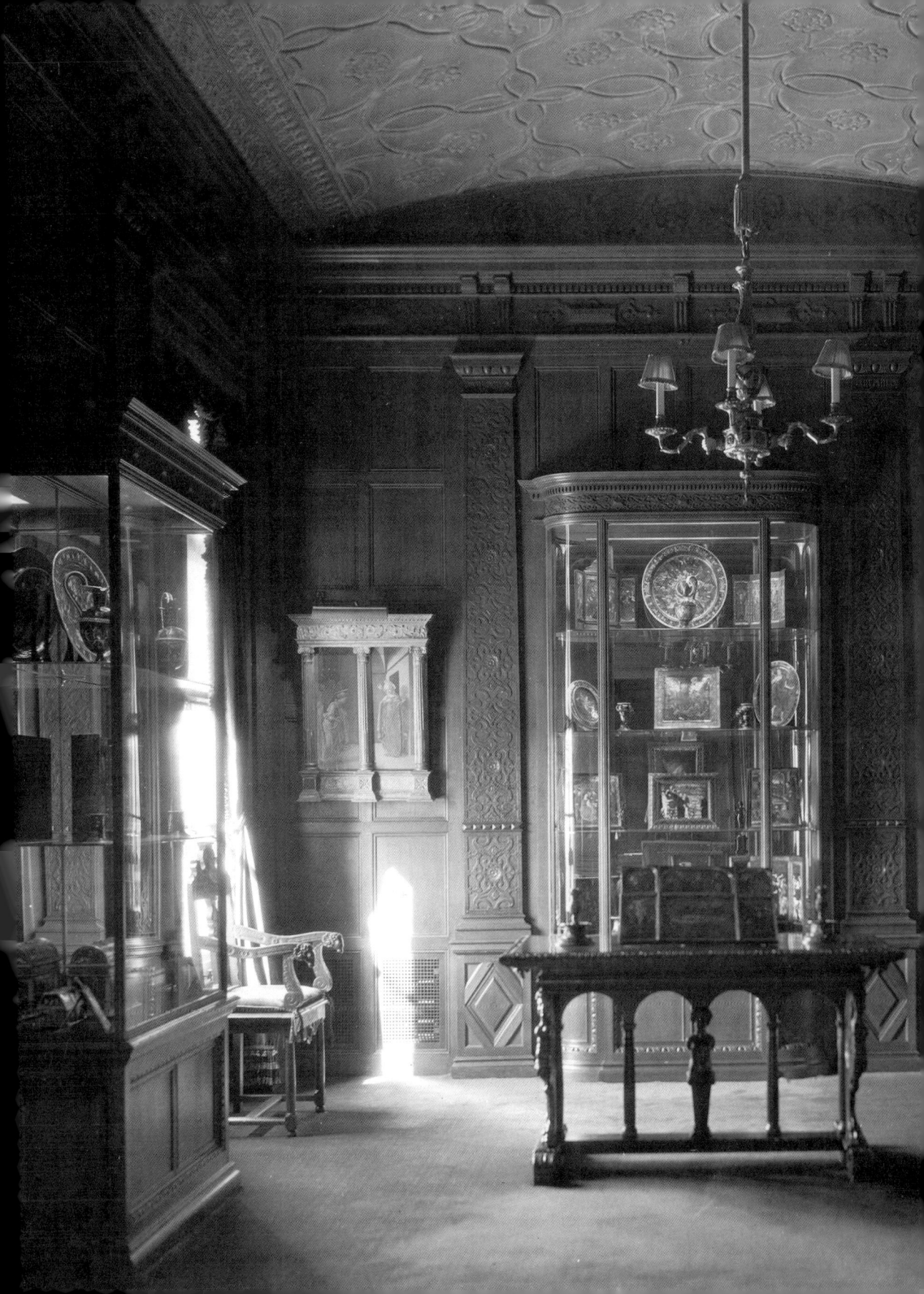

FIG. 80
The north wall of the
Enamels Gallery, 1927.

crafts—its veneered wood case by Balthazar Lieutaud, bronze mounts by Philippe Caffieri, and clock movement by Ferdinand Berthoud—the clock illustrates the artistry of three of the foremost artisans in their respective fields. On top, a statue of the god Apollo driving his horses symbolizes the passage of the day, while reliefs representing the seasons decorate its sides. Within, Berthoud included movements of solar time and Greenwich Mean Time, as well as barometric and other gauges, reflecting scientific advances of the era (see fig. 65).

In addition to selecting individual works of great quality, Frick acquired through Duveen groups of rare pieces of Renaissance furniture intended to complement the decor and other works of art. The first grouping consists of three tables, two chairs, and eight Italian cassoni. Among the cassoni are a pair with vivid carving in high relief that illustrates episodes from the life of Apollo as depicted in Ovid's *Metamorphoses* (fig. 79). A long center table (1500–1550) is one of the largest of its kind to survive from the Renaissance. Duveen likely assembled these from various private family collections in Europe, selling them en bloc to Frick as suitable furnishings for the Art Gallery, where they remain today.

The other group is of French Renaissance furniture, some sixteen pieces, including cabinets, tables, and chairs. These Frick purchased to complement a collection of French Limoges enamels he acquired from the estate of J. P. Morgan in 1916. A number were shown that year in what became the Enamels Gallery when Frick gave up his office to display his latest acquisitions. Only a few pieces of furniture can be shown in the relatively small space (fig. 80). Most French Renaissance furniture has later additions, repairs to the inevitable deterioration of wood objects over five hundred years. The museum displays only the best and least altered of these rare and fragile pieces. The French Renaissance was in vogue when these entered Frick's collection, so there were rivals competing for the few pieces on the market; nonetheless, his purchase was one of the largest ever to enter an American collection.

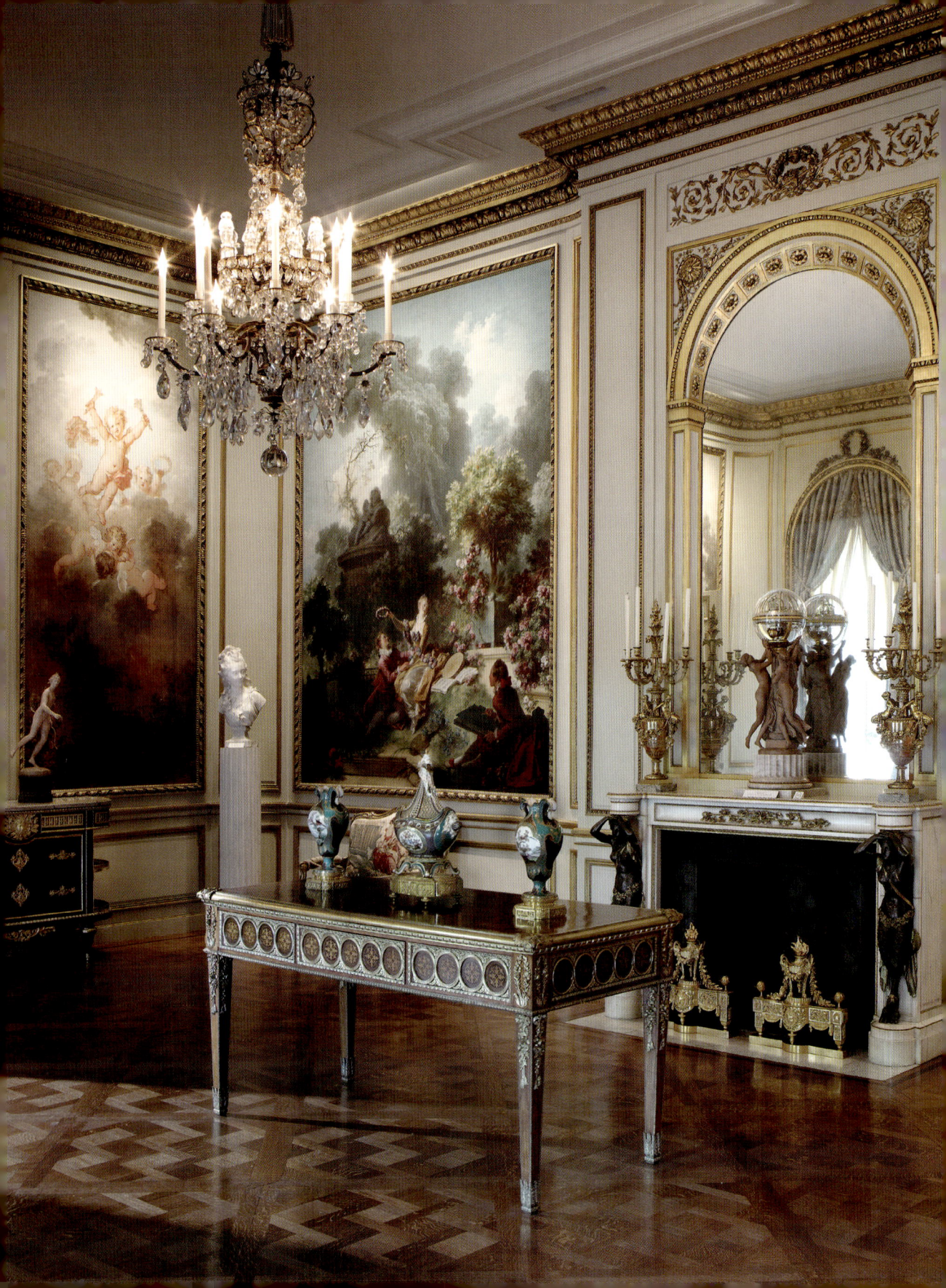

XI

DUVEEN AND
DECORATIVE ARTS

In the first quarter of the twentieth century, the Duveen Brothers—with showrooms in London, Paris, and New York—became the foremost art dealers in the world, famous for arranging many of the most expensive sales of art. The firm had a modest origin in Holland in the mid-nineteenth century. Joseph and his brother Henri expanded to England, and by the 1910s, Joseph's son, also named Joseph, had taken the firm to new levels. In the beginning, the focus was on decorative objects, particularly Delftware and Chinese porcelain, which were then highly desirable. In time, Joseph handled many of the most important painting deals of the era, as well as the major transactions of decorative arts (fig. 82).

While Duveen and Frick often garnered newspaper headlines for sales and purchases of paintings, it is worth noting that Frick also bought important Chinese porcelain from Duveen Brothers. Joseph's brother Henry Duveen sold Frick a group of miniature Asian porcelains, which had been in the George B. Warren collection in 1906, and a number of important Ming dynasty pieces from J. P. Morgan; most went to Eagle Rock. By 1915, Joseph Duveen could sell Frick finer pieces for much higher prices. A group of four Qing dynasty blue-and-white covered jars (fig. 85), which his uncle had handled in the 1880s, subsequently dispersed to various collections, were repurchased and sold to Frick for $80,000 (by comparison, the same year Frick paid $170,000 for Giovanni Bellini's *St. Francis in the Desert*). In 1918, Frick paid Duveen $117,000 for two Qing dynasty *Figures of Ladies on Stands*, for which Morgan had paid $14,860 in 1903. While Frick negotiated diligently over paintings, a market he knew well, he often accepted the asking price for porcelain, about which he knew less. Frick did not concentrate on this area in the way more specialized collectors such as James Garland or Charles Lang Freer did; rather he followed the lead of others, such as Morgan, Altman, and Widener, in rounding out his collection with highly sought-after objects. To Frick's blue-and-white and enameled wares was added a group of 147 pieces acquired by Childs Frick over his lifetime and bequeathed in 1966. While not a highlight of The Frick Collection, Chinese porcelain nonetheless

FIG. 81
The Fragonard Room
(looking east), 2020.

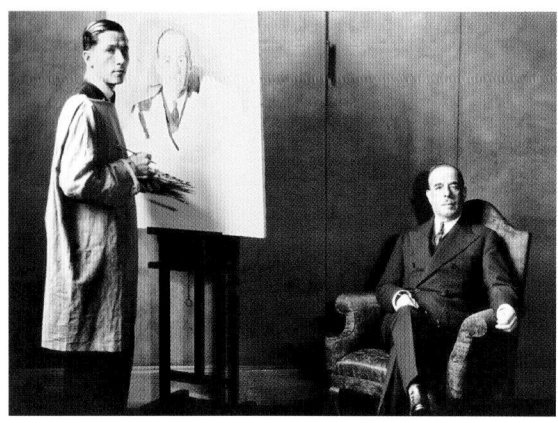

FIG. 82
Joseph Duveen sitting for
his portrait, ca. 1930.

FIG. 83
Sèvres Porcelain
Manufactory, model by
Jean-Claude Duplessis,
painted by Louis-Denis
Armand the Elder,
Pot-pourri à Vaisseau, 1760.

constitutes a distinguished group; it appears to have been an aspect Frick thought his collection should have rather than a personal passion, the kind of work that filled out many contemporary mansions.

While Joseph Duveen did sell notable paintings to Frick, his decisive influence was in the area of decor and decorative arts. Some of the paintings that came through the firm were arguably more important as decoration and served as backdrops for decorative arts. The single most important sale that Duveen made to Frick—and at $1.25 million the collector's costliest purchase—was the set of Fragonard paintings called *The Progress of Love* (fig. 81). The four original paintings had been commissioned in 1771 for the chateau at Louveciennes, belonging to Madame Du Barry, Louis XV's mistress. When she rejected them, perhaps because their luscious Rococo manner was at odds with the strict Neoclassicism of the chateau, Fragonard took them back. Fleeing to his hometown of Grasse during the French Revolution, Fragonard received a commission to place the paintings in his cousin's house and to fill out the sequence by adding ten new canvases. Over time, J. P. Morgan acquired the complete set and installed them in his town house at Prince's Gate, London. After Morgan's death in 1913, the paintings were shipped to New York and, together with thousands of his works of art, shown at the Metropolitan Museum of Art for two years.

Duveen's role in selling the set to Frick, overseeing the installation in the mansion, and providing furnishings for the room illustrates the dealer's methods. Duveen happened upon Roland Knoedler and his associates in front of the Fragonards at the Metropolitan Museum of Art and surmised that his competitors wanted to sell them to Frick. Forestalling this, Duveen contacted Jack Morgan and negotiated the purchase for $1.25 million. As he later admitted to another dealer, he sold them without profit: "I didn't take a penny for commission."[34] What he did next, however, ensured his future relationship with Frick and laid the ground for many future sales. He engaged the interior decorator Charles Allom, already at work in the mansion and a frequent collaborator with the dealer; and, together with another designer, Auguste Decour, Duveen oversaw the building of frames by Allom's craftsmen to fit the paintings into Frick's Drawing Room. This room had already been finished by 1915, so its architecture had to be adapted to the paintings.

As Duveen explained in a telegram to his colleagues, "Important for our sake room should be marvelous success considerable benefit will accrue to us."[35] Indeed, Duveen filled the room with objects appropriate to the period of the Fragonard paintings, including a commode by Riesener and a grouping of porcelain—a *Pot-pourri* à *Vaisseau* and two *Vases "à Oreilles,"* made at the Sèvres porcelain manufactory (fig. 83). One of Duveen's favorite ploys was to find and place furnishings in a newly decorated mansion in whose design he had a hand. For Edward Stotesbury and his wife, Eva, in Whitemarsh Hall outside Philadelphia, for example, in 1921 he sent truckloads of antiques, adroitly positioning them in the rooms and succeeding in selling many of them to the couple. Frick bought most of Duveen's recommended objects at the listed

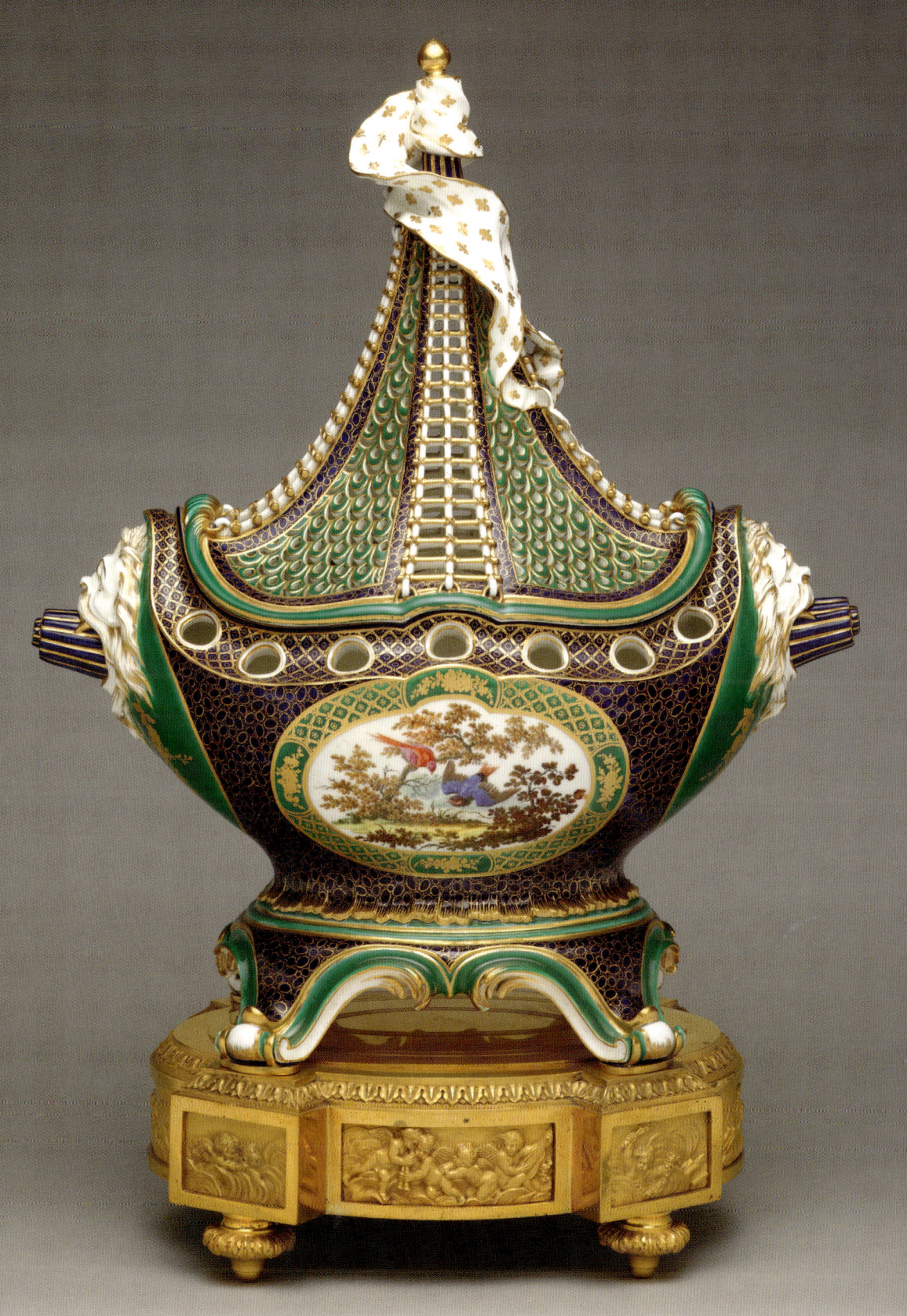

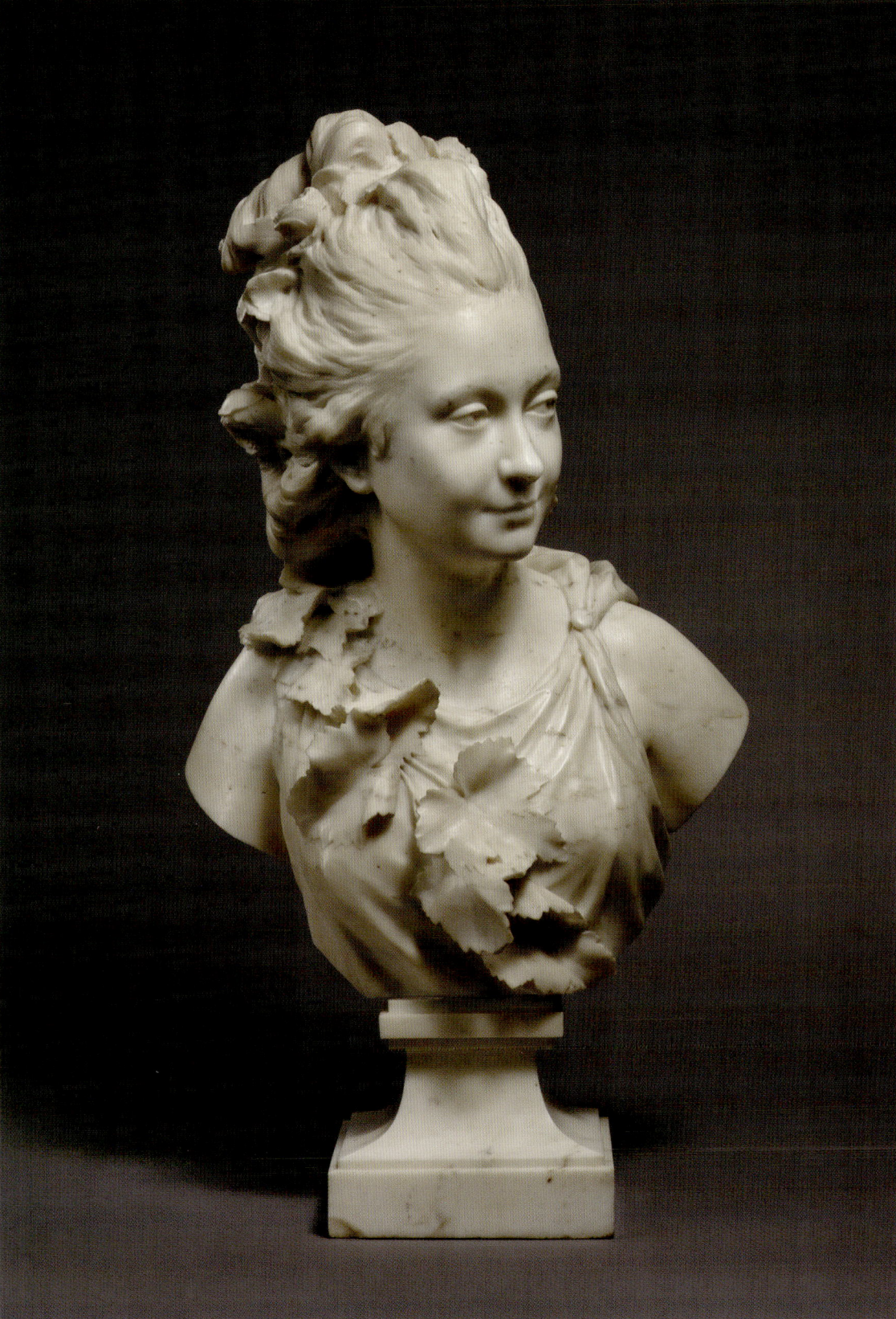

price. The dealer not only recouped his loss of a commission on the Fragonard paintings but also profited immensely.

A rare example of Duveen's cunning misfiring is the story of the marble bust intended for the Fragonard Room's mantelpiece. He searched for a chimneypiece suitable for the room and found a marble one decorated with bronze female satyrs that had been designed by the architect François-Joseph Bélanger in 1780–85. At the same time, Duveen knew that Frick wanted a marble bust to grace the Drawing Room. To make space for it, he ordered that the depth of the mantel be enlarged so that it could accommodate the bust. Frick, however, instead chose a bust of the comtesse du Cayla by Jean-Antoine Houdon, which was offered by rival dealers E. Gimpel and Wildenstein (fig. 84). Thus, an exquisite sculptural work did enter the room but not the one Duveen wished to sell his client. The sliver of marble inserted to expand the mantel is still visible. It is worth noting that to choose between the two busts, Frick insisted that both be delivered to the house so he could live with them and deliberate on which he preferred. Quite often, dealers would accommodate the wealthy collector by taking works of art to his home for him to see how they suited the space.

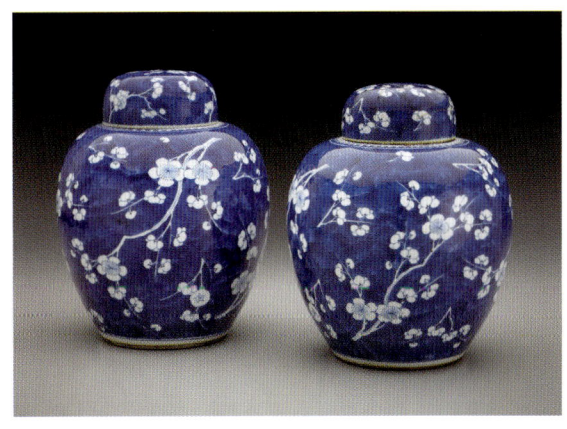

FIG. 84
Jean-Antoine Houdon, *Elisabeth-Suzanne de Jaucourt, Comtesse du Cayla*, 1777.

FIG. 85
Chinese, Qing Dynasty (1644–1911), Kangxi Period (1662–1722), *Covered Jars with Blue and White Decoration*, 18th century.

The success of the Fragonard Room gave Duveen an opening to supply Frick with furnishings for another room. De Wolfe had overseen the decoration of Adelaide's boudoir on the second floor, recommending for it some fine eighteenth-century French furniture and receiving a commission for these sales. In June 1916, the same month that Frick paid Duveen about $5 million for the furniture in the Fragonard Room and elsewhere in the house, the dealer was able to convince his client to add eight panels of allegorical paintings on the theme of the arts and sciences by Boucher and his studio. Duveen further persuaded him and Adelaide to dismantle the space that De Wolfe had created and commission French decorator André Carlhian to design wood paneling that would incorporate the Boucher paintings. Carlhian's interior included a mirrored wall cabinet, which was conveniently sized for a group of Sèvres porcelains. With this masterstroke, Duveen was able to sell more porcelain and small tables to complement the furnishings already present. When the mansion first opened as a museum in 1935, the panels by Boucher and his workshop were moved down to the first floor so the public could view them, their original site repurposed as the director's office. With the second floor now accessible to visitors, the Boucher panels have returned to their first location and the room's features, such as the porcelain cabinet and paint colors, restored to their original appearance (see fig. 67).

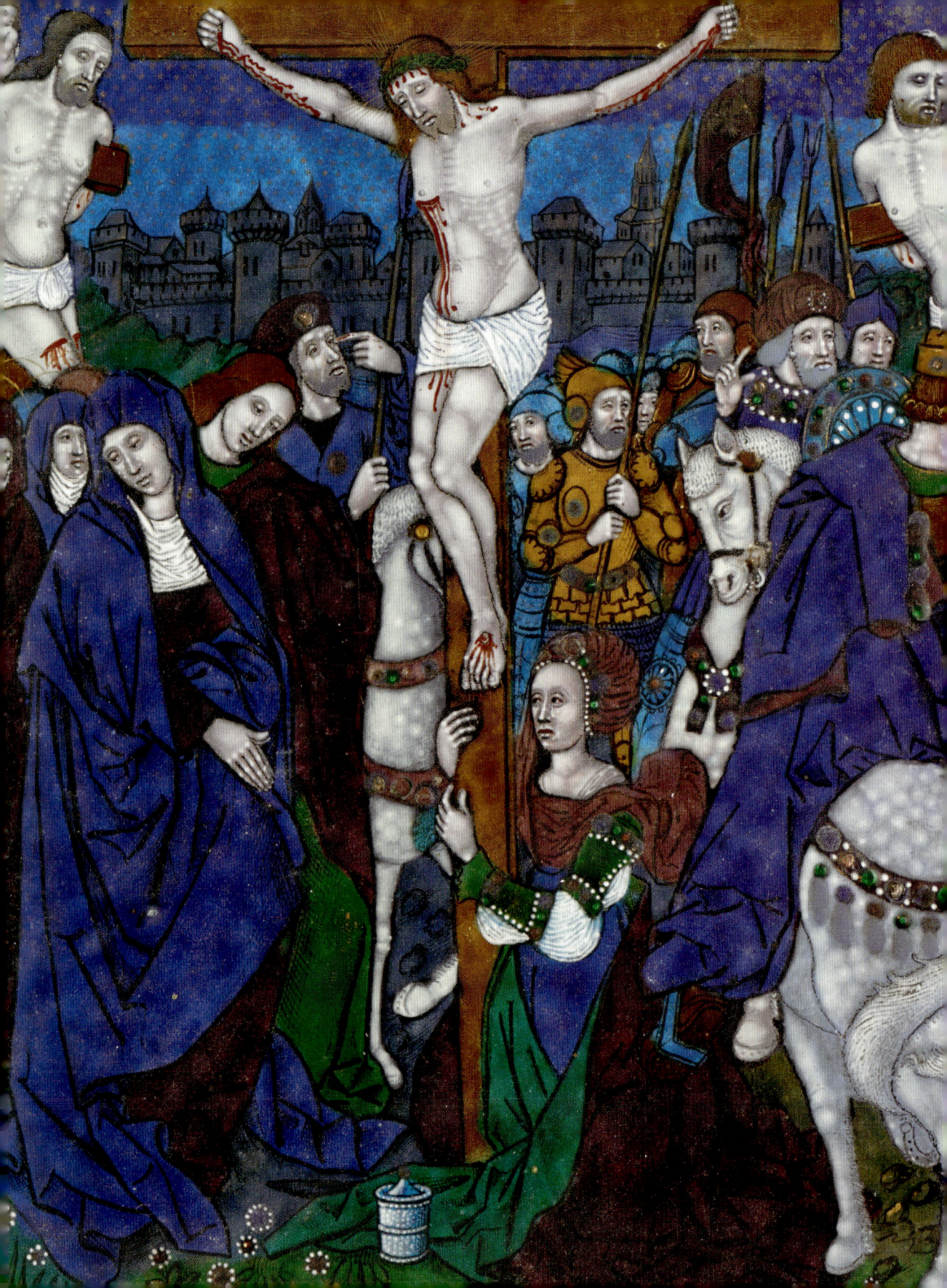

XII

CHOOSING WELL:
THE COLLECTION OF J. P. MORGAN

Banker and financier J. P. Morgan was a dominant figure in this dynamic period of American business, of such influence and stature that he organized a coalition to resolve a national economic crisis in 1907. Among corporate mergers that he engineered was the creation of the United States Steel Corporation, built on the Carnegie Steel Company; thus, he was entwined with Frick's former business. Morgan was also a philanthropist: as president of the Metropolitan Museum of Art from 1904 to 1913, he was instrumental in the museum's development. His gifts of art—including, in 1906, thousands of objects and architectural fragments from the Georges Hoentschel collection—enriched the museum and were foundational for its Department of Decorative Arts (see fig. 71). His rare books, manuscripts, and drawings are today housed in the Morgan Library & Museum. Morgan was the most voracious acquisitor of his day, often buying entire collections in his favorite media of ceramics, metalwork, tapestries, and sculpture from antiquity through the eighteenth century (fig. 86).

The timing of Morgan's death in 1913 proved providential for Frick. Just as the house at 1 East 70th Street was taking shape, its owner turning his attention to its furnishing, this great collection of objects became available. Morgan's son Jack arranged for four thousand of his father's objects to be displayed in thirteen galleries at the Metropolitan Museum of Art, and he was willing to sell them. Morgan's strength as a collector was not as much in paintings—though Frick did buy the important Fragonard *Progress of Love* series from the estate—as it was in books and manuscripts and in objects dating from antiquity through the eighteenth century. Two groups of Morgan's Renaissance objects, bronze statuettes and Limoges enamels, drew Frick's attention.

The casting and chasing of bronze statuettes flourished in Italy and Germany from the late fifteenth through early seventeenth centuries. These rare sculptures found their way into aristocratic and royal collections, which later became public in museums in Vienna, Paris, Berlin, Florence, London, and Dresden. By the turn of the nineteenth century, scholars such as Wilhelm von Bode, director of the Prussian

Detail of FIG. 89.

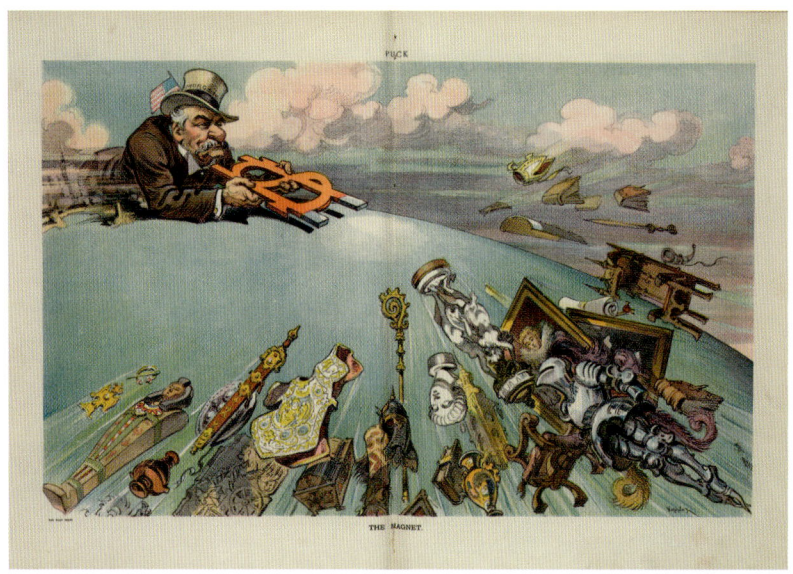

FIG. 86
Joseph Keppler Jr., "The
Magnet," from *Puck*
magazine, June 21, 1911.

Museums of Berlin (today known as the Berlin State Museums), were encouraging private art lovers to collect these works. According to Bode, Morgan's estate included "probably the most important collection of bronzes to be found in private possession."[36] Duveen arranged to represent all of them, and Frick had the opportunity to try out some of these sculptures in his house before making a significant purchase of eighty-six bronzes. While this was a large group, Frick took care that he could pick the best, as a letter of May 22, 1916, to Duveen makes clear: "The essence of our understanding . . . was, I was to have all the finest bronzes and Limoges in the collections purchased by you from the Estate of J. P. Morgan."[37]

Frick chose well. The finest of these rank among the very best produced by the foremost sculptors who practiced in this medium. One of the earliest, a relief of *The Resurrection* (1472), is the only signed work by Lorenzo di Pietro, the Sienese artist known as Vecchietta, outside of Italy (fig. 87). Another striking work is the *Shield Bearer* (ca. 1470–80) created by the influential master Bertoldo di Giovanni, a disciple of Donatello and teacher of Michelangelo, probably made for the Medici family in the 1470s. The great bronze master of the early sixteenth century, Andrea Brisoco, known as Riccio, is represented by an oil lamp, one of only three of this form that he created. Covered with small-scale reliefs, this deliberately antiquarian object was one of several fashioned for an intellectual clientele in the university town of Padua (fig. 88). A northern Italian rival of Riccio, Severo da Ravenna, or his workshop, produced no fewer than five works in the collection. One of his best represents the sea god Neptune standing on the back of a monster, his smooth, rippling musculature gleaming above the scaly creature he controls. These are only a few examples of what is one of the finest collections of Renaissance bronzes in the world.

The placement of these works reflects Frick's thinking of how they would fit in the decoration of the house. Several larger works, such as an early seventeenth-century bronze of Nessus and Deianira, attributed to Pietro Tacca, were of a scale to stand on tables in the large Picture Gallery. Likely at Duveen's suggestion, Frick positioned the smaller works on bookshelves in the Library, replicating the way Renaissance scholars displayed these works, or, idiosyncratically, below eye level, on cassoni in the Art Gallery. Frick acquired several larger sculptures, notably three important Renaissance bronze busts bought from Duveen in 1916. The finest of these is Jacques Jonghelinck's bust of Don Fernando Álvarez de Toledo, 3rd Duke of Alba (1571). Frick seems to have conceived of these, along with a fourth bust, as anchoring the corners of the Art Gallery. Their current placement in niches in the Garden Court returns to this concept. Frick even considered building a sculpture gallery. In 1915, Hastings drew up plans for one—for which elevations and renderings exist—adjacent to the Art Gallery on recently purchased land on East 71st Street. By 1917, however, Frick decided against this addition; he paid the architect only a portion of the bill rendered. While he bought several busts dating from periods that interested him—including an Italian Renaissance marble by Francesco Laurana and a French Rococo terra-cotta by Augustin Pajou—he did not favor full-length sculpture. One of Hastings's renderings includes an image of the large *Ugolino and His Children* by Jean-Baptiste Carpeaux (now in the Metropolitan Museum of Art), which suggests that Frick thought of acquiring full-length sculpture. If so, this appears to have been a passing fancy.

The art form of firing colored powdered glass onto copper sheets has been practiced in the French town of Limoges since the Middle Ages. In the sixteenth century, new techniques allowed this enameling to be more freely painted. The brilliant colors so well preserved by this method appealed to many nineteenth- and twentieth-century collectors, including Frick. Examples he might have seen in Europe or known about were those belonging to Sir Richard Wallace and to Baron Ferdinand de Rothschild, whose gift to the British Museum was known as the Waddesdon Bequest, as well as the 1909 gifts of George Salting to the Victoria & Albert Museum. In America, Henry Walters was among the first to collect Limoges enamels; others included William Randolph Hearst, Philip and Robert Lehman, Widener, and Charles Phelps Taft and Anna Sinton Taft. All of their enamels ended up in museums, the collectors gifting them to Baltimore, Los Angeles, New York, Philadelphia, and Cincinnati, respectively. While this art form is less widely recognized today, it was highly sought by collectors of Frick's time.

Morgan had acquired his enamels from dealers in Europe and New York, rapidly creating one of the most important groups in private hands, and he left it on loan to the Victoria & Albert Museum. In April 1916, Jack Morgan sold Duveen his father's Limoges for $750,000, together with the Renaissance bronzes for $1 million, and Italian maiolica for $500,000. (Curiously,

FIG. 87
Vecchietta (Lorenzo di Pietro), *The Resurrection*, 1472.

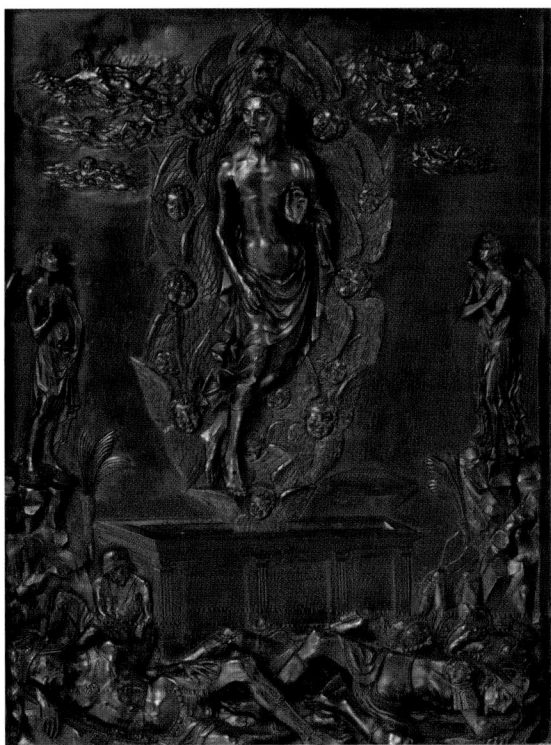

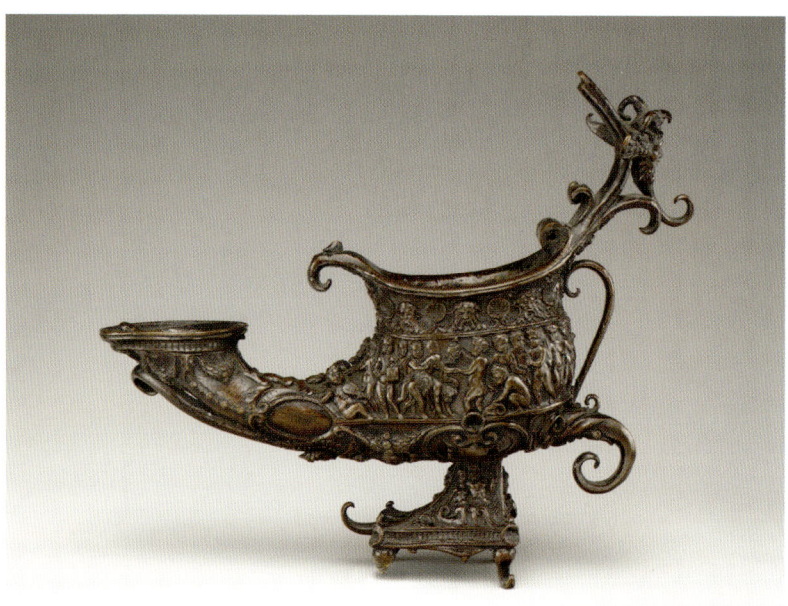

FIG. 88
Riccio (Andrea Briosco),
Lamp, ca. 1516–24.

maiolica—Italian tin-glazed pottery, much admired by collectors of the time—never appealed to Frick.) Within months, Duveen sold most of Morgan's Limoges, thirty-seven pieces, to Frick. The great masters Leonard Limousin and Pierre Reymond are represented along with other workshops, including that of Suzanne de Court, the only known female head of a workshop in Limoges. Religious and mythological subjects dominate, but also included are a number of portraits, which always appealed to Frick. While he rarely bought paintings with religious subjects, many of the early sixteenth-century enamels on copper are depictions of the life of Christ, including the *Triptych: The Way to Calvary, The Crucifixion, The Deposition* from the workshop of Nardon Pénicaud or Jean Pénicaud I, the most valuable of the lot, invoiced at $140,000 (fig. 89). Almost all the Limoges are polychrome in bright colors. The soberer yet sophisticated mid-sixteenth-century grisaille works (in tones of black, gray, and white) were not in fashion in the early twentieth century.

How Frick chose to display his latest acquisitions signaled, along with the high purchase price, his pride and interest in these works. As discussed, Frick gave up his office at the western end of the Art Gallery and ordered vertical display cases built for the enamels. While Duveen was negotiating the sale of the Limoges, he also bought a French collection, that of Maurice Chabrières-Arlès, famous for its Renaissance furniture and objects. Out of these, the dealer separated several pieces of furniture and, along with pieces from other sources, sold a group of sixteen to Frick on the same bill as the Limoges. It is likely that Duveen persuaded Frick that the Limoges would show well on furniture of the period, in the way that the Italian bronzes could be displayed on Italian Renaissance furniture. While a number of Americans assembled Italian Renaissance rooms, Frick was one of the few to create a French Renaissance environment; early photographs show the enamels resting on tables and *dressoirs*, as well as in the newly built cabinets (see fig. 80).

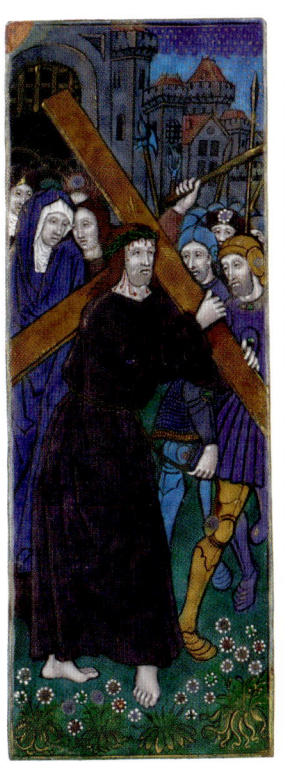

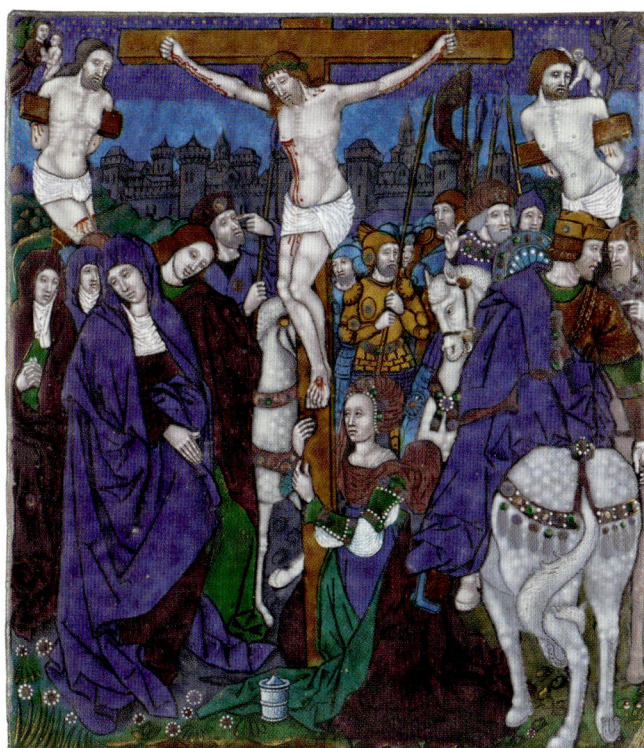

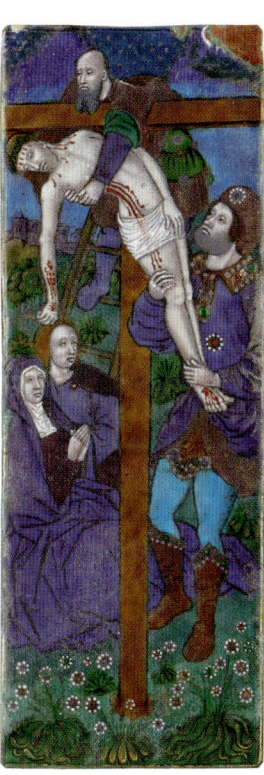

FIG. 89
Workshop of Nardon
Pénicaud or Jean Pénicaud I,
*Triptych: The Way to Calvary,
The Crucifixion, The Deposition*,
ca. 1520–25.

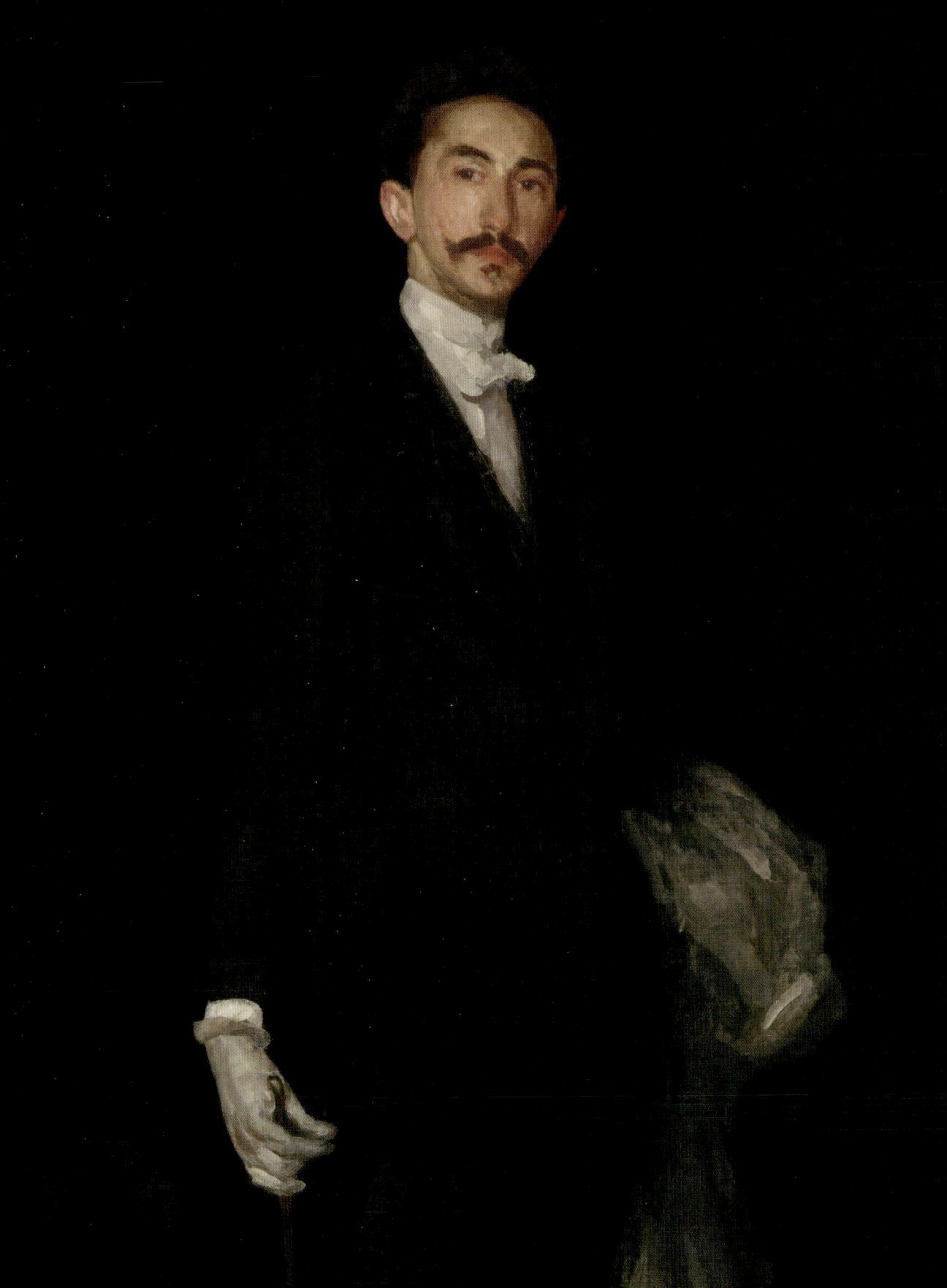

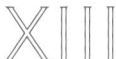

XIII

COLLECTING PAINTINGS,
1912–1919

By 1912, when Frick was able to take title to the property he had purchased at 1 East 70th Street, he was turning his attention to the design of a new house. As it became a reality, his artistic purchases were more often guided by the role they would play in the mansion. Just as the furnishings he bought, largely from Duveen or through De Wolfe, were often intended for specific rooms, the scale of the paintings he acquired increasingly measured up to the grand size of the house. At the same time, the major factor influencing the art market was the beginning of the world war. Economic need drove some European collectors to part with paintings, and, with the threat of destruction, many works of art were moved to America for safety. At the height of his power and wealth, Frick was well positioned to buy more art just as superb examples from across the Atlantic were becoming available.

He continued to buy what he liked, such as portraits, and sought work of increasing quality. One example, purchased in 1912, was the work of Hans Holbein the Younger, a German painter and designer whose precise portraiture appealed to those in the court of Henry VIII, among them the English statesman and author Sir Thomas More. More had welcomed Holbein into his home when the artist first arrived in England, and one senses a true sympathy between sitter and painter (fig. 90). Details, down to the glistening stubble of More's beard or the sheen of his red velvet sleeves, convince us of the exactitude of this image, yet his distant gaze offers a window into his idealism and vision.

Three years later, Frick found a companion to this painting—Holbein's *Thomas Cromwell* (1532–33). This was not a reunion, as had been the case for the portraits of Van Dyck's *Frans Snyders* and *Margareta de Vos*, but rather a face-off between two historical antagonists. Cromwell was the minister who interrogated More on behalf of the king and had More executed in 1535, when he refused to acknowledge Henry VIII as head of the Church of England. In turn, Cromwell was beheaded in 1540 for failing the king. That Frick was attuned to this parable of power is revealed in his placement of the two portraits, across from each another in the Living Hall, separated by yet another stern man, St. Jerome (see fig. 50).

Detail of FIG. 94.

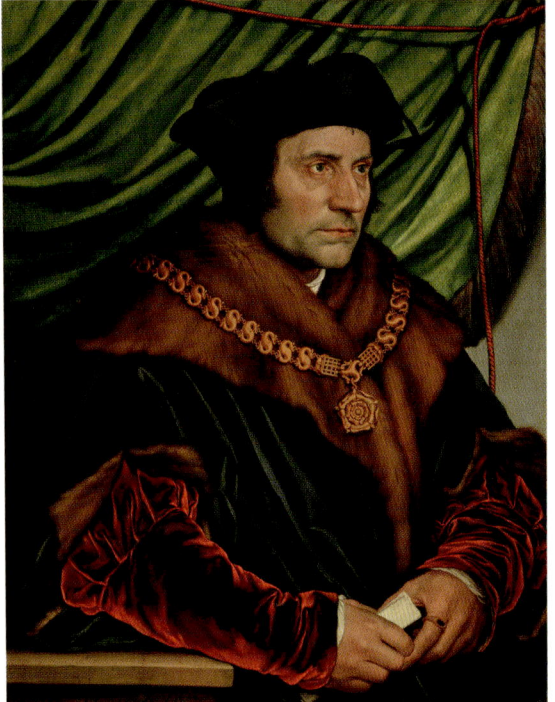

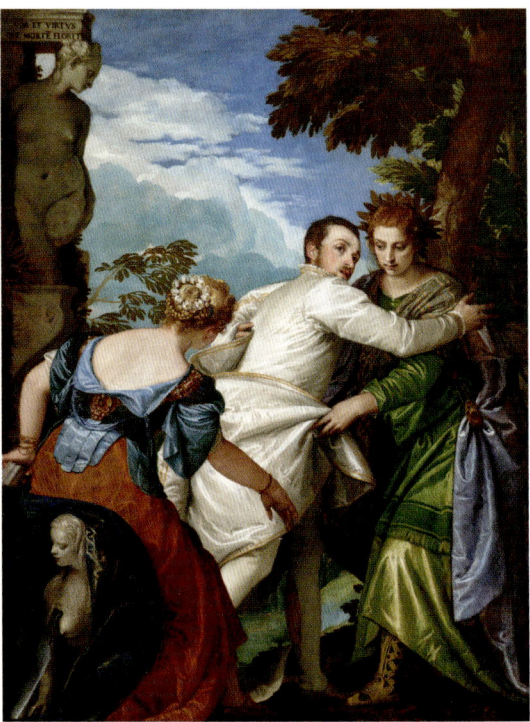

FIG. 90
Hans Holbein the Younger,
Sir Thomas More, 1527.

FIG. 91
Paolo Veronese (Paolo
Caliari), *The Choice Between
Virtue and Vice*, ca. 1565.

At the end of 1911, Carstairs moved two enormous paintings by Paolo Veronese to New York and hung them in the Vanderbilt mansion for Frick to consider. The canvases were just the right scale to command the large gallery Frick envisioned for his new house, and since their installation in 1914 at the western end of the gallery, they have never left (except during World War II and the 2020–25 renovation). The paintings are well matched to flank the door in the Art Gallery, but they may not have been originally intended as pendants. The first is *The Choice Between Virtue and Vice* (fig. 91), representing the myth in which Hercules is presented with a choice between good and evil. Here, however, Hercules is depicted as a contemporary aristocrat. Paolo's skill at rendering sumptuous, vividly colored cloaks and the elegant manners of those who wear them made him a favorite of Venice's elite. On a canvas of nearly the same dimensions, *Wisdom and Strength* represents another personification of abstract concepts. In this case, the fur-clad Hercules stands in for strength, while a richly dressed woman, an image of light beaming from her forehead, personifies wisdom. As with many of Paolo's paintings, details enrich the stories: Vice's claw-like fingernails reveal her malevolence, while the jewels and crown beneath Wisdom's feet remind the viewer that the qualities of the mind supersede the riches of the world. While the two paintings may not have been intended to hang beside one another, they have in fact traveled together through the palaces of some of the greatest art patrons. Emperor Rudolf II, Queen Christina of Sweden, and the Duke of Orléans—famous collectors all—are among the past owners of the two paintings. In addition to superb quality and condition, Frick prized the distinguished provenance of his artworks, none more elevated than these.

Size continued to matter as Frick acquired more paintings by a favorite, Van Dyck. Another large canvas, the eight-foot-tall *James Stanley, Lord Strange, Later 7th Earl of Derby, with His Wife, Charlotte, and Their Daughter* (ca. 1646) joins the beautiful, smaller portraits Frick had acquired of Frans Snyders and Margareta de Vos from Van Dyck's youthful period in Antwerp. This grand work is from the artist's mature period in England. The Earl of Derby owned lands in the north of England, as well as on the Isle of Man, which may be what he is indicating in the distance of the painting. A royalist, the earl was later beheaded during the English Civil War; however, in the idyllic moment depicted, the sweeping setting, flattering characterizations, and beautifully rendered costumes are ample evidence of the reasons why Van Dyck enjoyed popularity throughout Europe. Frick, too, was enamored. The following year, he bought another large Van Dyck painting—*Lady Anne Carey, Later Viscountess Claneboye and Countess of Clanbrassil* (ca. 1636)—and, in 1918, the portrait of the eccentric poet Sir John Suckling (ca. 1638).

As Frick prepared to occupy his house, finally taking possession in November 1914, he acquired still more impressive paintings. In mid-career, the great British landscape painter Joseph Mallord William Turner produced two of his most important works, *Harbour of Dieppe: Changement de Domicile* (fig. 92) and *Cologne, the Arrival of a Packet-Boat: Evening* (1826). When restrictions during the Napoleonic wars were lifted, European ports represented Britain's new freedom of travel. Capitalizing on their increased significance, Turner made numerous watercolors of European and British ports and had them engraved to reach a larger market. These two canvases were major statements by the artist when exhibited separately at the Royal Academy, one in 1825, and one in 1826. At its summer exhibition, *Dieppe* was criticized for depicting sunlight in a way that was more appropriate for southern climes than northern

FIG. 92
Joseph Mallord William Turner, *Harbour of Dieppe: Changement de Domicile*, exhibited 1825, but subsequently dated 1826.

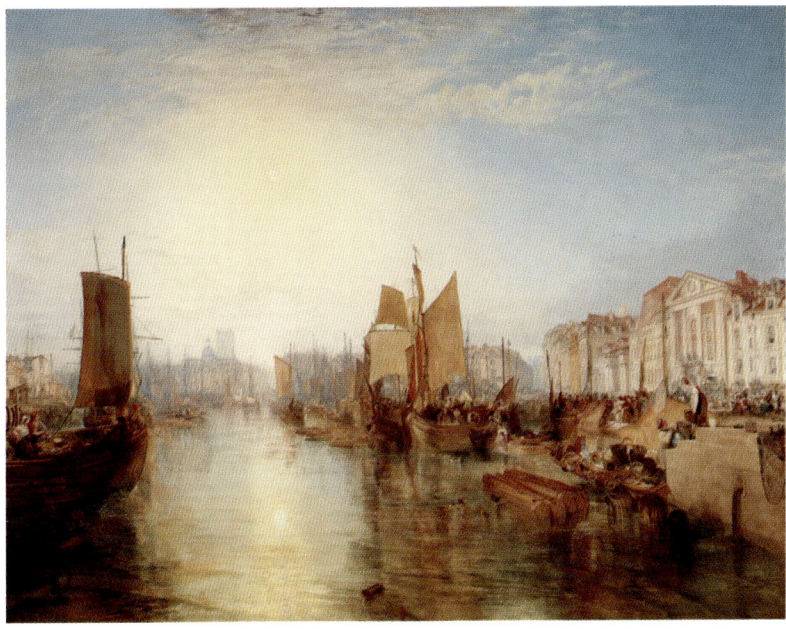

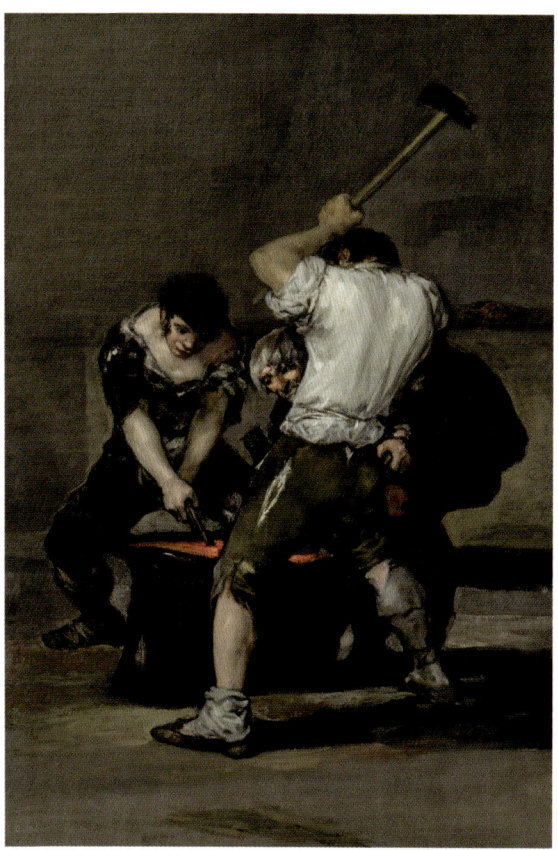

FIG. 93
Francisco de Goya y
Lucientes, *The Forge*,
ca. 1815–20.

France. For Turner, however, these represented a turning point, as he began to prime his canvases with a lighter ground color and brushed on newly invented pigments such as chrome yellow, to achieve a more infused form of light. Such experiments led to the increasing abstraction of the radiant sunlit scenes of his late work. Frick had been attracted to Turner before, in 1909 buying *Mortlake Terrace: Early Summer Morning*, a serene landscape that reflected his earlier taste for idyllic Barbizon School scenes (and which previously belonged to his friend Andrew Mellon). By comparison, these two striking port canvases represented a dramatic step forward in Frick's ambitions. Knoedler exhibited them in the New York gallery in January 1914; Frick bought *Cologne* first and *Dieppe* later that summer, hanging them under dust covers in the North and South Halls until construction was finished. It is surprising that their first location in the mansion was in narrow halls, where a viewer scarcely had space to stand back and admire them. Perhaps Frick thought they would not relate to the mainly seventeenth-century paintings then hanging in the Picture Gallery; once they took their place facing each other from the center of the long walls in the 1930s, they never left.

Another large canvas that arrived in 1914 is Goya's *Forge* (fig. 93). In a cavernous space, three figures surround an anvil: one holds the red-hot piece of metal to be worked, one pumps the bellows, and one hoists a large hammer to pound the metal into shape. A dramatic scene rendered in the expressive brushstrokes of Goya's late style, it is an atypical picture for Frick to have bought. Some writers conjecture that the painting reminded Frick of his coking and steel businesses. A visit to a steel mill or metal foundry confirms the intensity of this dangerous activity, brilliantly conveyed by Goya's brush. Frick rarely bought scenes of workers, and when he did, they were usually agrarian—farmers or shepherds. Given the disastrous events of the Homestead Strike, it seems unlikely that he would choose to be reminded of work in those factories. The quality of art came first in Frick's eye and mind. This is a superb painting by an artist he admired and of a scale that would fill his large, new house.

The same year saw the purchase of two significant portraits by James McNeill Whistler. Born in Massachusetts, but trained in Paris, Whistler moved to London in 1839 and made his name there as an expatriate painter. As early as 1901, Carstairs tried to interest Frick in Whistler and in 1911 offered him 250 Whistler etchings, which were turned down. When the Knoedler firm finally succeeded in convincing Frick to acquire Whistler, it was almost by chance.

After Charles Lang Freer, the greatest American collector of Whistler was Richard Albert Canfield, a former owner of gambling establishments. Imprisoned in

1885, Canfield claimed that his interest in art began during his time in jail. Having regained his fortune and established himself in New York, he proceeded to acquire as many Whistlers as he could. When, in 1914, Roland Knoedler happened on Canfield having a late breakfast at Delmonico's, he asked, "When are you going to sell your Whistlers, Dick?" Canfield replied, "You can have them today for $300,000."[38] Knoedler left to make a phone call and agreed to the sale when he returned. It is likely that he called Frick, since the next day several of the paintings were at the collector's house. As ever attracted to portraits, Frick purchased two of Whistler's monochromatic paintings, the first of them *Arrangement in Black and Gold: Comte Robert de Montesquiou-Fezensac* (fig. 94). Thought to be a model for Baron de Charlus, a principal character in Proust's *In Search of Lost Time*, this Parisian dandy was viewed through the painter's aesthetic lens. The sitter's black clothes submerge into the dark background, and his features have a nearly ghostly appearance. Two years later, Frick bought two more portraits, which also emphasize Whistler's practice of merging the colors of the figure with its surroundings. Most appealing of all is *Symphony in Flesh Colour and Pink: Portrait of Mrs. Frances Leyland* (1871–74), for which the artist controlled all aspects, even designing the sitter's gown. The Whistlers were among the most contemporary works Frick bought during this period; Montesquiou-Fezensac even outlived Frick. The collector added one more portrait and a landscape by Whistler, as well as several of his etchings, lithographs, and pastels. Numerically, more works by this artist than by any other entered the collection under Frick.

FIG. 94
James McNeill Whistler,
*Arrangement in Black
and Gold: Comte Robert
de Montesquiou-Fezensac*,
1891–92.

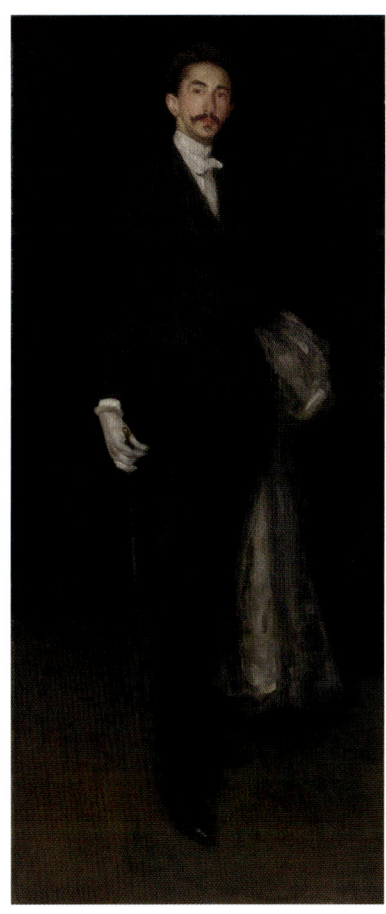

Seeing art placed throughout the house encouraged Frick's collecting passions, and 1915 was a banner year for acquisitions. In addition to the many decorative objects from Morgan's collection, and the Fragonard and Boucher panels that were installed that year and the next, Frick made some of his most important purchases of Renaissance painting. Financial instability brought on by the war flushed several paintings onto the market, and Frick was able to buy some of them. These included Bellini's *St. Francis in the Desert* and Titian's *Portrait of a Man in a Red Hat*, which the London merchant banker Arthur Morton Grenfell's bankruptcy forced him to sell back to Knoedler; another casualty of the stock market was James Dunn, who had to relinquish his *Lodovico Capponi* (ca. 1550–55) by Bronzino to Carstairs. Frick, too, was affected by the plunging stock market but was better positioned to surmount financial turbulence.

An extraordinary aspect of Bellini's *St. Francis in the Desert* (fig. 95) is its provenance, which stretches back to its very commission by Zuan Michiel, who

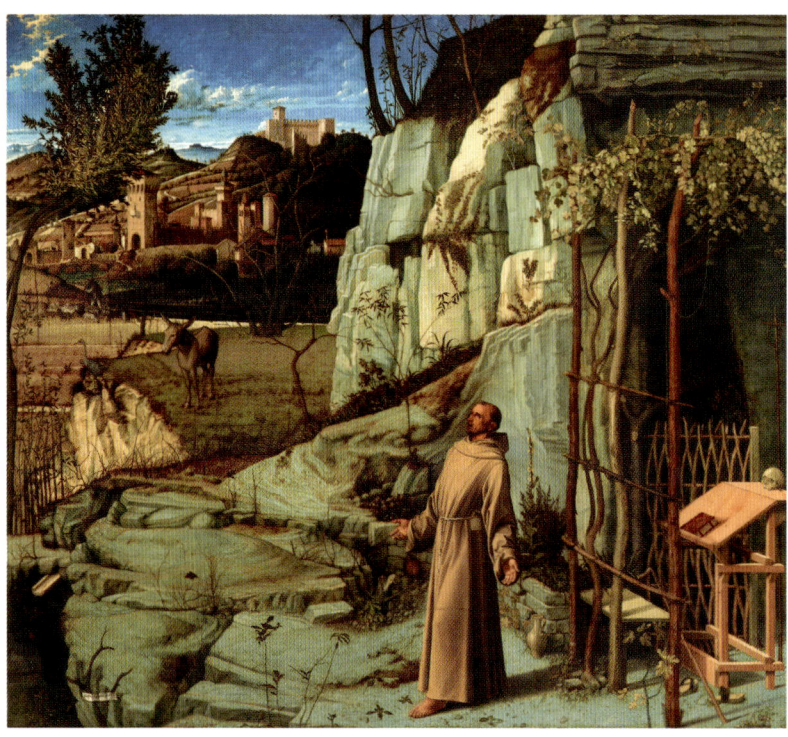

FIG. 95
Giovanni Bellini, *St. Francis in the Desert*, ca. 1475–80.

FIG. 96
Titian (Tiziano Vecellio), *Portrait of a Man in a Red Hat*, ca. 1520.

died in Venice in 1513, and its subsequent description in 1525 by the scholar and collector Marcantonio Michiel in the collection of Taddeo Contarini. The painting still bears Michiel's title for it. Bellini represents the saint receiving the stigmata at La Verna, omitting the image of the crucified Christ borne by angels, which is usually depicted as the source of the marks of the cross on the saint. Francis steps out of his rustic study to greet the day, standing before the monastic community he founded in 1224; while it is a moment of great religious significance, it is also a poetic study of man in nature.

Because Frick was not particularly drawn to religious subjects, the pure beauty of the landscape may have been the deciding factor in his buying the Bellini. Extra persuasion was needed to convince him to acquire what is today acknowledged to be one of the greatest paintings in his collection, indeed, one of the finest Italian Renaissance works in North America. Carstairs wrote to Frick a second time when the collector balked at buying it and the National Gallery in London expressed interest in it. In the end, the painting took pride of place in the Living Hall, where six Renaissance masterpieces hung.

Next to the Bellini, Frick placed another Venetian painting, one by Titian, an artist influenced by the older master. Like Bellini, Titian was official painter to the Republic of Venice. His flowing, sensuous manner, fully evident in this early work, *Portrait of a Man in a Red Hat* (fig. 96), dominated painting in the republic, known as La Serenissima, in the sixteenth century. The unidentified young man is lavishly dressed in a black coat lined with lynx fur that covers a gold garment, called a *saione*, and a white shirt. His red hat is associated with northern European styles of dress—such

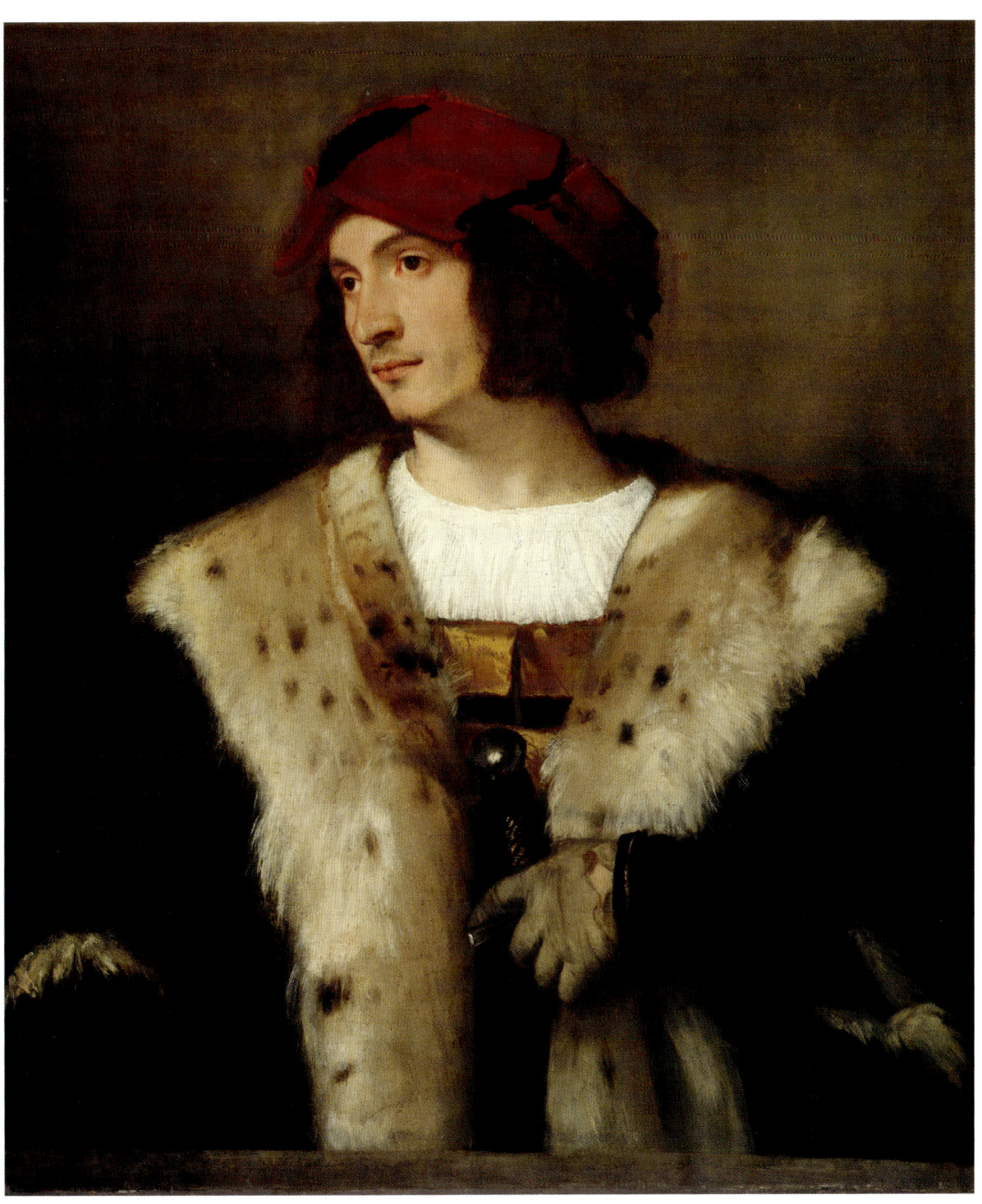

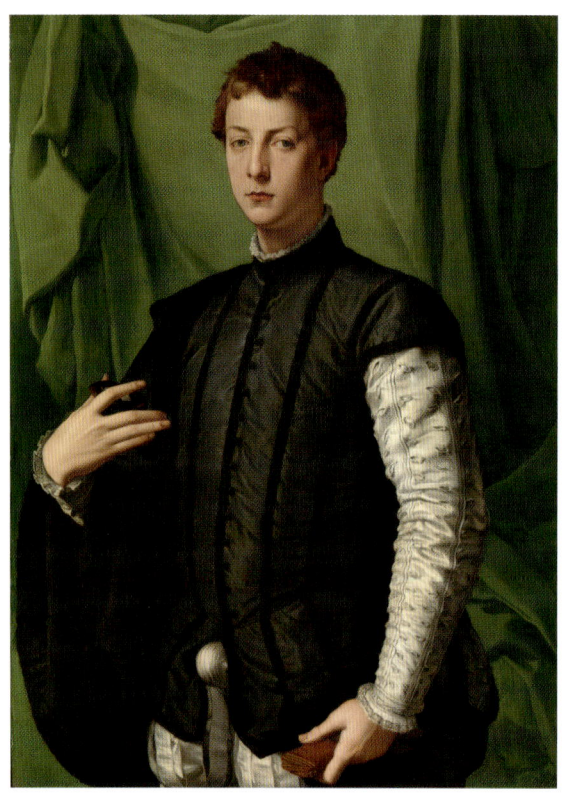

FIG. 97
Agnolo Bronzino (Agnolo
di Cosimo), *Lodovico
Capponi*, ca. 1550–55.

headgear was often worn by Germans living in this great trading city—perhaps a clue to the man's identity. The thrust of the man's sword hilt, contradicting his dreamy expression, adds tension to the painting.

Strikingly different in style is another Italian Renaissance portrait bought in 1915. Bronzino was court painter to the Medici in Florence, an artistic leader in this time and place as Titian was in his. While Titian's brush evokes the texture of fur and leather, Bronzino's, in his portrait of Lodovico Capponi (fig. 97), is explicit, rendering every stitch in the lace cuffs or wrinkle in the black satin jacket. Compared to Titian's visage, Bronzino depicts the sitter's features with crystalline precision. An implied narrative animates this severe, icy portrait. The medal or cameo he holds in his right hand bears a portrait of a woman and is inscribed with the Italian word *sorte*, meaning fate or fortune. An accomplished poet, Bronzino may have included the word to allude to Capponi's love affair with Maddalena Vettori, whom he wished to marry and did—but only after a dramatic delay—with permission finally granted by Duke Cosimo I de'Medici. All three of these purchases—the Bellini, the Titian, and the Bronzino—made in the same year, are masterpieces by some of the greatest Italian Renaissance painters. In a sense, they are also masterpieces of Frick's collecting, supreme works of art acquired at the height of his visual acumen and buying power.

Frick's last three years of collecting follow his earlier inclinations. Four paintings by Boucher, collectively titled *The Four Seasons* (1755), were bought in 1916. Ravishingly beautiful, these paintings complement the scenes of children enacting the arts and sciences from the panels of the Boucher Room. Both commissions were conceived as room decorations, since the *Seasons* were originally overdoors set into the architecture of an interior, just as the depictions of children were paired in the panels of a room. As such, both sets were conceived as series, for example, a range of professions, such as sculptor, painter, and architect, versus the four seasons, spring, summer, fall, and winter. Not surprisingly, Duveen nudged Frick to this purchase. Although the prominence of the Fragonard and Boucher Rooms in the mansion makes one think of Frick as having a proclivity for French art, he actually bought relatively few eighteenth-century French paintings, the *Seasons* being among the best. The Frick's canvases by Jean-Siméon Chardin, Jean-Baptiste Greuze, and Jean-Antoine Watteau all came into the collection decades after his death.

Frick continued to fulfill his love for Gainsborough, buying, through Duveen, the full-length *Mrs. Peter William Baker* (1781) to keep company with *The Hon. Frances Duncombe* that he had acquired six years earlier. More unusual was *The Mall in St. James's Park* (ca. 1783), which combines Gainsborough's facility with portraiture (although none of the figures are clearly identifiable) with his talents as a landscapist. A group of women accompanied by a soldier march down the center of the mall, while clutches of other women stare at them and chatter. A critic described the brushwork for the trees as if the artist were waving a fan, much as the ladies depicted might. Their fashionable attire is set against the pastoral scene of dairy cows, still necessary in central London before pasteurization enabled milk to be transported into the city without spoiling. Frick collected few drawings, but he did have a landscape sketch by Gainsborough, reflecting his interest in the British artist's depiction of nature.

Toward the end of his life, Frick made a few purchases of what might be termed modern art, returning to his earlier taste for contemporary French canvases of the Barbizon School but now seeking out more progressive Impressionist masters. Earlier in his life, he had bought paintings by Claude Monet. In 1914, he bought canvases by Manet, Pierre-Auguste Renoir, and Edgar Degas. The largest and most important of the three is Renoir's *La Promenade* (1876). It was later thought to represent a mother with children and was retitled as such, but a 2011 scientific study reveals that an older woman was painted out by the artist; so these are likely two sisters accompanied by a nanny or older sister. Degas's *Rehearsal* (1878–79) is a fine example of the many evocations the painter made behind-the-scenes of a dance studio, with an angle of vision and cut-off figures that thrust the viewer into the composition. The most innovative is Manet's *Bullfight* (fig. 98), which is the upper portion of a larger painting that the artist cut in pieces after a bad critical review. Manet's flat passages of color and summary depictions of the audience were startling at the time. Frick kept the Manet and Degas in his sitting room on the second floor, an indication that these canvases were more private expressions of his taste. This late excursion into modern art makes one wonder whether he might have continued to collect in this area were it not for his sudden death in 1919.

Poignantly, Frick's final purchase was another work by a favorite artist, Vermeer. One of the largest of the Delft master's paintings, *Mistress and Maid* (ca. 1666–67) is a variant on the artist's theme of love letters, showing a maid passing a note to the well-dressed woman seated at the table. The artist emphasized this ambiguous social exchange, as we know from recent scientific research, by painting out a rather busy interior background. Evidently, Frick was much taken with the painting, even moving his dinner-table chair at Eagle Rock to face it. To the end, Frick showed his deep love of art.

FIG. 98
Edouard Manet, *The Bullfight*, 1864.

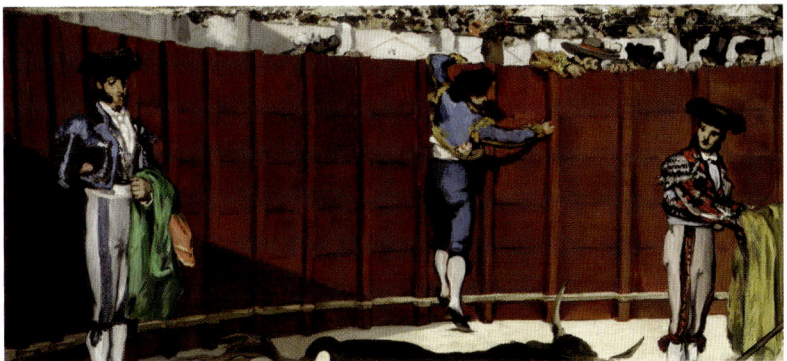

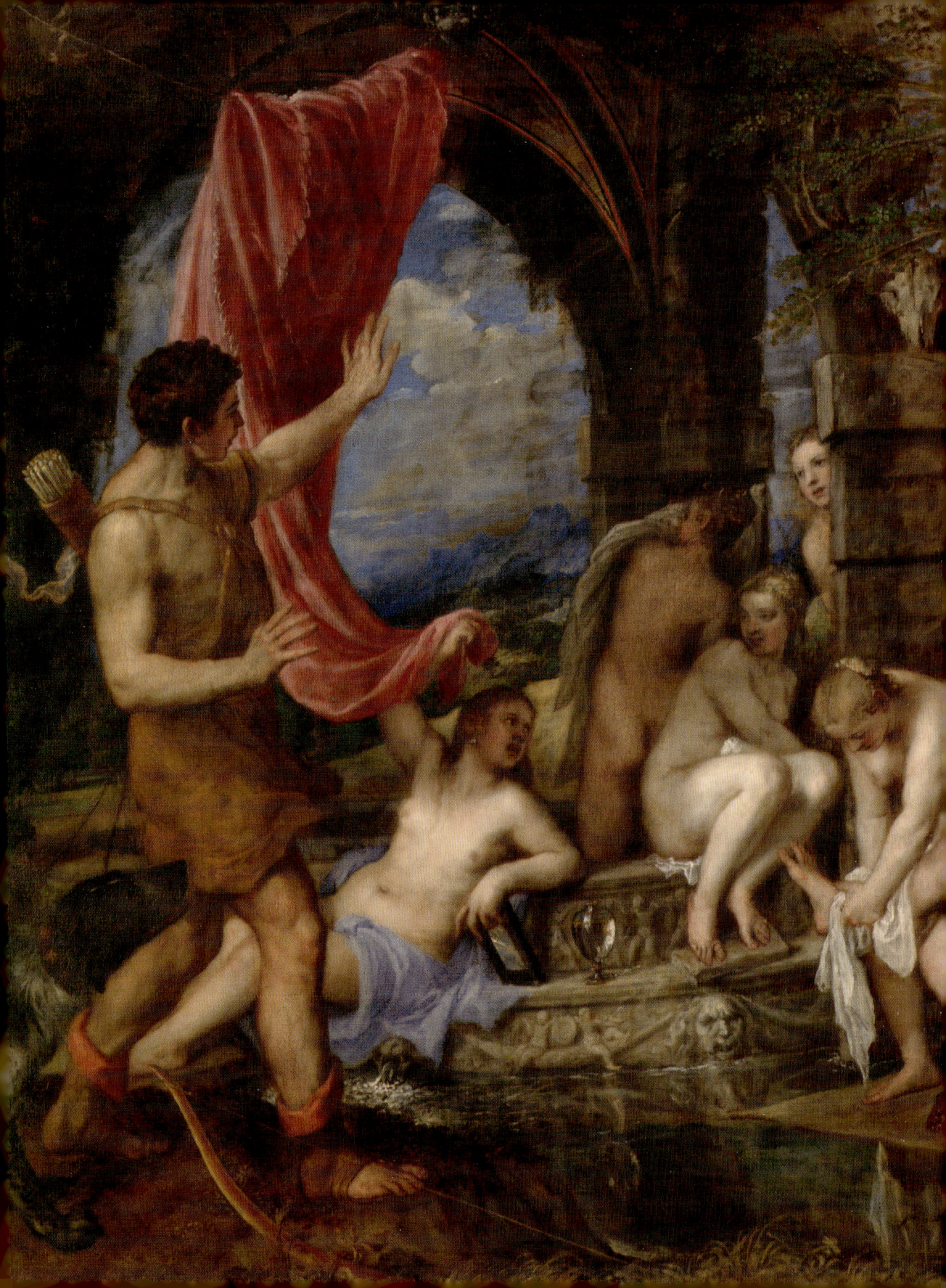

THE ONES THAT GOT AWAY

Frick's competitive nature sharpened when other collectors or institutions were vying for the same painting that he was. He did not lose gracefully, and failing to get a work he coveted often spurred him on to acquire others by the same artist. Examining the cases of some paintings that he failed to purchase also gives a sense of his ambitions and of the scope he aimed at in collecting.

The most famous of these misses was Holbein's full-length portrait *Christina of Denmark, Duchess of Milan* (fig. 99). Belonging to Henry Fitzalan-Howard, 15th Duke of Norfolk, it had been lent to the National Gallery in London for years. Though Christina was Danish and Holbein German, both subject and painter were much admired in Britain. Holbein had enjoyed special stature as painter to Henry VIII, who had commissioned the portrait in 1538, when he was considering Christina as a marriage prospect. In the spring of 1909, Frick contracted with Carstairs to purchase the picture from the duke for £72,000. It would have been a major step forward for his collection. The only condition of the sale was that the National Gallery had the option of acquiring it first, if it could raise funds for the purchase price by June 1.

The celebrity of the Holbein portrait and the nation's consternation at possibly losing such a masterpiece is summed up by a cartoon that appeared in *Punch* magazine on May 12, 1909 (fig. 100). A malevolent Uncle Sam, in striped trousers and a starred hat, clutches a money bag in one hand and attempts to drag Christina out of the picture with the other. Resisting, she braces herself with one foot and one hand on the frame. A note on the wall behind her reads, "Please spare £70,000." Parliamentary laws increasing death duties in Britain pressured many noble families to sell art in order to pay taxes; this also made it more difficult to raise funds to save works for the nation. By 1913, a government account noted that dozens of works by Rembrandt and Rubens, as well as by Holbein and Vermeer, had left the country. The National Gallery director Charles Holroyd despaired at raising the money needed. By the weekend before the option ran out, only £32,000 had been raised, and the painting appeared to be Frick's. Dramatically, however, Carstairs cabled Frick on June 1:

Detail of FIG. 102.

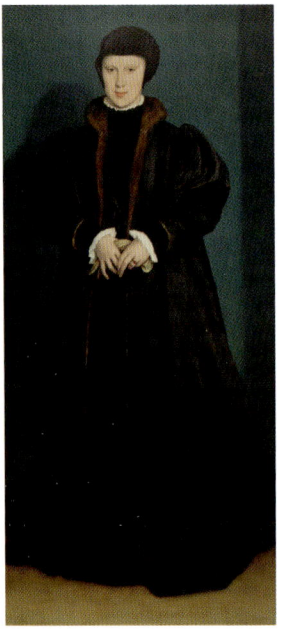

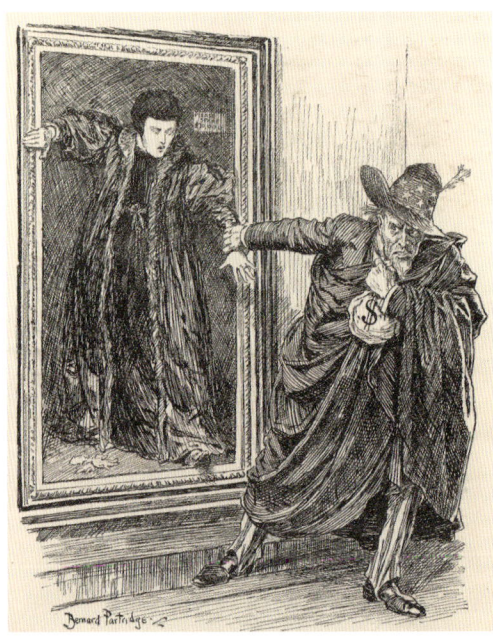

"NATION RETAINS HOLBEIN BALANCE MONEY SUBSCRIBED TODAY REGRET CANT BE YOURS." Angrily, Frick replied, "CONSIDER HAVE BEEN TRIFLED WITH. NO AUTHORITY EXTEND OPTION WHICH EXPIRED YESTERDAY."[39] In the aftermath of the affair, it was revealed that an anonymous donor had cabled over the weekend that she would contribute the needed £40,000. The money did not arrive until weeks later, and there was a misunderstanding over the legal deadline of the option. Frick was right to be upset. But the Holbein remained in England.

Failing to get the portrait of Christina only whetted Frick's appetite for a Holbein. His rivals Isabella Stewart Gardner and J. P. Morgan had already bought paintings by the artist. When another famous Holbein, the abovementioned portrait of Sir Thomas More (see fig. 90), became available and Roger Fry approved of the picture, Frick acted through Carstairs to buy the painting for £55,000 in January 1912. While Frick did not get the first Holbein he tried for, he did in time succeed in acquiring one of the finest of all paintings by the artist.

Another missed opportunity for Frick had occurred in 1907 with Van Dyck paintings of the Genoese Cattaneo family. Carstairs, along with the dealer Otto Gutekunst, represented a group of paintings of which the most spectacular was of Marchesa Elena Grimaldi Cattaneo (fig. 101). Frick was given the first opportunity to choose from the paintings, and he traveled to Paris to see them. Carstairs wrote him, "There is no question, no argument, from every standpoint it is Van Dyck's masterpiece."[40] It is an exaggeration to say that it is the artist's absolute best painting, but it is certainly one of them. The year 1907 was a financially difficult one in the United States and for Frick too, so he declined the pricey painting (offered at $490,000). Carstairs instead sold it to Peter Widener, ruefully writing Frick in 1908, "My feelings on the subject are somewhat mixed. I always expected you to take this great picture."[41]

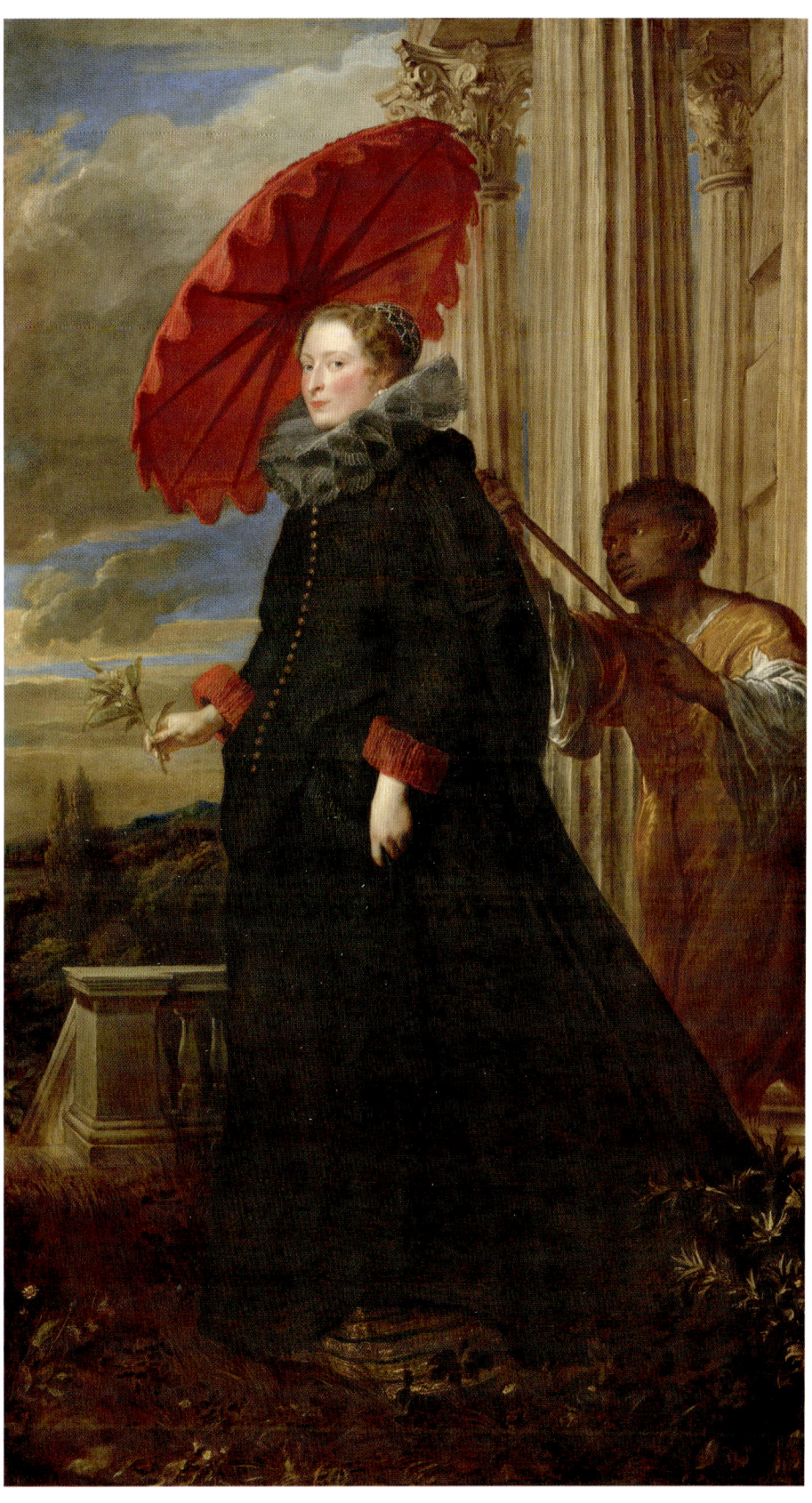

Over time, the collector made up for the loss by acquiring eight works by Van Dyck, one of the most important groups in the United States.

Two famous paintings by Titian, sought by Frick, would have dramatically reshaped the collection. *Diana and Actaeon* (fig. 102) and *Diana and Callisto* (both 1556–59, now owned jointly by the National Gallery, London, and the National Galleries of Scotland) were part of a series of six mythological subjects known as the *poesie* that Titian painted late in his career for Philip II of Spain. Long chains of letters and telegrams dating 1916–18 and 1921–25 in the Frick Archives reveal an intense campaign involving a number of dealers and parties interested in their acquisition.[42] On February 19, 1916, Alfred Anson wrote Frick that he had sent a letter to his cousin Violet Ellesmere to inquire whether the Titians might be for sale. Together with two other Titians—*The Three Ages of Man* and *Venus Anadyomene*—the paintings were held by the Ellesmere family, heirs to the dukes of Sutherland, in Bridgewater, their house in London. In reply, Frick clarifies that he is interested in the two "Dianas." At this point, the dealers Lockett Agnew and Joseph Duveen became involved, with Duveen recommending to Frick that the paintings would be "reasonable at 200,000 pounds, but we would give 220,000. At 250,000, they would be too dear." The owners at Bridgewater refused to accept less than £400,000 for the four, "fancy prices" that Frick found "ridiculous." His offer of £160,000 was rejected.

What makes this story even more interesting is that, in 1921, Helen Clay returned to the effort. In a letter to her of March 30, 1921, the artist and art dealer

FIG. 102
Titian (Tiziano Vecellio),
Diana and Actaeon, 1556–59.

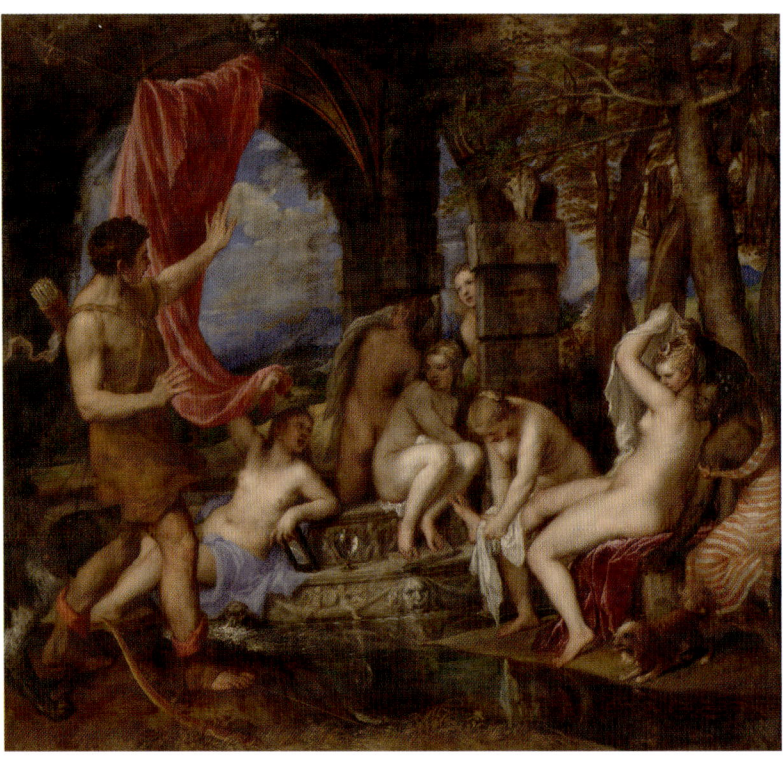

Alice Creelman (1858–1952) attempted to be an intermediary and urged Helen Clay to buy the Titians: "Do forgive me for writing so freely about a matter entirely your affair but I do feel a certain affection and pride in seeing the museum develop and take the place in the world Mr. Frick wished—a second great Wallace Collection." A different coalition of dealers, including the London-based Arthur J. Sulley and the agent Henriette Lewis Hind in London, interceded and recommended an offer of £250,000. On December 20, 1922, the Frick trustees voted to provide £180,000, up to 200,000. What would have been one of Helen Clay's first great acquisitions was again rebuffed by the family.

Only in 2012 were the Diana paintings sold to the National Gallery in London and National Galleries of Scotland. In 2020, the six paintings were reunited for the first time in exhibitions that traveled to Edinburgh, Madrid, Boston, and London. Two paintings of the series that Frick would have known well and coveted—Isabella Stewart Gardner's *Rape of Europa* (1559–62) and the Wallace Collection's *Perseus and Andromeda* (1554–56)—were, for the first time in the institution's history, lent to this historic exhibition.

A lost opportunity of a different nature concerned the artist John Singer Sargent, widely recognized at the time as one of the greatest living portraitists. Frick had admired Sargent's portrait of Gardner, and he went to Sargent with a request for the artist to paint him; but Sargent flatly turned him down. This was late in the artist's career, and he had begun to tire of commissions. Frick did buy two Sargents in the last years of his life—*Sheepfold in the Tirol* (private collection) and *Corner of the Church of St. Stae, Venice* (Museum of Fine Arts, Boston)—but gave them three years later to Lewis Cass Ledyard, who had helped him draft his will. Three years after his death, in 1922, Helen Clay, then head of the Frick's Acquisitions Committee, received a letter offering one of Sargent's most important paintings, *Gertrude Vernon, Lady Agnew of Lochnaw* (National Galleries, Scotland). She responded, "I regret very much that we are not purchasing just now."[43] She did not even bring it to the committee's attention.

As an active collector, Frick was offered numerous works of art, and for various reasons he turned down many of them—too expensive, not good enough, not to his taste. His discernment is the reason his collection is celebrated. Nonetheless, it is interesting to note what he failed to acquire and how those experiences motivated him to double down on his collecting activity.

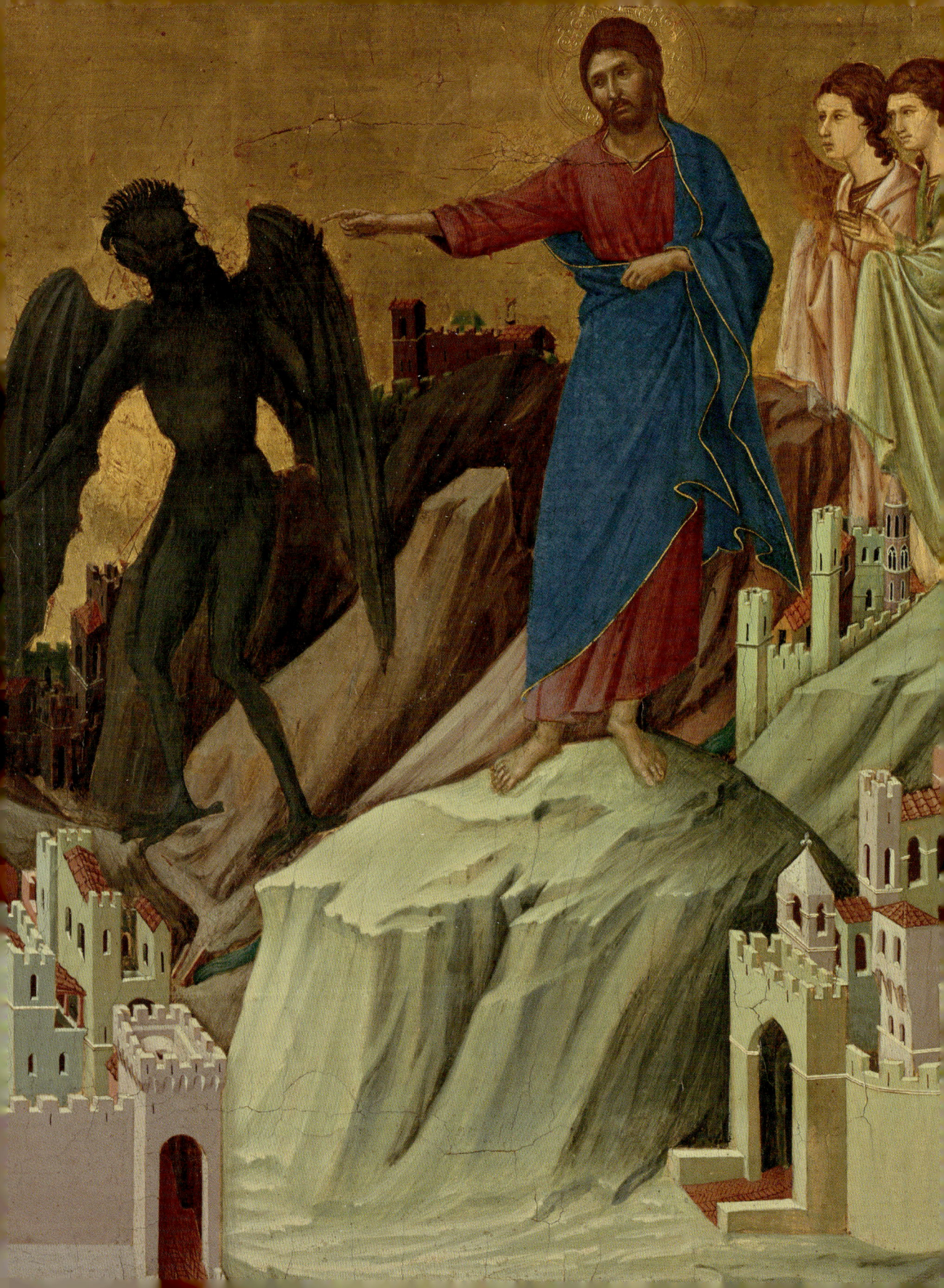

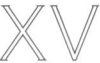

XV

FURTHERING THE FRICK COLLECTION: HELEN CLAY FRICK

Henry and Adelaide's third child, Helen Clay Frick, was born in Pittsburgh in 1888. Helen Clay was educated by a Swiss governess; after the move to New York, she attended the Spence School. An inclination to philanthropy began early, when, for her debutante gift in 1908, she asked her father for the donation of land as a public park, now Frick Park, in Pittsburgh. Interest in art came quite naturally through her father on visits to artist studios and travel to Europe. Her travel diaries overflow with postcards of paintings she saw in European museums alongside her penned observations. She continued these diaries throughout her life; seven scrapbooks of her trips to Italy in the 1920s and '30s are filled with her snapshots, postcards, and prints of artworks she purchased from photography firms such as Fratelli Alinari, Florence, alongside musings on and lists of what she had seen. A visit to The Hague in 1932, for example, is recorded by a card of Vermeer's *Girl with a Pearl Earring* (fig. 104).

A desire to help others combined with her affection for Europe when she established, in November 1917, a Frick unit under the Red Cross in France and worked to aid refugee women and children (fig. 103). On her return to New York, she resided with her family at the Fifth Avenue house. Following her father's death in 1919, she inherited a considerable portion of his fortune—$38 million—making her the country's wealthiest unmarried woman at that time. She never married or had children.

Helen Clay devoted herself to furthering The Frick Collection and knowledge about it. In the process, she acquired art for the museum, as well as for her personal holdings. She also established the Frick Art Research Library (FARL), which would become one of the foremost repositories of books and photographs for the study of art history. Even before her father's death, she had begun cataloguing the family art collection. In 1920, she traveled to Europe on her first independent trip and in London met Robert Witt, who had founded a library for photographic reproductions of works of art. The ease of finding images on the internet today makes it hard to imagine how difficult securing images was then. Helen Clay purchased photographs and commissioned photographers to reproduce paintings in churches, private

Detail of FIG. 106.

homes, and other out-of-the-way locations. In 1926, for example, she commissioned photographer Mario Sansoni to take advantage of temporary scaffolding in the upper church of San Francesco in Assisi to photograph frescos by Cimabue for the library. Wartime destruction of monuments, and the need to retain images of works that might be lost, added urgency to this endeavor. By the time of World War II, the resources of the Frick Art Research Library (FARL) served to annotate hundreds of maps that Allied bomber pilots used to avoid attacking monuments of cultural significance. Over several years, Helen Clay assembled an archive of thirteen thousand photographic records. Having since grown to 1.4 million, this resource is in the process of being digitized and joined with fourteen other photo archives around the world—in a consortium known as PHAROS—to make twenty-five million images and associated texts available to the public on the internet.

When the boxes of photographs and shelves of books outgrew their temporary quarters (in the mansion's bowling alley) in 1924, Helen Clay commissioned Thomas Hastings, who designed the Fifth Avenue mansion, to design a building on East 71st Street. In the 1930s, at the same time that the mansion expanded to become a public museum, Pope demolished Hastings's library and, on the site of two former town houses purchased by the Frick, erected the present structure (fig. 105). At a moment when the library's total holdings numbered 90,000 books, the larger library was designed with unusual foresight to hold 350,000. Not until 2002, sixty-seven years later, was capacity reached and off-site storage for less-in-demand books deemed necessary.

Alongside bibliographic activities, Helen Clay harnessed her wealth and knowledge to enhance the Frick's art collection. Between 1924 and 1935, before the collection opened as a museum, she headed the Acquisitions Committee and was the sole member who could propose works of art to be considered for purchase. Of profound effect on the collection was her decision to follow her own tastes into

FIG. 103
Helen Clay Frick (center) visiting soldiers in France during her Red Cross service, 1918.

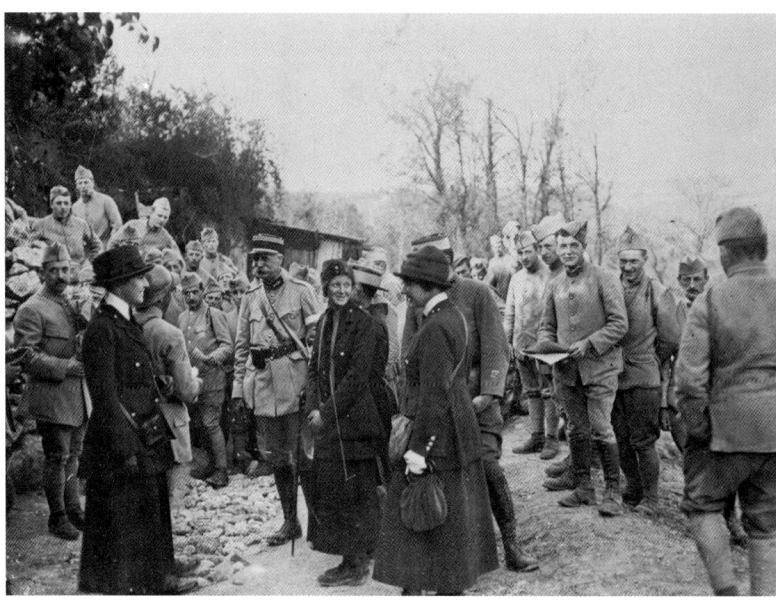

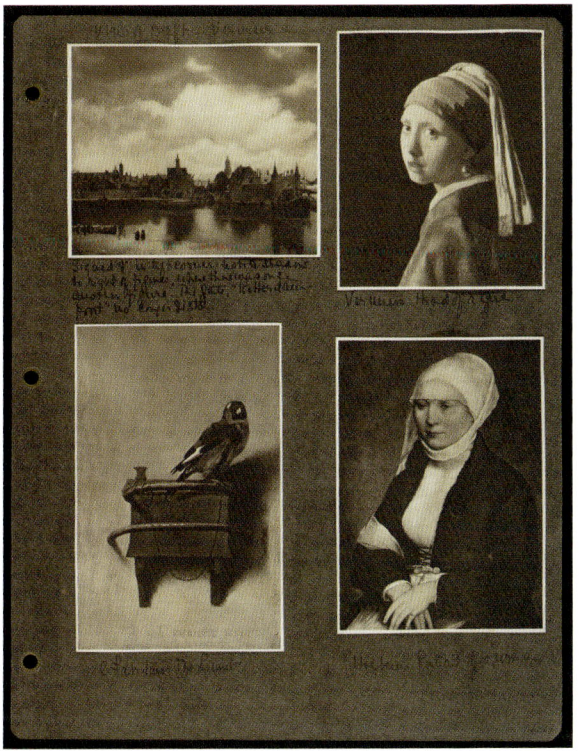

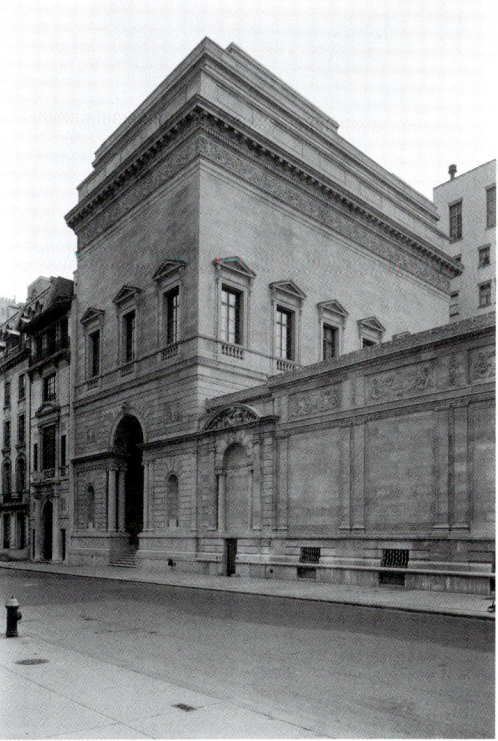

areas of little or no interest to her father. Two paintings that she bought in a single year, 1927, illustrate this new direction and offer evidence of the exceptional level of quality she sought. First is Duccio di Buoninsegna's *Temptation of Christ on the Mountain* (fig. 106), a rare panel from the Maestà, the Siena Cathedral altarpiece (now in the adjacent Museo dell'Opera del Duomo) and the masterpiece of this forerunner of the Renaissance. In the painting, Christ is shown rejecting the Devil's bribe of all the cities of the world, which are detailed in miniature below the craggy setting. Henry had shown little inclination to buy works with religious subjects or paintings from the early Renaissance. Helen Clay continued to acquire works by other masters of this period, including Paolo and Giovanni Veneziano and Piero della Francesca, creating a foundation of one of the most distinguished groups of trecento and quattrocento paintings in America.

Helen Clay's other masterstroke of 1927 was purchasing Jean-Auguste-Dominique Ingres's *Louise, Princesse de Broglie, Later the Comtesse d'Haussonville* (fig. 107). This beguiling portrait of the accomplished woman writer seen in her intimate quarters is today one of the artist's most important pictures in the United States. Henry had a decided taste for French works of the later nineteenth century—Barbizon School, especially, and Impressionism—but he did not seek out artists from the Neoclassical era, such as Jacques-Louis David and Ingres.

Through her own scholarly interests, Helen Clay also deepened the museum's strength in areas her father had collected. Henry had purchased Houdon's enchanting

FIG. 104
Page from Helen Clay Frick's scrapbook, showing Johannes Vermeer's *Girl with a Pearl Earring* (1665), recorded during a trip to France and the Netherlands, 1932.

FIG. 105
The Frick Art Reference Library (now the Frick Art Research Library), 1936.

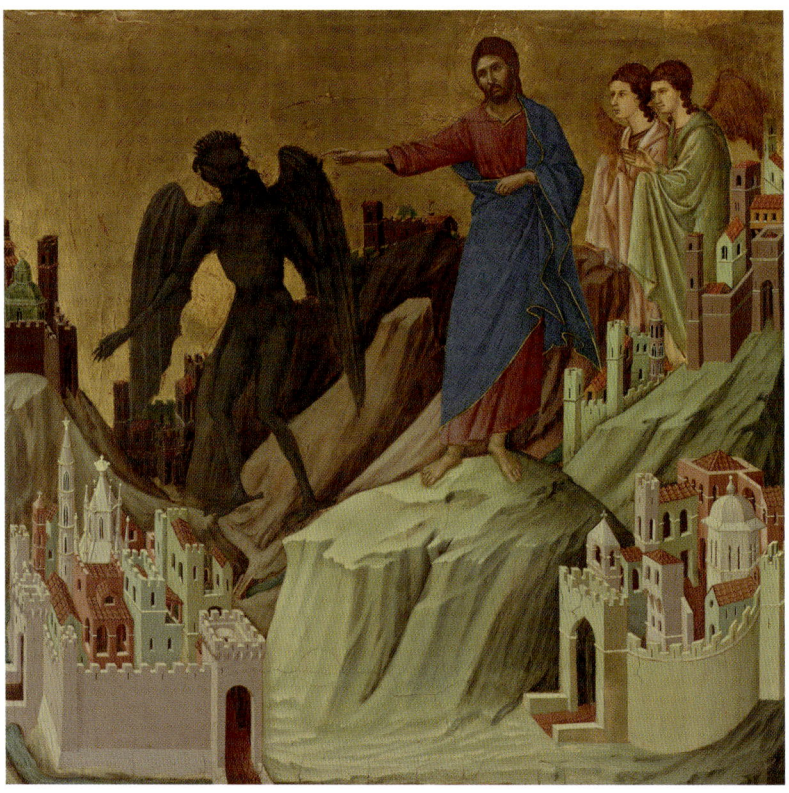

Élisabeth-Susanne de Jaucourt, Comtesse du Cayla (1777), and Helen Clay made herself an expert on this eighteenth-century French sculptor, writing a biography (unpublished) and two short articles for scholarly journals. In 1935, she bought another superb bust, *Armand-Thomas Hue, Marquis de Miromesnil* (1777), of which her father would have likely approved, and the life-size terra-cotta *Diana* (1776–95), a statue he would probably have shunned as too forthright in its nudity.

Father and daughter shared an admiration for Houdon, although a bust of Helen Clay that Frick commissioned problematizes this. As Frick wrote to the sculptor Malvina Hoffman: "Come and take a look at the Houdons in my collection: it might be suitable to do my daughter in the eighteenth-century manner."[44] A marble bust was completed but later destroyed, it was thought, by Helen Clay's own hand. This rumor was confirmed in 2016 with the gift from Hoffman's estate of a painted plaster of the lost bust, which arrived with a tag reading, "Carved in marble for Mr Frick—destroyed by H.F. after her father's d[eath]." The plaster (fig. 108) does share the flowered décolletage and upswept hair of Houdon's comtesse du Cayla, indications that Henry's suggestion was followed. Helen Clay was skittish at being portrayed, and she had a close personal relationship with Hoffman; either factor could have somehow led to the destruction of the marble. It seems less likely that the historical style would have so enraged her. We cannot be sure why or when she took a hammer to the marble, but it is further evidence of her fiery temper.

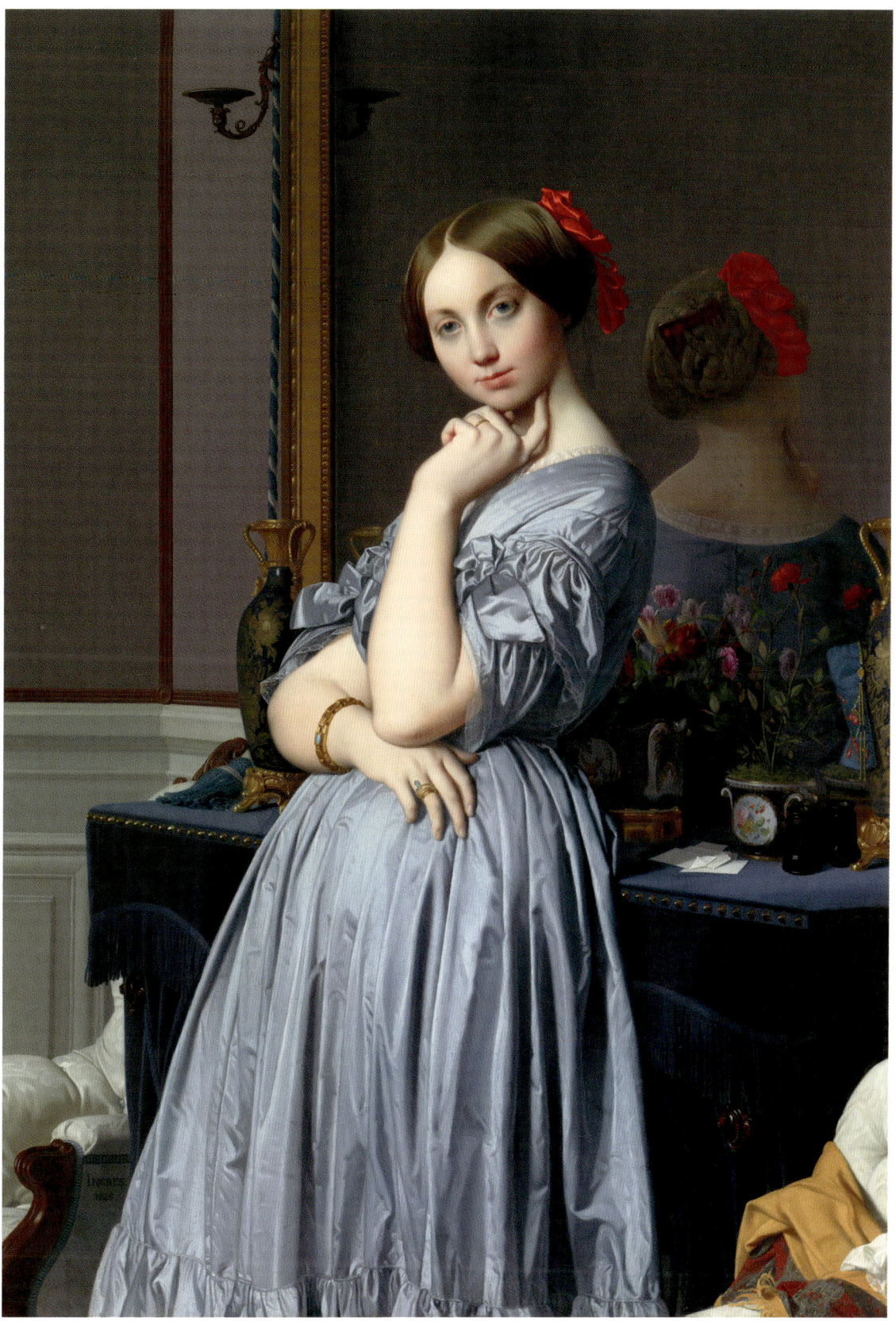

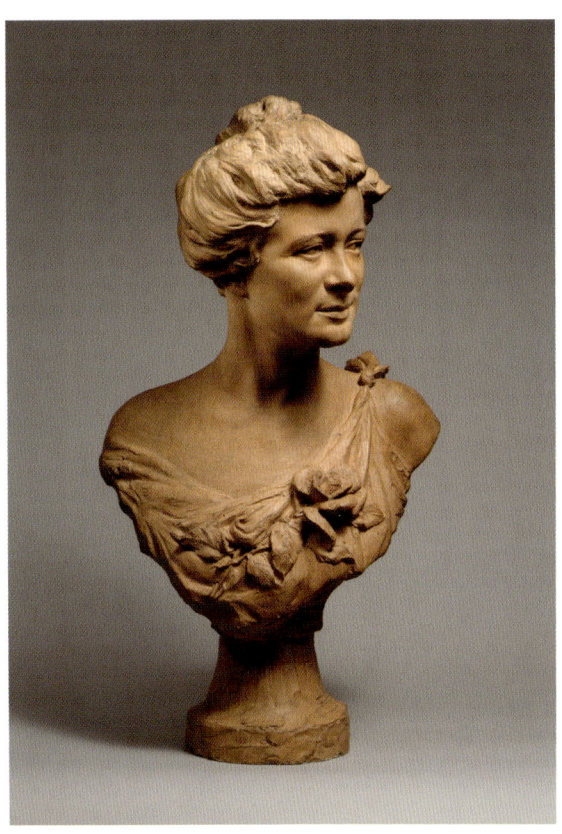

FIG. 108
Malvina Cornell Hoffman,
Bust of Helen Clay Frick, 1919.

Helen Clay's very first acquisition for the museum after her father's death reveals a certain daring yet, at the same time, a dependence on academically grounded experts. Her father preferred instead to listen to dealers he knew well. In 1924, Fra Filippo Lippi's *Annunciation* (fig. 109), an unpublished and undocumented painting, was offered to Helen. Today, it is acknowledged as one of the Italian Renaissance painter's greatest early works. At the time, Lippi had received scant scholarly attention; Helen relied on Robert Langton Douglas, one of the first art historians to ground his studies in period documents. The attribution and assessment of quality have proved to be correct, and Helen Clay showed courage in proposing a little-known work as one of her first acquisitions. Other scholars she relied on include Bernard Berenson, Isabella Stewart Gardner's principal advisor, and the academics Frederick Mason Perkins and Walter Friedländer.

No collector has a perfect record. Mistakes can be made, especially in little-studied fields, yet once made, they may sharpen one's ability to avoid repeating them. This was the case with two large marble statues thought to be by the Renaissance painter Simone Martini. Helen Clay purchased them in the same year as the Lippi, but they were later proven to be contemporary forgeries and were banished to Pittsburgh to be used as case studies for art students.

In 1931, with Helen Clay's support, The Frick Collection hired its first professional director, Frederick Mortimer Clapp, an art history professor in Pittsburgh. Clapp's primary objective was to orchestrate the collection's display in the enlarged building complex designed by Pope. Inevitably, his vision of the expansion of the art collection came into conflict with Helen's strong opinions. In 1936, Vermeer's *Allegory of Painting* (ca. 1666–68) was offered to the Frick, but Helen summarily rejected the great painting (Kunsthistorisches Museum, Vienna) with the marginal note "Have 3 V's."[45] The museum has the good fortune to hold three of the master's rare paintings, yet one may still regret the loss of this masterpiece. Obsessively, Clapp also tried to interest Helen Clay in Giorgione's *Adoration of the Shepherds* (1505–10)—one of the great Venetian Renaissance paintings, now in the National Gallery in Washington— but he failed: "I weep to think that we have lost the great Titian-Giorgione. I doubt whether a similar picture will be seen again," he wrote in 1938.

Following Henry's purchases of Degas and Renoir paintings, Clapp proposed, reasonably, several Impressionist works, but Helen consistently rejected them, citing lack of space and the wish to confine the collection's scope of modern art to the nineteenth century. *L'Arlésienne* (1888), one of Van Gogh's greatest portraits and now a treasure of the Metropolitan Museum of Art, was rejected in 1939.

The greatest trove of paintings and sculptures to enter the Frick after the founder's death came in 1943, when six masterful works formerly in Morgan's collection were negotiated through Knoedler. Among them were Constable's first "six-footer," *The White Horse*, a canvas that was so important to this painter of the English countryside that he bought it back toward the end of his life; a stirring Reynolds portrait of the English general John Burgoyne (ca. 1766), who lost the critical battle of the American Revolution; Rembrandt's portrait of Nicholas Ruts (1631), from early in the painter's career; a brilliant portrait of the Duke of Osuna by Goya (ca. 1790s); and a charming *Wool Winder* (ca. 1759) by Jean-Baptiste Greuze. Rounding out this group is an angel by Jean Barbet (1475), one of the only large-scale bronzes to have escaped the fate of so many fifteenth-century works—to be melted down and cast into cannons or bells. While Helen Clay still ruled over the Acquisitions Committee, a few more paintings of great quality entered the collection—in 1945, Chardin's beautiful *Still-Life with Plums* (ca. 1730); in 1950, Cimabue's *Flagellation of Christ*, the only painting by this seminal figure of the Italian Renaissance outside of Europe (fig. 110); and *The Sermon on the Mount* (1656), an unusual composition by the great French landscapist Claude Lorrain, whose poetic renderings of the Italian *campagna* made him one of the most revered of all seventeenth-century artists. While the Frick did not enter the art market frequently during these years, it maintained its reputation for acquiring the very best.

FIG. 109
Fra Filippo Lippi,
The Annunciation,
ca. 1440.

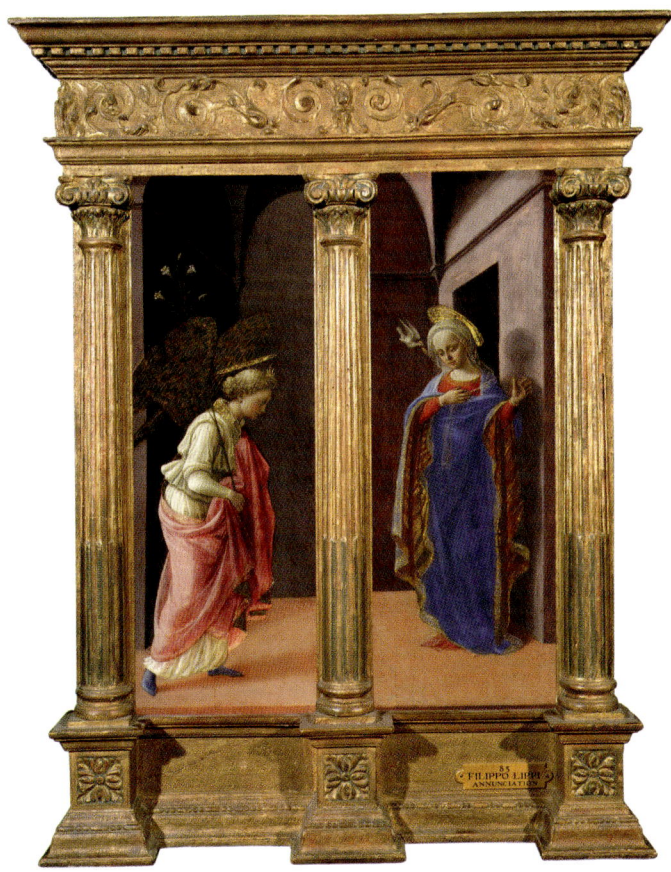

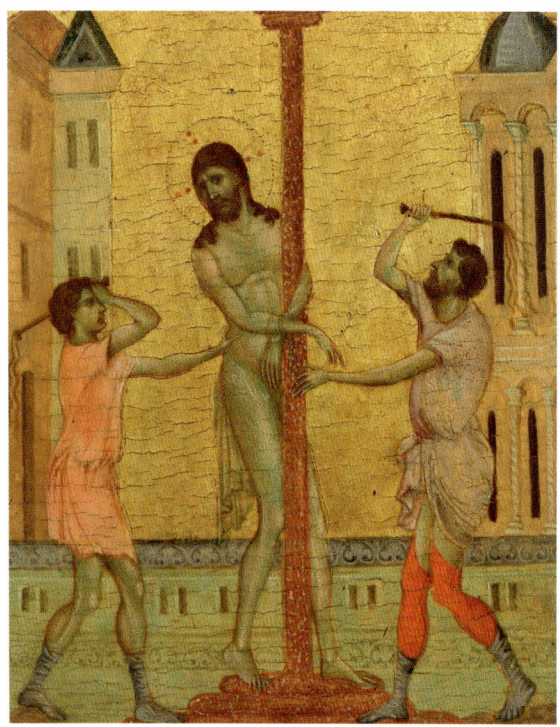

FIG. 110
Cimabue (Cenni di Pepo),
The Flagellation of Christ,
ca. 1280.

In her later years, Helen Clay increasingly saw herself as the arbiter of her father's taste, even though her primary contributions were in great paintings of a kind her father might not have bought. Some board members chafed at narrowing the limits of acquisition to early paintings by Old Masters. Three paintings of more recent date that had slipped in—two by Cézanne and one Gauguin—she later succeeded in purging from the Frick (now in major museums, the Minneapolis Institute of Art and the Metropolitan Museum of Art). These tensions came to a head in the late 1950s, when John D. Rockefeller Jr. proposed giving a Piero della Francesca predella panel along with two marble busts of the 1470s, one by Laurana and one by Verrocchio. Helen adamantly opposed accepting the gift, arguing that her father intended that the collection be increased only by purchase or by a family gift, even though the terms of the bequest have no such stipulations. Helen Clay sued the board of trustees and lost; she appealed the decision and lost again. When Rockefeller's gift was finally accepted in 1961, she stepped down from the board. As a consequence, the Frick was free to accept gifts from outside collectors, though this has always been done with care and circumspection, ensuring that the quality of accessioned works match that of art already in the museum.

With newfound wealth and independence after her father's death, Helen Clay also collected for herself. Many of her personal purchases in the 1920s complemented the Italian Primitives she pursued for the museum. Among the finest of these gold-ground paintings on panel were a polyptych by Bernardo Daddi (ca. 1335–40) and a *Nativity* by Giovanni di Paolo (ca. 1450). Since we know so little of Adelaide's taste in art, it is intriguing that she had a hand in encouraging her daughter's interest in painting. In 1922, Adelaide bought *Madonna and Child with Saints and Scenes from the Life of Christ and the Virgin*, a tempera on panel by the Master of the Scrovegni Chapel Presbytery (ca. 1308). She also acquired an Annunciation by Sassetta, part of an altar-piece whose panels are now scattered to Berlin and Washington (fig. 111). Together, the women bought Sassetta's *Virgin of Humility Crowned by Two Angels* (ca. 1438). What Helen Clay was looking for in her acquisitions may be characterized by her description of another Sassetta she saw in Italy in 1923–24: "Human and refreshing; perfect in its delicacy yet full of character with a beautiful line and an avoidance of the obvious."[46] Her love of early Italian painting extended to commissioning copies to decorate her libraries. She asked Russian artist Nicholas Lochoff to paint copies of works by Masaccio, Mantegna, and Botticelli for the courtyard of the Fine Arts Building, as models for art students at the University of Pittsburgh. In 1928, he made a copy of Pietro Lorenzetti's *Madonna and Child with Saint Francis and Saint John* from the church of St. Francis in Assisi for Hastings's 1924 library. When this building was demolished to make room for the larger library in 1934–35, the fresco was transferred to the present reading room in Pope's building.

Helen continued to acquire, though her increasing absorption in the library (FARL) left her less time for this pursuit. Sometimes, she bought works related to the New York collection, such as a study by Fragonard for *The Progress of Love*. Terra-cotta and plaster busts by Houdon, her favorite sculptor, attracted her. Dutch, northern French, and Flemish art by painters such as Jean Bellegambe and Rubens represents choices not found in the New York house. Some were fine works by French masters of the second tier, such as Antoine Le Nain and Carle van Loo, paintings that were unlikely to have found favor in her father's eyes. Among her personal acquisitions were some excellent works, but her collection rarely rose to the level established by her father. In 1970, she opened the Frick Art and Historical Center (now called The Frick Pittsburgh), built primarily for her personal collection. Most of the work that she inherited from her father was displayed nearby in Clayton, where many had been originally. Other works from Eagle Rock, such as period-room wall panels and Chinese porcelains, were installed in the new museum building alongside her personal collection.

Helen's contributions to The Frick Collection in New York were of a high order of magnitude. As the primary acquisitor in the 1920s and '30s, she set standards for the quality of what entered the collection. Strongly opinionated, she expanded the collection in areas that she liked—Italian early Renaissance and French early nineteenth century—but at the same time, she excluded more modern work, such as Impressionist and Post-Impressionist paintings, in which her father had shown an interest. In addition, the foundation of the library established a resource for the scholarly study of the museum, which has significantly added to its reputation. Alongside the direction she set for future acquisitions, the library was her great contribution to this institution.

FIG. 111
Sassetta (Stefano di Giovanni),
The Annunciation, ca. 1435–40.

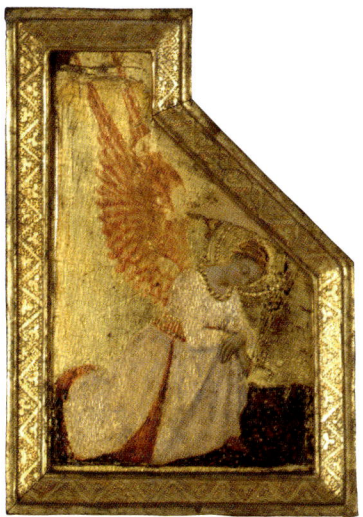
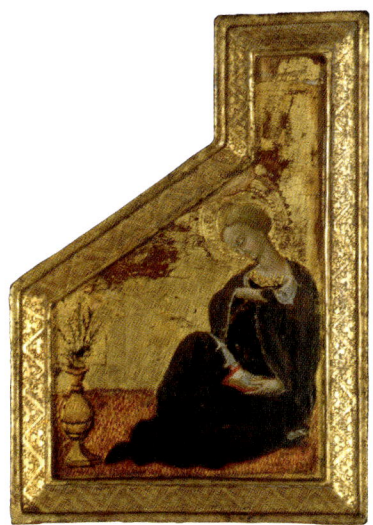

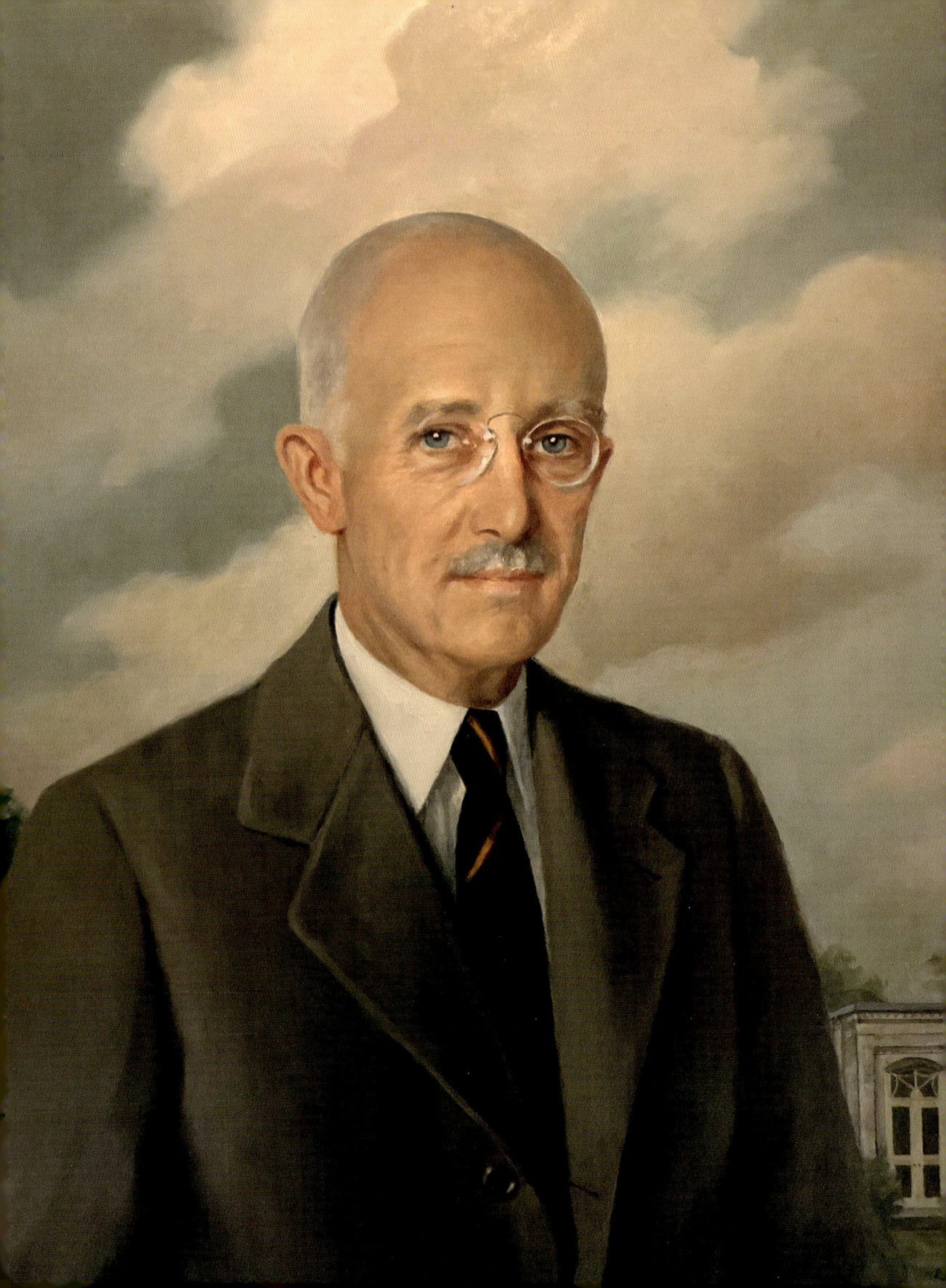

XVI

CHILDS FRICK, COLLECTOR AND PALEONTOLOGIST

Frick founded The Frick Collection, and his daughter Helen Clay added to its art holdings and established The Frick Art Reference Library. Typically left out of the picture is Frick's son, Childs (fig. 112). Although Childs is rarely acknowledged as a collector, his bequest of Chinese blue-and-white porcelain in 1965 was the first collection, other than his father's, to enter the Frick, and it set a precedent for other private collections to follow. Earlier, in 1906–7, the Duveen firm sold Frick a number of important pieces of Chinese porcelain, mostly brightly colored wares: *famille vert*, distinguished by its green glazes; *famille rose*, with deep pink colors; and *famille noire*, with black; along with some larger and miniature blue-and-white. Later, in 1915, Frick bought only one set of blue-and-white, an important group of four plum-blossom-decorated covered jars, made in the eighteenth century for the European market (see fig. 85). Childs exclusively sought blue-and-white porcelain, ranging in date from the Ming dynasty in the early sixteenth century to the Qing period at the beginning of the nineteenth. While it is a good collection, featuring many excellent examples, Childs did not approach this activity with the same intensity as his father (fig. 113). Many of these were gifts to and from his wife, Frances, a pleasant activity over the years until her death in 1953. (His bequest of the collection was made in her memory.) Childs's collection was pursued consistently and in depth but without the insistence on acquiring the very best that his father maintained. As president of the Frick Board of Trustees from 1920 to 1965, he oversaw the transition from private collection to public institution. Less known is that Childs was the most voracious of all the family in amassing museum collections, albeit in a totally distinct field, paleontology. Childs's passion for natural history, particularly mammals and birds, living and extinct, began shortly after his graduation from Princeton in 1905. This interest originated in hunting big game in East Africa, followed by a 1911 expedition to Kenya and Ethiopia that focused on collecting specimens of birds. He presented them to the Carnegie Museum in Pittsburgh, where some fifty-two hundred specimens were catalogued. By 1915, his primary focus had become fossils of mammals, and he led field expeditions to the American West, beginning in southern California, resulting in his first publication (fig. 114).

FIG. 112
Elizabeth Shoumatoff,
Childs Frick, 1952.

Childs had the financial means to subsidize field trips that, as a scientist in the Department of Vertebrate Paleontology, Thomas D. Nicholson wrote in 1975, "built up the collection of fossil specimens probably unequalled anywhere in the world."[47] The Frick Laboratory was established at the American Museum of Natural History (AMNH) in the mid-1930s. Childs appears on the registers of museum staff from 1923 to 1929 as Research Associate in Paleontology and in 1930 as Honorary Curator of Late Tertiary and Quaternary Mammals. His most important publication was *Horned Ruminants of North America* (1937), a 669-page study based on specimens his expeditions had gathered.

Although Childs established a laboratory for personal research at his estate in Roslyn on Long Island, his goal was to make the AMNH a center for fossil research. Early on, he recognized, as a later article by Thomas D. Nicholson and colleagues in the Department of Vertebrate Paleontology put it: "Large paleontology collections offer documentary proof of evolutionary change by sampling many successive stages in the history of the population of organisms."[48] The numerous expeditions he sponsored were a major factor in assembling this research collection. When his 250,000 fossil specimens were formally given to the museum after his death, in 1968, they could no longer be contained within the existing space. In 1972, construction finished on the Childs Frick Building, a ten-story, 60,000-square-foot edifice inserted into one of the museum's interior courtyards. Since the AMNH is listed as a city landmark, the new wing was designed so it would not be visible from outside. In addition to donating the collections and providing funds for the building, Childs left a considerable endowment that continues to support research and other activities.

A modest and quiet man, Childs left a significant legacy through his collections and the building to house them. Buried within the vast complex of the AMNH, his

FIG. 113
Chinese, Ming Dynasty (1368–1644), Wanli Period (1573–1620), *Stem Bowl*, 1573–1620.

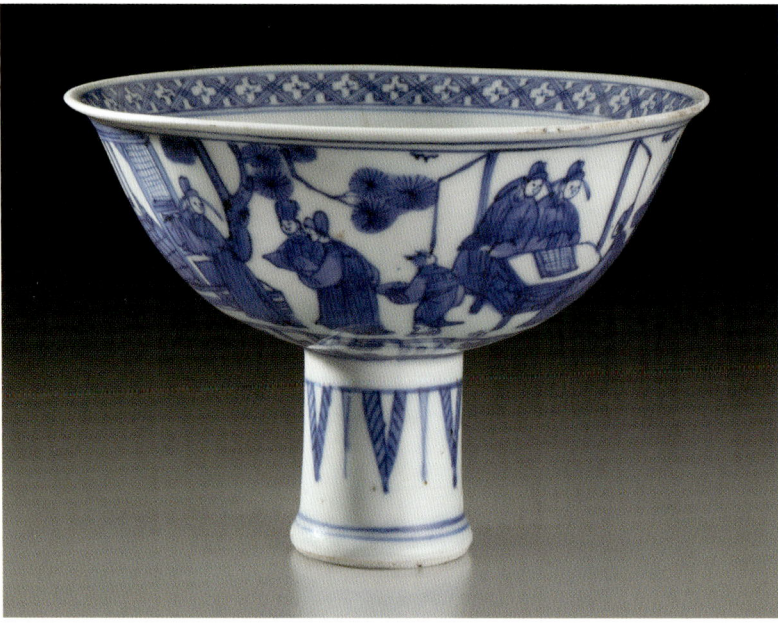

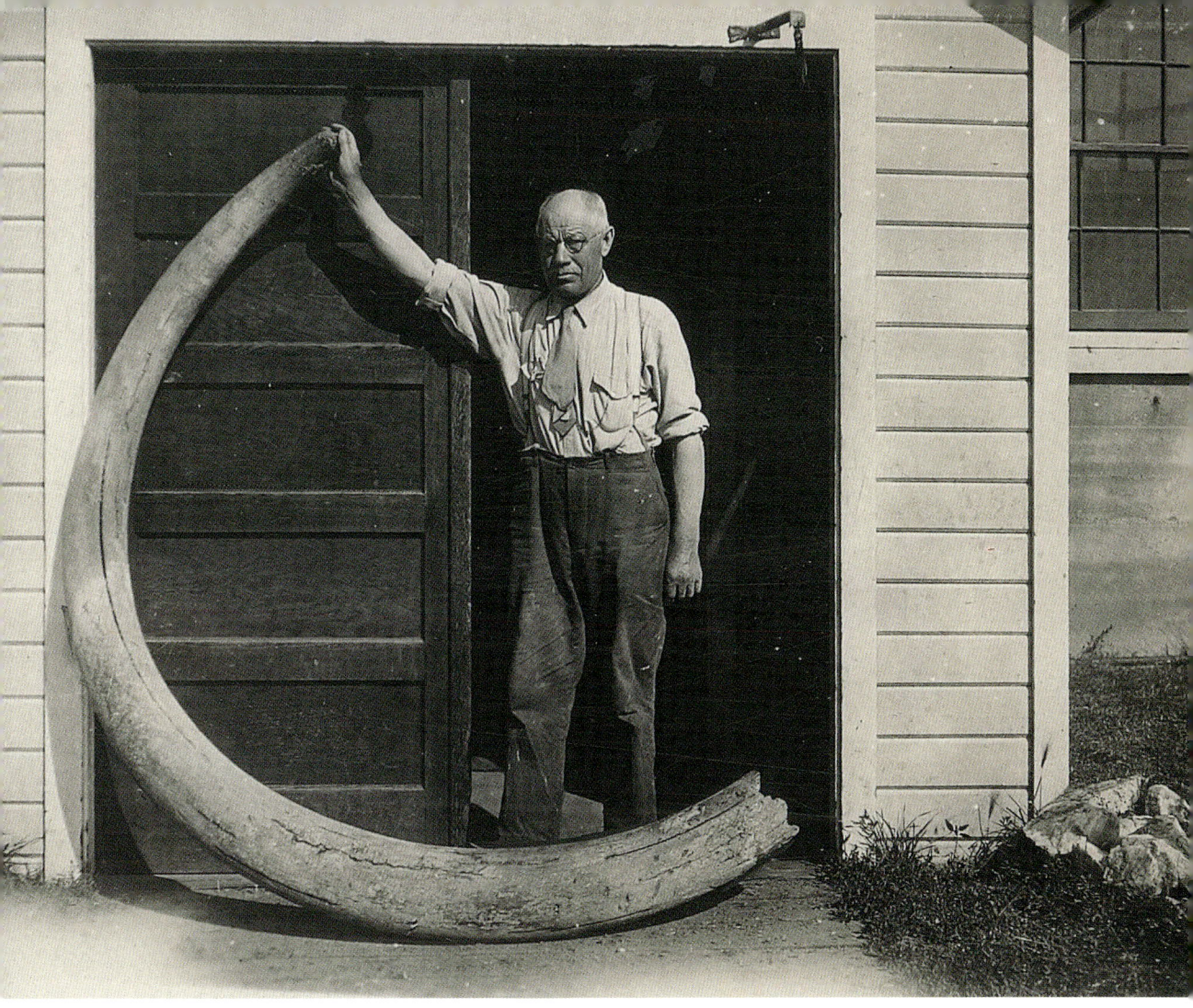

FIG. 114
Childs Frick with tusk,
Cripple Creek, Alaska,
1938–39.

impact can be overlooked. Recognizing that quantities of specimens were necessary to formulate scientific results, Childs had an approach to collecting that was the opposite of his father, who sought the best of kind rather than large numbers of works. Childs's collections are not nearly as famous as those of his father but are perhaps as important for science as Henry's for art. In an article of 1975, Theodore Galusha, also of the AMNH, wrote, "No collection better illustrates the results of long-term dedication than the Frick Collection of late Cenozoic fossil mammals accumulated under the direction of Childs Frick during a lifetime of research. This collection is recognized as the largest single assemblage of fossil mammals ever made in North America, and it is considered the most important collection by paleontologists dealing with the later Tertiary."[49]

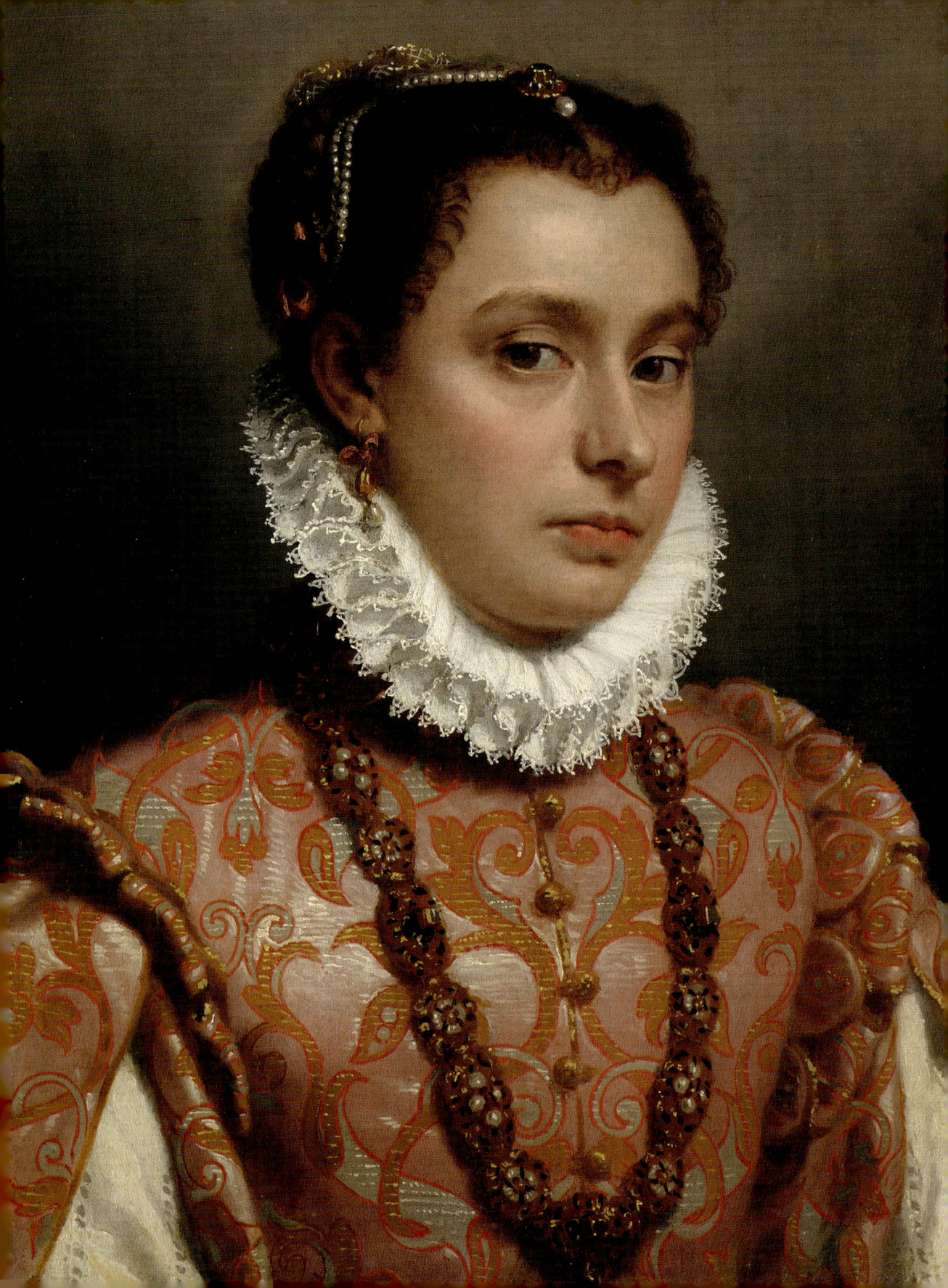

XVII

GILDING THE LILY:
THE FRICK COLLECTS

Henry Clay Frick's will anticipated that works would be added to the collection after his death. In the era when Helen Clay's was the decisive voice in making acquisitions, the museum bought art, mostly paintings, of the highest quality, consistent with that of the existing collection. Over time, buying at the top of the market brought pressure on the institution's endowment. As the museum became more active with programs and exhibitions and the staff grew commensurately, the endowment could no longer cover operating expenses, and the trustees decided that it should cease to be used to purchase works of art. Since 1968, the acquisitions fund has been modest, and the relatively few purchases made have come through funds specifically earmarked or raised for each. That year, the entrancing *Portrait of a Man* by Hans Memling entered the collection (fig. 116). The 1970s and '80s saw few acquisitions, but an unusual scene of soldiers by the master of the outdoor aristocratic *fête champêtre*, Jean-Antoine Watteau, *The Portal of Valenciennes* (ca. 1710–11) came in 1991.

Some superb paintings have arrived by way of gifts. In 2014, Dr. and Mrs. Henry Clay Frick II gave the Murillo *Self-Portrait* (see fig. 61), one of only two by the artist, an inheritance from Henry Clay Frick, who had bought it in 1904. In 2022, from the estate of Aso Tavitian, a trustee and remarkable collector of Old Master paintings and sculpture, came one of the finest works of his collection—*Portrait of a Woman* by Giovanni Battista Moroni, an artist who focused on representations of citizens of Bergamo, near his native Albino (fig. 115). This is the first painted Renaissance portrait of a woman in the Frick's collection. Finally, in 2017, an important purchase was made of a painting by François Gérard, the preeminent painter of Napoleon's family. Gérard portrayed the emperor's brother-in-law, Camillo Borghese, governor of northern Italy (fig. 117). Because a new lining was never ironed on to the back, which would have flattened the paint surface—often the fate of large canvases in the nineteenth century—it retains its brilliant colors and impasto layers of pigment.

Many of the Frick's most recent acquisitions have been in the field of decorative arts, where it is more feasible to afford an object that is best of class than among the

FIG. 115
Giovanni Battista Moroni,
Portrait of a Woman, ca. 1575.

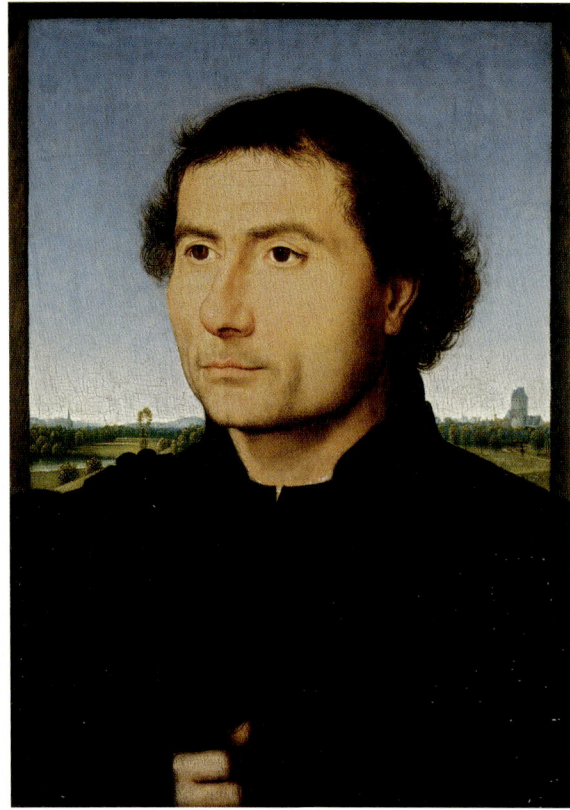

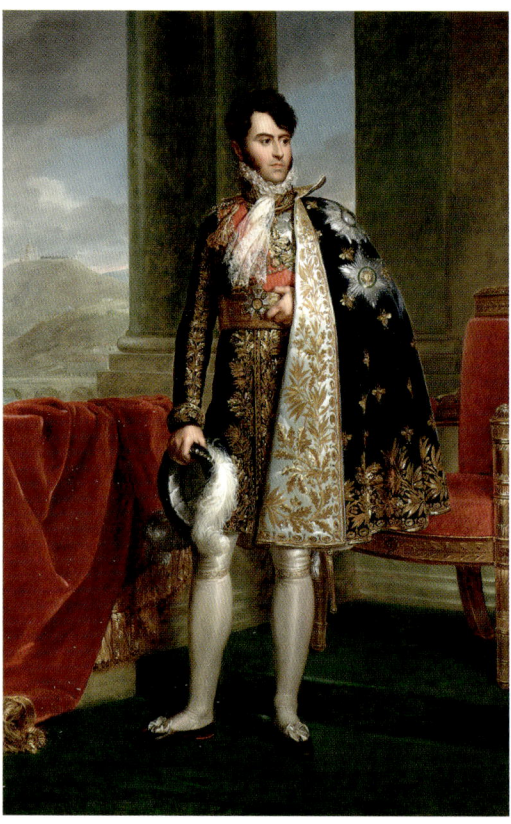

FIG. 116
Hans Memling, *Portrait of
a Man*, ca. 1470–75.

FIG. 117
François Gérard, *Camillo
Borghese*, ca. 1810.

FIG. 118
Saint-Porchaire ware,
attributed to Bernard
Palissy, *Ewer*, mid-16th
century.

stratospheric prices that the top Old Master paintings can command. A remarkable globe clock supported by terra-cotta figures modeled by the sculptor Clodion arrived in 1999, acquired by then-director Anne Poulet, an expert on the sculptor. Thanks to trustee Sidney R. Knafel, an extremely rare Saint-Porchaire ceramic ewer (fig. 118) was purchased in 2015. It is now one of three the institution owns, from only several dozen known to have been produced. Alongside the first-ever exhibition on the great *bronzier* Pierre Gouthière, which the Frick organized in 2016, came the purchase, also with the support of Knafel, of a pair of Meissen vases that the master bronze-caster and gilder mounted as candelabra.

Where the Frick has been truly fortunate is in having been honored to choose from some of the finest collections of European decorative arts and sculpture in the world. Over the last quarter century, several primarily New York–based collectors have enhanced our holdings with works that build on what Frick had acquired in the early twentieth century. They include works in horology, ceramics, and medals.

The first of these was a group of thirty-eight clocks and watches from Winthrop Kellogg Edey, acquired in 1999, who was fascinated by timekeeping in earlier eras. A serious student of this field, Edey carefully selected clocks and watches from the early sixteenth through the early nineteenth centuries. These range from a small table clock shaped like a building, by the French Renaissance master Pierre de Fobis, to

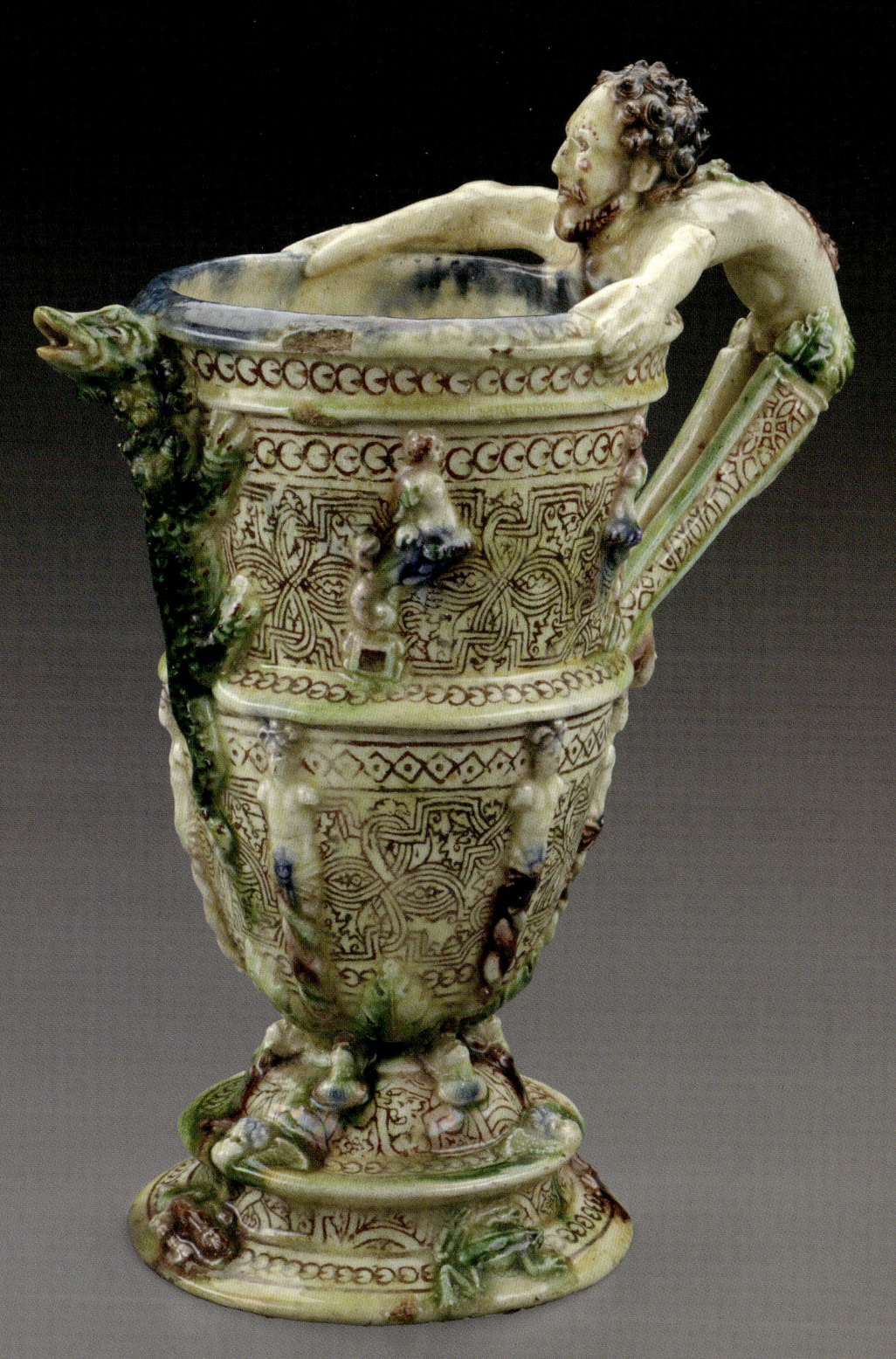

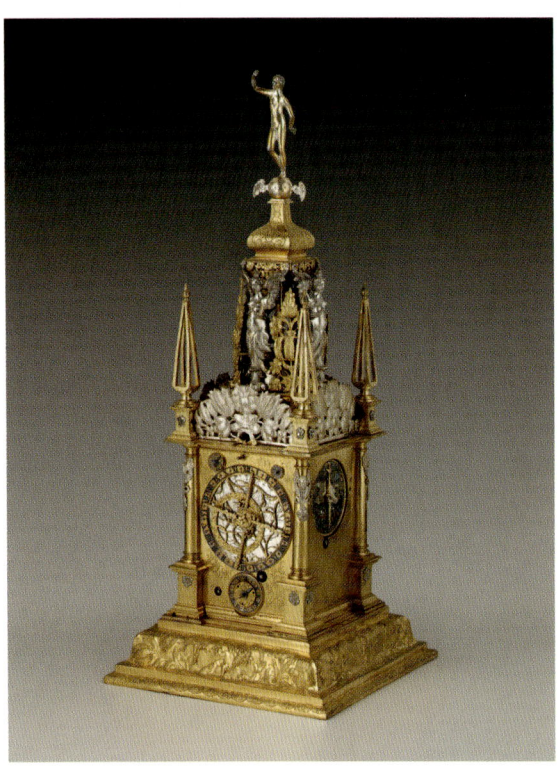

FIG. 119
David Weber, *Table Clock
with Astronomical and
Calendrical Dials*, probably
1653.

FIG. 120
Meissen Porcelain
Manufactory, after Johann
Gottlieb Kirchner, *Great
Bustard*, 1732.

the mid-seventeenth-century masterpiece (literally, the work assigned to an artisan to make for acceptance into a guild) by David Weber in Augsburg (fig. 119). A longcase clock and a barometer clock, by or attributed to André-Charles Boulle, whose works of furniture Frick so admired, came with the bequest. A new gallery on the second floor now permits the display of a majority of these works for the first time.

In the decade between 2014 and 2024, more extraordinary works of decorative art, particularly ceramics, entered the collection. Frick's tastes in this area ran mainly to Chinese and Sèvres porcelain. Some of Henry Arnhold's superb collection of Meissen porcelain arrived during his lifetime, with most of 134 pieces coming to the museum following his death in 2018. Meissen was the first manufactory in Europe to discover the technique of making porcelain, which had been imported from China for centuries. Meissen porcelain bridges Frick's interests in Chinese and French porcelain in the sense that from Meissen technical knowledge spread to other European centers, such as Sèvres, and its decoration was inspired, at least in the beginning, by Asian work. The first of Arnhold's objects to come to the Frick was the *Great Bustard* (fig. 120), part of an ambitious undertaking at the manufactory to make life-size animals and birds for a pleasure palace of the Elector of Saxony in Dresden. Some of the earliest production of Meissen, works in red stoneware—called Böttger stoneware after Johann Friedrich Böttger, the alchemist who discovered the secret formula for making porcelain in 1708—are in the collection. Through a range of vessels and a few figures, the Arnhold Meissen gift highlights the best productions of the manufactory through the eighteenth century. The quality of these works establishes the Frick as one of the premier collections of Meissen in this country, and it is displayed in a daylit Portico Gallery designed specifically for it.

In 2016, Melinda and Paul Sullivan gave the Frick fourteen pieces of Du Paquier porcelain. Theirs is the finest private collection of this porcelain made in Vienna from 1725 to 1750, in a production started by artisans lured away from Meissen. The Sullivans invited the museum to choose a group that represents some of the principal achievements of this porcelain manufactory. More whimsical in form and eccentric in color than Meissen, Du Paquier is invariably inventive (fig. 121).

In 2018, the Frick mounted an exhibition of seventy-five pieces of French faience from Knafel's extraordinary collection of tin-glazed earthenware. Immigrant Italian maiolica painters spread a new tradition that spanned the sixteenth through eighteenth centuries and radiated from Lyon to cities such as Nevers and Rouen in the north and Moustiers and Montpellier in the south. This production of pottery, as opposed to porcelain, has a delightful range of color, pattern, and form, reflecting

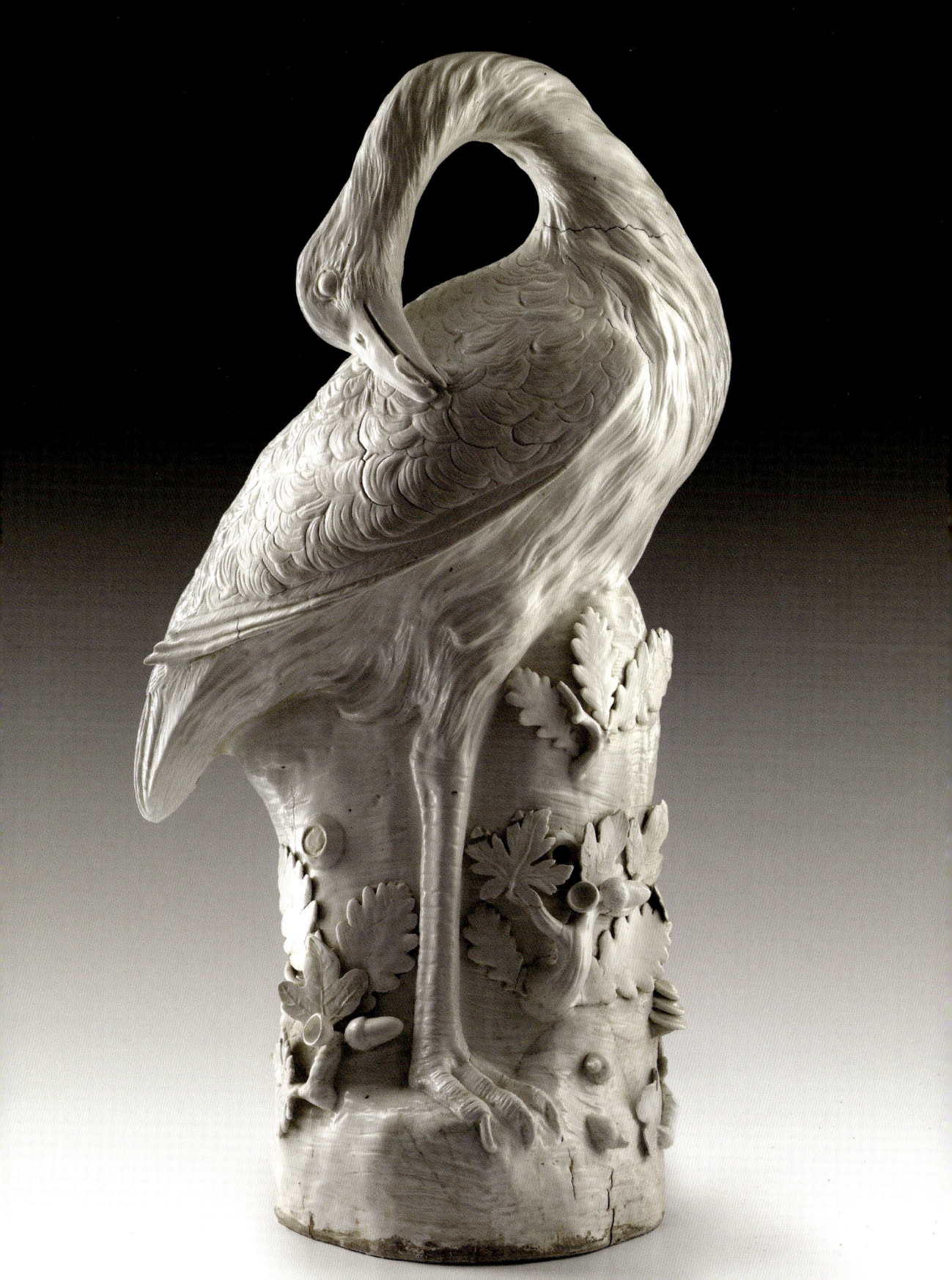

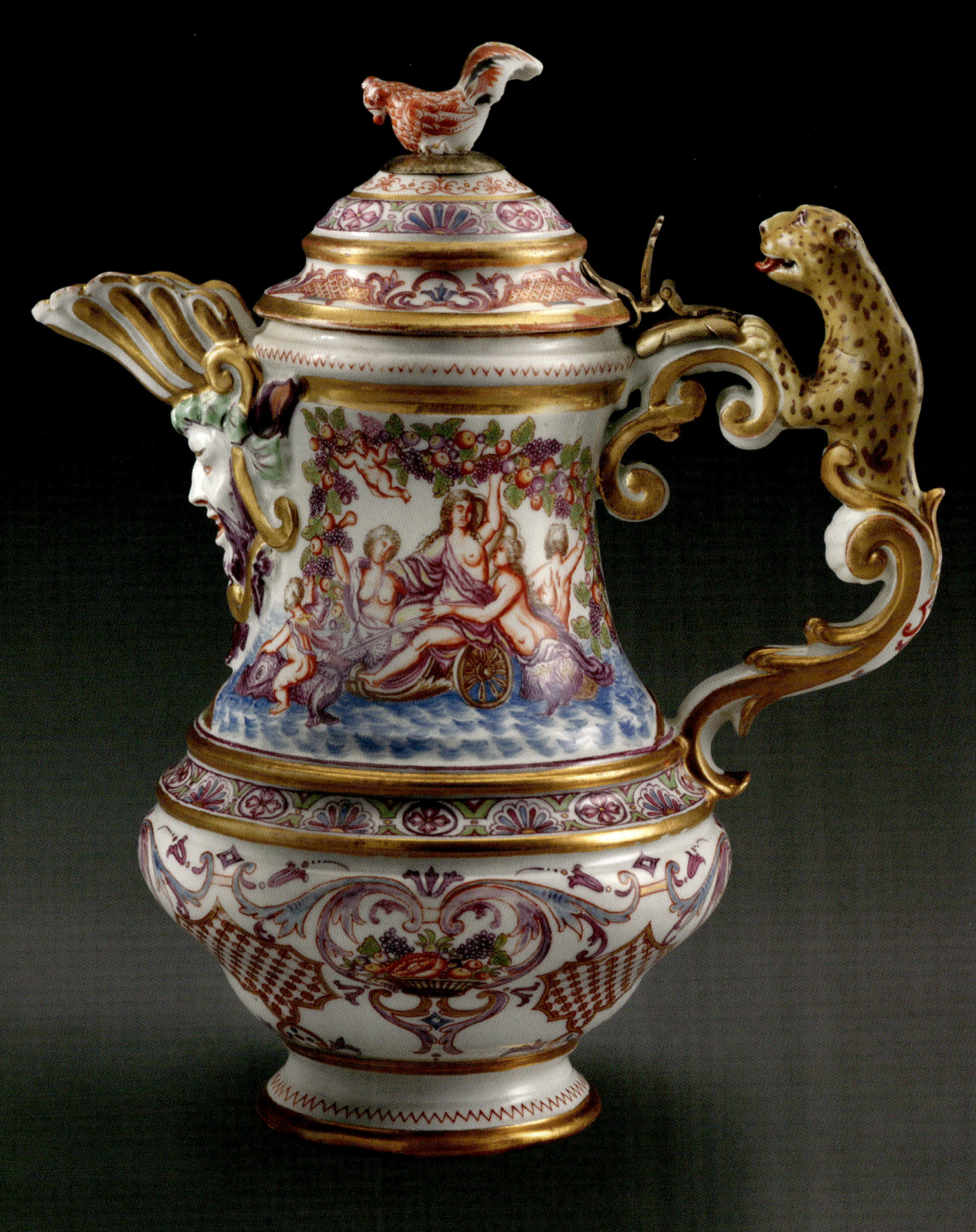

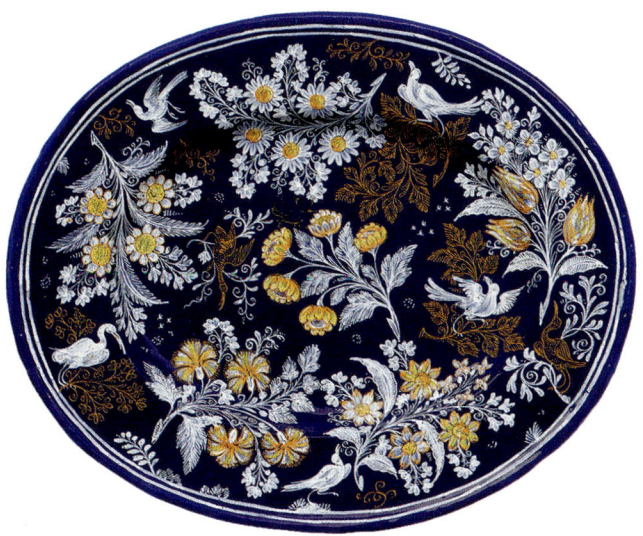

FIG. 121
Du Paquier Porcelain
Manufactory, *Ewer*,
1725–30.

FIG. 122
Nevers, *Platter*,
ca. 1660–70.

regional variations and changes of taste from era to era. A charming complement to the many forms of French art in the Frick, the collection, which came in bequest in 2022, is the centerpiece of a new second-floor gallery dedicated to ceramics (fig. 122).

A more varied decorative arts collection, predominantly French but including some German and Italian pieces, arrived in 2021 as a bequest from Alexis Gregory. One of the foremost collectors of Renaissance decorative arts in the United States, Gregory had a deep interest in Limoges enamels. His taste ran to grisaille enamels (painted in shades of black, gray, and white), an area that Frick's collection distinctly lacked (fig. 124). This collection joins Frick's Limoges works in the Enamels Room; Gregory's other works—clocks, objects in ivory, pottery, gold, stone, and pastel on paper—enrich the collection in many areas.

Numerically, the largest collection ever to enter the museum comprises some of the smallest objects. The Stephen K. and Janie Woo Scher collection of commemorative medals, eventually numbering several hundred pieces, is displayed in a specially designed gallery on the second floor. Like coins, medals are generally two-sided, with a portrait on the obverse and an emblem or figural scene on the reverse. Though made of bronze, silver, or gold, their value lies in the artistry with which the miniature reliefs are made and the interest in their historical subjects. The Scher collection ranges from the reinvention of the medal in the mid-fifteenth century by Pisanello and other Italian artists to its maturity as an art form in France, Germany, the Netherlands, and other European centers. The medals match the Frick's holdings particularly well, since their basis is portraiture, the great strength of the museum in other media. Many of them were devised by sculptors of the Frick's bronze statuettes, such as Bertoldo and Antico. A long-standing friend of the Frick and a scholar on the subject, Stephen Scher organized two distinguished exhibitions on medals at the museum. One of the strongest holdings of its kind in the world, the Medals Room and endowed programs making use of it give this captivating art form the attention it deserves (fig. 123).

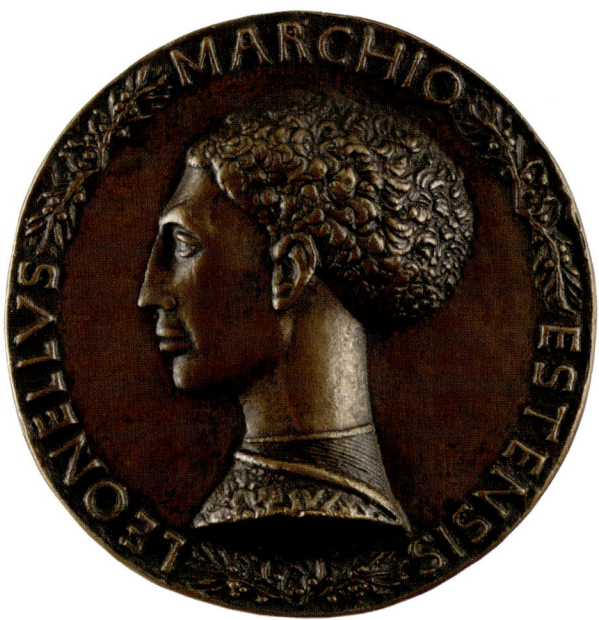

FIG. 123
Pisanello (Antonio di
Puccio Pisano), *Leonello
d'Este, Marquis of Ferrara*
(obverse); *Allegory of the
Blessings of Peace* (reverse),
ca. 1445.

FIG. 124
Pierre Reymond, *Covered
Tazza (One of a Pair)*, late
16th century.

In recent years, the Frick has also been given or pledged drawings collections. In 2010, the first was a group of ten sheets belonging to a former director, Charles Ryskamp. Ryskamp's taste was founded in British art—represented by oil-on-paper studies of clouds by Constable—but also turned to artists such as Giovanni Battista Tiepolo, Eugène Delacroix, and Degas. Most recently, chair of the board of trustees Betty Eveillard and her husband, Jean-Marie, have pledged twenty-six works on paper, ranging from a late fifteenth-century Venetian drawing to a late nineteenth-century Sargent pencil study. The Eveillards have always been attracted to images of the human face, so their promised works on paper will find good company at the Frick. Many of their finest are French, such as Maurice-Quentin de La Tour's portrait of Madame Rouillé (fig. 125), which joins a superb group of pastels at the museum and others promised by former Board Chair Margot Bogert and her husband, Jeremiah. Before these gifts, The Frick Collection had small but choice holdings of drawings. These works will greatly augment what is already here; a new first-floor gallery dedicated primarily to drawings signals the institution's intent to build further on this superb foundation.

* * *

In November 1915, when the mansion was complete and the family had taken possession of it, the magazine *Architecture* published a photograph with the caption "The most costly and sumptuous house in the United States has been turned over to its owner."[50] Frick lived to enjoy it for fewer than five years. How did others respond to the collection he had assembled and so beautifully housed? Some were less than

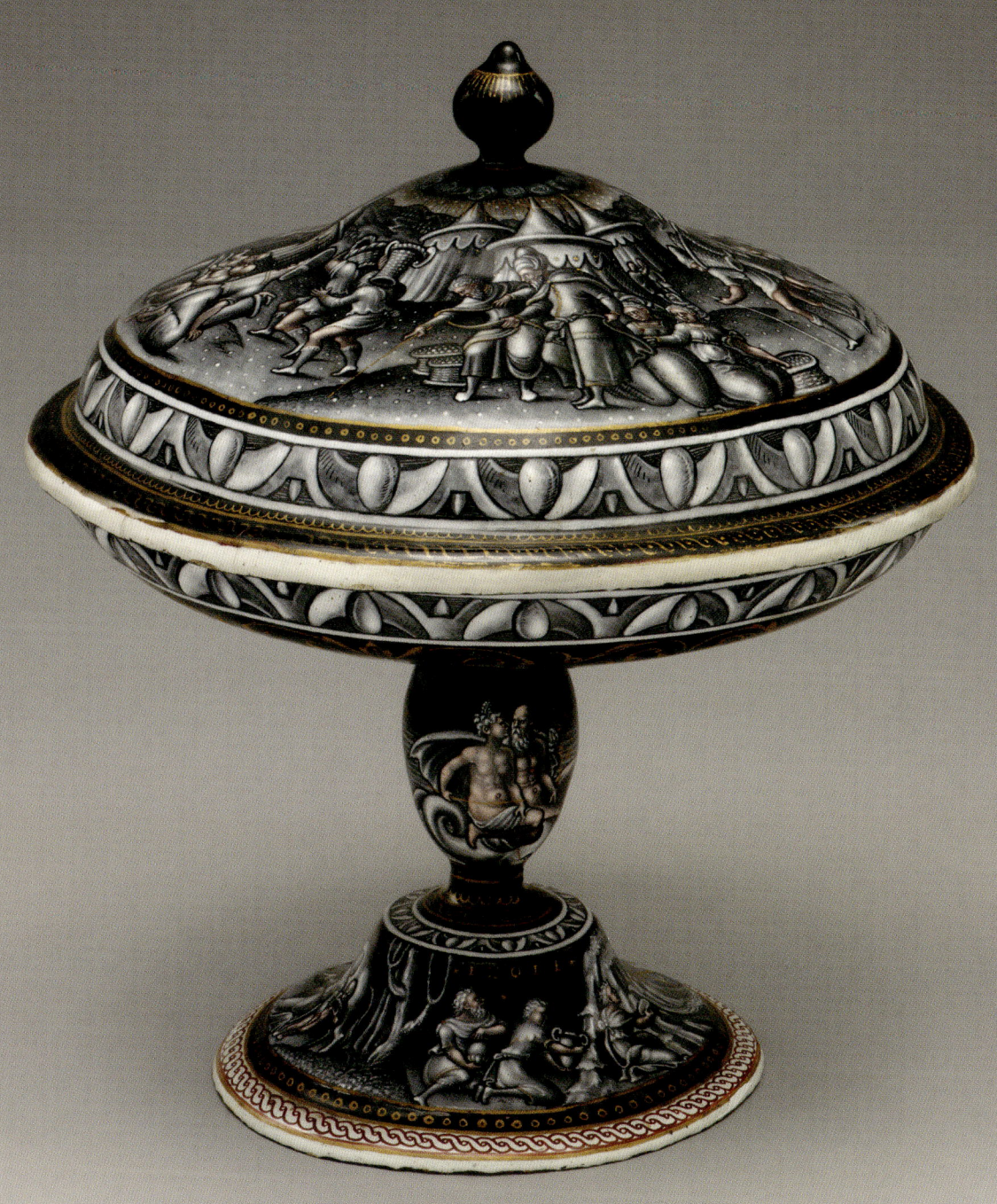

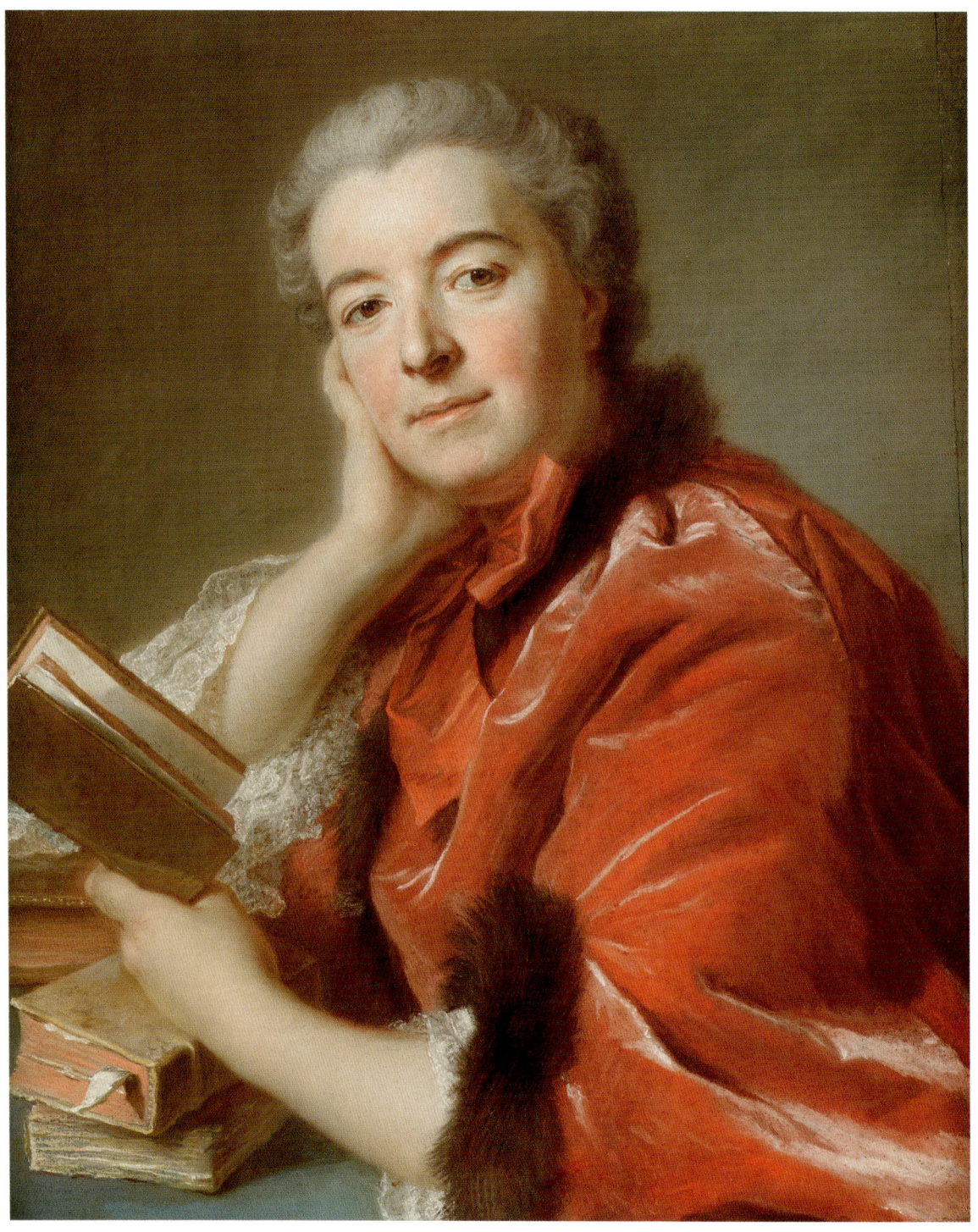

charitable. Bernard Berenson referred to it as a "mausoleum," though he also grudgingly sent a telegram in 1915, saying, "Congratulate Frick Bellini which one Masterpieces all Italian art."[51] Most, however, were awed by the experience. This is perhaps best captured in a piece by the art historian and critic Royal Cortissoz published in 1919 in the *New-York Tribune* the week of Frick's death: "The Special Value of the Frick Gift," subtitled "A Noble Landmark in Our Art History." Cortissoz writes:

> The independent gathering of masterpieces, isolated in a building of their own, is a boon for which we are always bound to be grateful, and it takes on a particularly rare atmosphere when it reduces to a minimum the institutional character independent from the public museums. . . . We would be lost without museums, but we are trebly enriched when the museum idea is camouflaged, so to say, by the atmosphere of an individual's home.[52]

By 1915, when Frick had already written the will that committed his house to the public, the family noted that he often would slip downstairs to commune with his collection at night, sometimes with a cigar (fig. 126). The paintings were his to enjoy, but he knew that after his passing, the public would too. In the week before his death, Helen Clay discovered her father lying on a couch in the West Gallery facing Goya's *Forge* and Velázquez's *King Philip IV of Spain*. The sense of a dying wish fulfilled is conveyed after the mansion opened to the public in a *New York Times* article of December 19, 1935: "The house with all its art is more than a museum. It is a potential addition to the home of every person, whether it is tenement, apartment, or mansion, who becomes intimately acquainted with what it holds of beauty—away from all the ugliness of the world." The poignancy of this dream is embedded in the house.

Henry Clay Frick had a passion for art. He began hanging framed prints on his walls as soon as he had an office in Pennsylvania, and he was still buying paintings for his New York mansion just weeks before his death. Using financial terms, in 1895 the tough businessman expressed the value that art held for him: "It seems to me better to have a certain amount of such things [paintings] than the same value in bonds in the Safe Deposit Company, as you can draw your dividend daily." In another letter to the same correspondent, the industrialist J. C. Morse: "I get more real pleasure out of this than anything I have ever engaged in outside business."[53]

For some, this was a cold calculation. Charles M. Schwab, president of the Carnegie Steel Company and less a friend of Frick's than an antagonist, wrote of him: "the most methodical thinking machine I have ever known. . . . He seemed to lavish on art all the passion he might have bestowed on human beings."[54] To the contrary, Frick clearly enjoyed art as an antidote to business, and it was not an activity devoid of humanity. He liked sharing art with others, whether talking with artists, giving art to friends, or bestowing his entire collection on the public.

As a collector, Frick began as a follower and ended as a leader. His earliest acquisition was a painting by a local artist; like other Pittsburgh collectors, he broadened his net to pull in American artists more generally. At that stage, he preferred precise, finished work such as still lifes and more meditative landscapes. Purchases in the 1890s included George Waters's *Still Life with Peaches* and Harnett's *Still Life* (both Frick Pittsburgh), both scrupulously observed and faithful to their subjects. It was

FIG. 126
Gerald Kelly, *Portrait of
Mr. Frick in West Gallery*,
1925.

not a far leap to Jan van Os's still life, the first Old Master picture he bought, in 1896. While he soon lost interest in still life as a genre, he continued to appreciate linear precision in some of his later acquisitions. Witness Holbein's sharp portrayal of Thomas More or Bronzino's crystalline rendering of Lodovico Capponi.

Of long duration was Frick's instinctive response to more meditative, even moody landscapes. His first acquisition, a landscape by Hetzel (see fig. 11), is a quiet picture that draws one in slowly to contemplate the sylvan glen. A decade later, he fell hard for Inness, a painter who wields a broad brush and conjures an almost visionary quality to his landscapes (see fig. 19); Frick began to privilege feeling over fidelity to representation. Somewhat surprisingly, he wrote comparing Inness to Turner before he ever bought a work by the British artist. He concentrated on Barbizon School landscapes by Corot, Rousseau, and others—in fact, he traded his Innesses for them. These are canvases evoking the mood of a place, and the spectacular pastel drawings by Millet that he bought in the late 1890s are suffused with the spirit of the land. Millet's drawings of peasants call out another incongruity in Frick's taste, what historian Neil Harris has called a "divided sensibility, a dual consciousness that separated art from life."[55] These images of noble workers of the land reveal a nostalgia for a way of life that was being displaced by the very industrial factories Frick was building. One can well imagine that images of farmers in the fields were a pleasing association to his West Overton childhood, before factories and cities filled his frame of reference. Still, it is these images of figures in the landscape that seemed to draw Frick's attention, more than the actual subject. He preferred to engage with line, color, and form more than with a religious scene or historical subject. The exception was portraiture, where he could both take the measure of the person portrayed and also assess the artist's success in achieving it.

Frick's collecting was certainly bound up with his wealth. He truly became a collector in the mid-1890s, when, now a rich man, he stepped back from chairing the Carnegie Company and had the time to focus on art. It is then that he began to buy heavily. Turning toward making his private passion public, this was also about social image. He was aware of his civic presence, that such gestures can burnish his stature in society. In New York, his collecting moved to another level. His love of the deal— trading, consolidating, and building businesses—was part of what he enjoyed in the art market. He learned and bought from dealers such as Carstairs and Duveen. While they made huge profits off of Frick, he bought the best. He knew what he was doing, and the decisions of what to acquire were entirely his. The collection is famous today because he trusted his instincts and was willing to pay large sums for first-rate works of art. Like all collectors, he thrived on the game of bidding, and especially outbidding his competitors, and he liked the endorsement of rivals who appreciated what he was doing. He sought status by measuring himself against Morgan, Rockefeller, and Mellon in an arena that he truly loved. The point is that his response to art was instinctive. His social and economic milieu certainly informed and encouraged his collecting, but his lifelong love of art was not simply to impress his peers. It was a pleasurable activity that he wanted to make available to others at all levels of society. Like other business tycoons of his time, the so-called robber-barons Rockefeller and Carnegie, among others, he left most of his wealth to charitable causes that continue to enrich American life to this day. One can debate whether these acts compensate for the ruthless business practices that led to their fortunes. In Frick's case, it can at least be said that his passion for art and desire to share it were genuine.

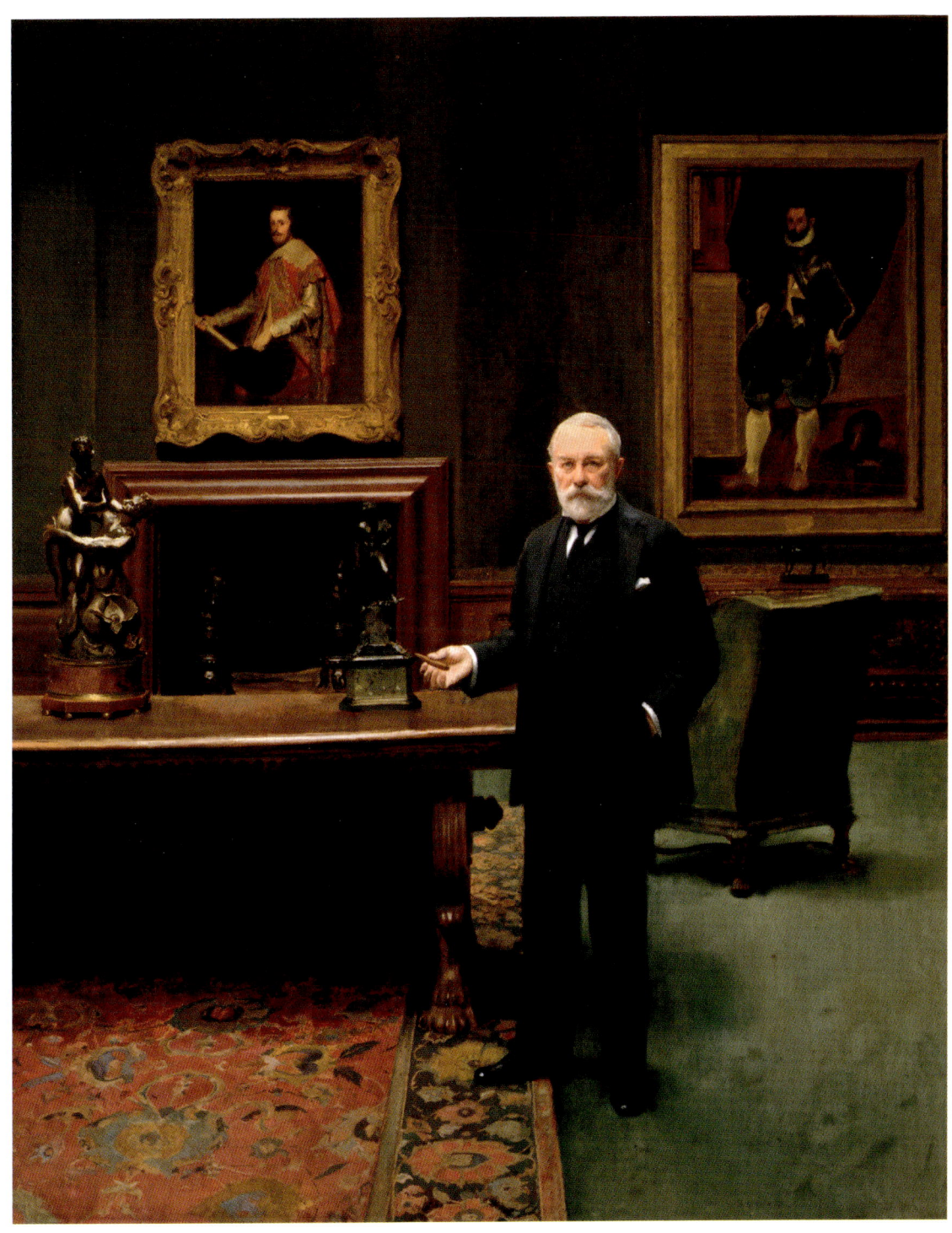

Some of his purchases were daring; for instance, the El Greco *St. Jerome*. Spanish paintings in general were not at the top of many collectors' lists, so he was one of the pioneers of the North American taste for Iberian art. Helen Clay wrote that he bought pictures "that were pleasant to live with,"[56] and it is true that he shunned works that were disturbing or overly expressive. Yet he did acquire the occasional challenging picture, particularly among his Spanish selections. Goya's *Forge* and El Greco's *Purification of the Temple* are striking and provocative. In the end, it is the mansion that pulls them all together. He had been buying what he liked and, in depth, artists he favored, such as Vermeer, Van Dyck, Gainsborough, and Whistler. Increasingly, he bought larger paintings to suit the grand scale of his new house and particular furnishings for its rooms. It is the mansion, too, that convinced him to acquire the great furnishings that must stand up to the masterpieces of paintings. Often overlooked beneath or around the canvases on the walls, the decorative arts and sculpture are magnificent, and his achievement in this area is impressive, considering the scant few years in which he assembled them. Their role in completing the atmosphere of the mansion is critical.

An American collector at a time of great national wealth, Frick's taste evolved alongside his fortune. His turn toward Old Masters, the most expensive area of the market, was propelled by his increased wealth. Yet his beginnings buying local artists were critical, as this helped to train his eye and directed him toward contemporary art in Europe. By the time he turned to older periods, he had become a skilled collector. Frick was fortunate that his children supported and enhanced his lifelong passion. Helen Clay had an eye of her own, and she oversaw the acquisition of great works that filled out and deepened the collection in different areas. Her library built a foundation for the scholarship that supports better understanding of the collection and of art history in general. As president of the board of trustees, Childs had a role in establishing the Frick as a public institution. Yet it was their father who had the vision of a great collection in a great house, one that he wished to share, as his will stipulated, with "all persons whomsoever."[57] In conversation with a friend shortly before his death, Frick stated quite clearly: "I want this collection to be my monument."[58]

1   Typical of the opprobrium newspapers heaped on Frick was the *New York World* headline of July 7, 1892: "While Blood Flowed, Frick Smoked." For a full account of public reaction to the Homestead Strike, see Standiford 2005.

2   Harvey 1936, 139.

3   Harvey 1936, 42.

4   Cannadine 2006, 262.

5   Mellon with Baskett 1992, 25–26.

6   Helen Clay Frick, *My Father, Henry Clay Frick, as Told to Mary O'Hara* (Pittsburgh, 1959), 27.

7   Reist 2011, 166n.4.

8   Harvey 1936, 71–72.

9   Letter from Carnegie to Frick, August 2, 1887, see Harvey, 88.

10   Diana Strazdes, *American Painting and Sculpture to 1945 in the Carnegie Museum of Art*, (New York, 1992), p. xiv.

11   The Frick Collection Archives; Finocchio 2013, 101.

12   Finocchio 2013, 241.

13   *Chicago Tribune* (6 February 1898); see Ross Finocchio, "Frick Buys a Freak: Dagnan-Bouveret and the Development of the Frick Collection," *Burlington Magazine* 155, no. 1329 (December 2013): 25–48.

14   In reference to the mansion, see Edith Wharton letter to the decorator Ogden Codman, spring 1897: "I wish the Vanderbilts didn't retard culture so very thoroughly. They are entrenched in a sort of Thermopylae of bad taste, from which apparently no force on earth can dislodge them."

15   Letter from Isabella Stewart Gardner to Bernard Berenson, August 26, 1907, in *The Letters of Bernard Berenson and Isabella Stewart Gardner 1887–1924*, edited by Rollin van N. Hadley (Boston, 1987), 405.

16   The original cable is in The Frick Collection/Frick Art Reference Library Archives; for the illustration, see Saltzman 2008, 181.

17   Henry Clay Frick Papers, Series: correspondence, The Frick Collection/Frick Art Reference Library Archives.

18   Salzman 2008, 214.

19   Johnson Collection Curatorial Records, Philadelphia Museum of Art, Johnson Contemporary collector, 1988–89, online.

20   Louisine Waldron Havemeyer, *Sixteen to Sixty: Memoirs of a Collector*, edited by Susan Stein (New York, 1998), 32.

21   Letter from Frick to Carstairs, July 29, 1908. The Frick Collection/Frick Art Reference Library Archives Letterpress.

22   Finocchio 2013, 73.

23   See Salzmann 2008, 180–93.

24   Salzmann 2008, 191.

25   Letter from Thomas Gerrity to Charles Carstairs, October 4, 1905, Knoedler Gallery Archive; Salzman 2006, 176.

26   *New York Times*, July 3, 1910.

27   Helen Clay Frick Papers, The Frick Collection Archives; see Bailey 2006, 18.

28   Burton J. Hendrick, "The New Fifth Avenue," *Metropolitan Magazine* 23, no. 2 (November 1905), 233–47; see Matthew Worsnick, "'A Gilded Stall' for the Progressive Era: Fabricating Aristocracy on Fifth Avenue," in *Tastemakers, Collectors, and Patrons: Collecting American Art in the Long Nineteenth Century*, edited by Jean-Louis Cohen et al. (Leiden and Boston, 2022), 88.

29   Helen Clay Frick Papers, The Frick Collection / Frick Art Reference Library Archives.

30   Quoted in Richard Saunders, "Caveat Emptor, The Trade in American Historical Portraits in the Early Twentieth Century," in *Tastemakers, Collectors, and Patrons: Collecting American Art in the Long Nineteenth Century*, edited by Linda S. Ferber and Margaret R. Laster (New York, 2024), 139n.13.

31   Bailey 2008, 47.

32   Helen Clay Frick Papers, The Frick Collection / Frick Art Reference Library Archives; see Bailey 2008, 49.

33   The Frick Collection / Frick Art Reference Library Archives; see Penny Sparke, *Elsie de Wolfe: The Birth of Modern Interior Decoration* (New York, 2005), 169.

34   Recorded by René Gimpel in his diary entry for July 3, 1918, in *Journal d'un collectionneur, marchand de tableaux* (Paris, 2011); see Vignon 2019, 59.

35   Vignon 2019, 60–62.

36   See John Pope Hennessy, in *The Frick Collection, An Illustrated Catalogue*, vol. 3 (New York, 1970), xxv-xxvi.

37   Letter from Frick to Duveen, May 22, 1916, and from Duveen to Frick, June 24, 1916, box 453, folder 1, Duveen Brothers Records, 1876–1988, Getty Research Institute, Los Angeles.

38   Perrin and Salomon 2022, 62.

39   Henry Clay Frick Papers, The Frick Collection / Frick Art Reference Library Archives; see Finocchio 2008, 92.

40   Letter from Charles Carstairs to Henry Clay Frick, February 18, 1907, Helen Clay Frick Papers, The Frick Collection / Frick Art Reference Library Archives; see Saltzman 2008, 205.

41   Letter from Charles Carstairs to Henry Clay Frick, July 2, 1908, Helen Clay Frick Papers, The Frick Collection / Frick Art Reference Library Archives; Saltzman 2008, 207.

42   Art Collecting Papers of Henry Clay Frick, The Frick Collection / Frick Art Reference Library Archives.

43   Letter from Cyril Maude to Helen Clay Frick, September 9 and December 12, 1922, Helen Clay Frick Papers, Art Files, The Frick Collection / Frick Art Reference Library Archives; see Reist 2011, 176.

44   The Frick Collection / Frick Art Reference Library Archives; see "A Bust Destroyed, #92," in Bury 2022.

45   "Paintings Offered for Sale to The Frick Collection, 1936," Helen Clay Frick Papers, The Frick Collection / Frick Art Reference Library Archives; Reist 2011, 176.

46   Helen Clay Frick Diary, trip to Italy 1923–24; see Pittsburgh 2016, 55.

47   Nicholson et al. 1975, 18.

48   Nicholson et al. 1975, 38.

49   Galusha 1975, 5.

50   "Henry Clay Frick Residence, New York City: Thomas Hastings," *Architecture: The Professional Architectural Monthly*, November 1914, 251–52.

51   Saltzman 2008, 250.

52   Royal Cortissoz, "The Special Value of the Frick Gift," *New-York Tribune*, December 7, 1919, 43.

53   Henry Clay Frick letterpress book, vols. 10, 11, dated September 26, 1895, and October 25, 1895, The Frick Collection / Frick Art Reference Library Archives.

54   Quoted in Kenneth Warren, *Triumphant Capitalism: Henry Clay Frick and the Industrial Transformation of America* (Pittsburgh, 1996), 374.

55   Neil Harris, "The Gilded Age Reconsidered Over Again," *Archive of American Art Journal* 23, no. 4 (1983): 8–18. Finocchio (2013) raises this point and offers many insights into Frick's taste.

56   Edgar Munhall, ed., *The Frick Collection: A Tour* (New York, 1999), 102.

57   Henry C. Frick, Last Will and Testament, dated June 24, 1915, Henry Clay Frick Estate Records, The Frick Collection / Frick Art Reference Library Archives.

58   Harvey 1936, 336.

Included here are readings organized by chapter.

I   THE FRICKS OF PENNSYLVANIA

George Harvey. *Henry Clay Frick, The Man.* New York, 1936.

Paul Krause. *The Battle for Homestead, 1880–1892: Politics, Culture, and Steel.* Pittsburgh, 1992.

Robin Nicholson, Sarah J. Hall, and Dawn Reid Brean. *The Frick Pittsburgh: A Guide to the Collection.* Pittsburgh, 2016.

Martha Frick Symington Sanger. *Henry Clay Frick: An Intimate Portrait.* New York, 1998.

Les Standiford. *Meet You in Hell: Andrew Carnegie, Henry Clay Frick, and the Bitter Partnership that Transformed America.* New York, 2005.

Kenneth Warren. *Triumphant Capitalism: Henry Clay Frick and the Industrial Transformation of America.* Pittsburgh, 1996.

II   HENRY CLAY FRICK,
BECOMING A COLLECTOR

David Cannadine. *Mellon: An American Life.* New York, 2006.

Anne de Courcy. *The Husband Hunters: American Heiresses Who Married into the British Aristocracy.* New York, 2017.

Ross Finocchio. "Henry Clay Frick: The Making of an American Collector, 1880–1905." PhD diss., New York University, Institute of Fine Arts, 2013.

Neil Harris, Wim de Wit, James Gilbert, and Robert W. Rydell. *Grand Illusions: Chicago's World Fair of 1893.* Chicago, 1993.

Sam Hunter, Charles Henschel, and Melissa de Medeiros. *The Rise of the Art World in America: Knoedler at 150.* New York (Knoedler & Company), 1996. Exhibition catalogue.

Paul Mellon with John Baskett. *Reflections in a Silver Spoon: A Memoir.* London, 1992.

Edgar Munhall. *Henry Clay Frick: The Young Collector.* New York (The Frick Collection), 1988. Exhibition catalogue.

Kenneth Neal. *A Wise Extravagance: The Founding of the Carnegie International Exhibitions, 1895–1901.* Pittsburgh, 1996.

Elizabeth Pegram. "Collecting in the United States: William F. Davidson and the Westward Expansion of M. Knoedler & Co." *Colnaghi Studies Journal* 12 (March 2023): 114–27. Online.

Agnès Penot. *La maison Goupil: galerie d'art internationale au XIXe siècle.* Paris, 2017.

III   CLAYTON, THE FIRST HOME,
THE FIRST COLLECTION

Dawn Reid Brean. "Clayton: Evolving Portrait of a Home." In *The Frick Pittsburgh, A Guide to the Collection* by Robin Nicholson, Sarah J. Hall, and Dawn Reid Brean, 25–48. Pittsburgh, 2016.

Mary Brignano. *The Frick Art and Historical Center: The Art and Life of a Pittsburgh Family.* Pittsburgh, 1993.

Ross Finocchio. "'Frick Buys a Freak': Dagnan-Bouveret and the Development of the Frick Collection." *Burlington Magazine,* 155, no. 1329 (December 2013): 827–31.

Helen Clay Frick. "Clayton" memoir in the Helen Clay Frick Papers. The Frick Collection / Frick Art Reference Library Archives.

IV   THE VANDERBILT MANSION AND
ITS ART COLLECTION

Melanie Linn Gutowski. "Aspiration and Obsession: Henry Clay Frick and the W. H. Vanderbilt House and Collection." *Nineteenth Century* 32, no. 1 (spring 2012): 27–30.

Robert B. King and Charles O. McLean. *The Vanderbilt Homes.* New York, 1989.

"Mr. Vanderbilt's Pleasures. Adding to His Picture Gallery and Building a Conservatory." *New York Times,* March 24, 1883.

Nathaniel Silver and Diana Seave Greenwald. "Countries Visited by Isabella," Appendix 1, p. 153. In *Isabella Stewart Gardner: A Life.* Princeton, 2022.

Gabriel Weisberg, DeCourcy E. McIntosh, and Alison McQueen. *Collecting in the Gilded Age: Art Patronage in Pittsburgh, 1890–1910,* p. 184. Pittsburgh (The Frick Pittsburgh), 1997. Exhibition catalogue.

Gabriel P. Weisberg. *Redefining Genre: French and American Painting, 1850–1900.* Memphis (Dixon Gallery and Gardens), Palm Beach (Society of the Four Arts), Santa Barbara (Santa Barbara Museum of Art), and Washington, DC (Meridian International Center), 1995–96. Exhibition catalogue.

David Wilkins, Jean McCullough, and Evangeline Beldecos. *Art in Nineteenth-Century Pittsburgh.* Pittsburgh (University of Pittsburgh), Latrobe, PA (Saint Vincent College), Slippery Rock, PA (Slippery Rock State College), and Washington, PA (Washington & Jefferson College), 1977. Exhibition catalogue.

V   RIVAL COLLECTORS

Natalie Dykstra. *Chasing Beauty: The Life of Isabella Stewart Gardner.* New York, 2024.

Linda S. Ferber and Margaret R. Laster, eds. *Tastemakers, Collectors, and Patrons: Collecting American Art in the Long Nineteenth Century.* New York, 2024.

David Finley. *Painting and Sculpture from the Widener Collection.* Washington, DC, 1948.

Alice Cooney Frelinghuysen et al. *Splendid Legacy: The Havemeyer Collection.* New York, 1993.

Neil Harris. "Collective Possession: J. Pierpont Morgan and the American Imagination." In *Cultural Excursions: Marketing Appetites and Cultural Tastes in Modern America,* 250–75. Chicago and London, 1990.

Cynthia Saltzman. *Old Masters, New World: America's Raid on Europe's Great Pictures, 1880–World War I.* New York, 2008.

Flaminia Gennari Santori. *The Melancholy of Masterpieces: Old Master Paintings in America, 1900–1914.* Milan, 2003.

VI   CHARLES CARSTAIRS AND
M. KNOEDLER & CO.

Inge Reist, *British Models of Art Collecting and the American Response: Reflections Across the Pond.* New York, 2014.

VII   COLLECTING PAINTINGS,
1900–1911

Stijn Alsteens and Adam Eaker et al. *Van Dyck: The Anatomy of Portraiture.* New York (The Frick Collection), 2016. Exhibition catalogue.

Dorota Juszczak and Xavier F. Salomon. *"The Polish Rider": The King's Rembrandt.* Warsaw (Royal Łazienki Museum), 2022. Exhibition catalogue.

Maira Kalman and Xavier F. Salomon. *Rembrandt's Polish Rider.* New York and London, 2019.

Javier Portús et al. *Diego Velázquez: The Early Court Portraits.* Dallas (Meadows Museum), 2012. Exhibition catalogue.

Francine Prose and Xavier F. Salomon. *Titian's Pietro Aretino.* New York and London, 2020.

Pieter Roelofs et al. *Vermeer.* Amsterdam (Rijksmuseum), 2023. Exhibition catalogue.

Edward Strahan (Earl Shinn). *Mr. Vanderbilt's House and Collection.* 10 vols. Boston, New York, and Philadelphia, 1883–84.

Ernst van de Wetering. *A Corpus of Rembrandt Paintings, VI: Rembrandt's Paintings Revisited: A Complete Survey*. Dordrecht, 2014.

VIII EAST COAST HOUSES

Colin B. Bailey. *Building The Frick Collection: An Introduction to the House and Its Collections*. New York, 2006.

Hilary Ballon. *Mr. Frick's Palace*. New York, 2009.

David Gray, ed. *Thomas Hastings, Architect: Collected Writings, Together with a Memoir*. Boston, 1933.

Jan Cigliano Hartman and Sarah Bradford Landau. *The Grand American Avenue, 1850–1920*. San Francisco, 1994.

Laurie Ossman, Heather Ewing, and Steven Brooke. *Carrère & Hastings: The Masterworks*. New York, 2011.

Xavier F. Salomon. "Frances Cotes's Portraits of Sir Griffith and Lady Boynton." *Burlington Magazine* 158, no. 1358 (May 2016): 349–57.

Xavier F. Salomon and Letizia Treves. *Murillo: The Self-Portraits*. New York (The Frick Collection) and London (National Gallery), 2017. Exhibition catalogue.

Martha Frick Symington Sanger. *The Henry Clay Frick Houses: Architecture, Interiors, Landscapes in the Golden Era*. New York, 2001.

IX THE DECORATORS: WHITE, ALLOM & CO. AND ELSIE DE WOLFE

White Allom and Diana Brooks. *Thomas Allom (1804–1872)*. Appendix on Sir Charles Allom. London (Royal Institute of British Architects Heinz Gallery), 1998. Exhibition catalogue.

Daniëlle Kisluk-Grosheide, Deborah L. Krohn, and Ulrich Leben. *Salvaging the Past: Georges Hoentschel and French Decorative Arts from the Metropolitan Museum of Art*. New York (Bard Graduate Center), 2013. Exhibition catalogue.

Penny Sparke. *Elsie de Wolfe: The Birth of Modern Interior Decoration*. New York, 2005.

X COLLECTING FINE FURNITURE

David DuBon and Theodore Dell. In *The Frick Collection: An Illustrated Catalogue*. Vol. 5, pt. 1, *Furniture Italian & French*. New York, 1992.

Charlotte Vignon. *The Frick Collection: Decorative Arts Handbook*. New York and London, 2015.

Charlotte Vignon and Christian Baulez. *Pierre Gouthière: Virtuoso Gilder at the French Court*. New York (The Frick Collection), 2016. Exhibition catalogue.

XI DUVEEN AND DECORATIVE ARTS

Colin B. Bailey. *Fragonard's Progress of Love at the Frick Collection*. New York and London, 2011.

Alan Hollinghurst and Xavier F. Salomon. *Fragonard's Progress of Love*. New York and London, 2021.

Charlotte Vignon. *Duveen Brothers and the Market for Decorative Arts, 1880–1940*. New York and London, 2019.

XII CHOOSING WELL: THE COLLECTION OF J. P. MORGAN

Denise Allen with Peta Motture, eds. *Andrea Riccio: Renaissance Master of Bronze*. New York (The Frick Collection), 2008. Exhibition catalogue.

James Fenton and Ian Wardropper. *Riccio's Oil Lamp*. New York and London, 2022.

Flaminia Gennari-Santori. "'I was to have all the finest', Renaissance bronzes from J. Pierpont Morgan to Henry C. Frick," *Journal of the History of Collections* 22, no. 2 (2010): 207–324.

Aimee Ng, Alexander J. Noelle, and Xavier F. Salomon, eds. *Bertoldo di Giovanni: The Renaissance of Sculpture in Medici Florence*. New York (The Frick Collection), 2019. Exhibition catalogue.

Philippe Verdier. "Limoges Painted Enamels." In *The Frick Collection: An Illustrated Catalogue*. Vol. 8. New York, 1977.

Ian Wardropper with Julia Day. *Limoges Enamels at The Frick Collection*. New York and London, 2015.

XIII COLLECTING PAINTINGS, 1912–1919

Colin B. Bailey. *Renoir, Impressionism, and Full-Length Painting*. New York (The Frick Collection), 2012. Exhibition catalogue.

Elizabeth Cleland et al. *The Tudors: Art and Majesty in Renaissance England*. New York (Metropolitan Museum of Art), Cleveland (Cleveland Museum of Art), and San Francisco (Legion of Honor), 2022–23. Exhibition catalogue.

Giulio Dalvit and Elizabeth Peyton. *Titian's Man in a Red Hat*. New York and London, 2022.

Susan Grace Galassi et al. *Turner's Modern and Ancient Ports: Passages through Time*. New York (The Frick Collection), 2017. Exhibition catalogue.

Hilary Mantel and Xavier F. Salomon. *Holbein's Sir Thomas More*. New York and London, 2018.

Daniel Mendelsohn and Aimee Ng. *Bronzino's Lodovico Capponi*. New York and London, 2023.

Paul Perrin and Xavier F. Salomon. *James McNeill Whistler (1834–1903): Chefs-d'oeuvre de la Frick Collection, New York*. Paris (Musée d'Orsay), 2022. Exhibition catalogue.

Esmée Quodbach. *America and the Art of Flanders: Collecting Painting by Rubens, Van Dyck, and Their Circles*. University Park, PA, 2020.

Christine Riding, Thomas Ardill, and Aimee Ng. *Turner on Tour*. London (National Gallery), 2022. Exhibition catalogue.

Susannah Rutherglen and Charlotte Hale, eds. *In a New Light: Giovanni Bellini's "St. Francis in the Desert."* New York and London, 2015.

Xavier F. Salomon. *Bellini and Giorgione in the House of Taddeo Contarini*. New York (The Frick Collection), 2023. Exhibition catalogue.

Xavier F. Salomon. *Veronese, 1527–1588*, pp. 176–79. London (National Gallery), 2014. Exhibition catalogue.

Anne T. Woollett et al. *Holbein: Capturing Character*. Los Angeles (J. Paul Getty Museum) and New York (Morgan Library & Museum), 2021–22. Exhibition catalogue.

XIV THE ONES THAT GOT AWAY

Michael Clarke, ed. *Masterpieces from the Scottish National Gallery*. New York (The Frick Collection), 2014–15. Exhibition catalogue.

Ross Finocchio. "Saving Face: Henry Clay Frick's Pursuit of Holbein Portraits." *Burlington Magazine* 150, no. 1259 (Feb. 2008): 91–97.

Matthias Wivel et al. *Titian: Love, Desire, Death*. London (National Gallery of Art), Edinburgh (National Galleries of Scotland), Madrid (Museo Nacional del Prado), and Boston (Isabella Stewart Gardner Museum), 2020. Exhibition catalogue.

XV FURTHERING THE FRICK COLLECTION: HELEN CLAY FRICK

Stephen J. Bury, ed. *One Hundred Objects in the Frick Art Reference Library*. Axminster, UK, 2022.

Stephen J. Bury. "Fresco." Number 31 in *One Hundred Objects in the Frick Art Reference Library*, edited by Stephen J. Bury. New York, 2022.

Katharine McCook Knox. *The Story of the Frick Art Reference Library: The Early Years*. New York, 1979.

Edgar Munhall. *Ingres and the Comtesse d'Haussonville*. New York (The Frick Collection), 1998. Exhibition catalogue.

Inge Reist. "Helen Clay Frick: Charting Her Own Course." In *Power Underestimated: American Women Art Collectors*, edited by Inge Reist and Rosella Mamoli Zorzi, 163–83. Venice, 2011.

Charlotte Vignon. *Masterpieces of French Faience: Selections from the Sidney R. Knafel Collection*. New York (The Frick Collection), 2018. Exhibition catalogue.

Aaron Wile. *Watteau's Soldiers: Scenes of Military Life in Eighteenth-Century France*. New York (The Frick Collection), 2016. Exhibition catalogue.

XVI CHILDS FRICK, COLLECTOR AND PALEONTOLOGIST

Theodore Galusha. "Childs Frick and the Frick Collection of Fossil Mammals." *Curator* 18, issue 1 (March 1975): 5–15.

Thomas D. Nicholson et al. "The Fossil Mammal Collections of the American Museum of Natural History." *Curator* 18, issue 1 (March 1975): 16–38.

John A. Pope. "Oriental Porcelains." In *The Frick Collection: An Illustrated Catalogue*. Vol. 7. New York, 1974.

XVII GILDING THE LILY: THE FRICK COLLECTS

Till-Holger Borchert, Maryan Wynn Ainsworth, and Lorne Campbell. *Memling's Portraits*. Madrid (Museo Thyssen-Bornemisza), Bruges (Groeningemuseum), and New York (The Frick Collection), 2005. Exhibition catalogue.

Marie-Laure Buku Pongo. *The Gregory Gift*. New York (The Frick Collection), 2023. Exhibition catalogue.

Meredith Chilton, ed. *Fired by Passion: Vienna Baroque Porcelain of Claudius Innocentius Du Paquier*. 3 vols. Stuttgart, 2009.

Giulio Dalvit, Aimee Ng, and Xavier F. Salomon. *The Eveillard Gift*. New York (The Frick Collection), 2022. Exhibition catalogue.

Edmund de Waal and Charlotte Vignon. *Gouthière's Candelabras*. New York and London, 2019.

Aimee Ng. *The Pursuit of Immortality: Masterpieces from the Scher Collection of Portrait Medals*. New York (The Frick Collection), 2017. Exhibition catalogue.

Aimee Ng, Simone Facchinetti, and Arturo Galansino. *Moroni: The Riches of Renaissance Portraiture*. New York (The Frick Collection), 2019. Exhibition catalogue.

Xavier F. Salomon and Letizia Treves. *Murillo: The Self-Portraits*. New York (The Frick Collection) and London (National Gallery), 2017. Exhibition catalogue.

Stephen K. Scher and Aimee Ng, eds. *The Scher Collection of Commemorative Medals*. New York and London, 2019.

Please note that most of the images have been provided by the owners or custodians of the works. Any separate credits that are due can be found at the end of the caption.

Page 2: Henry Clay Frick and Helen Clay Frick, 1910. Photo Henry Havelock Pierce. The Frick Collection / Frick Art Reference Library Archives

Page 4: View of the Garden Court, 2015. The Frick Collection

Page 10: Walter Gay, *The Living Hall (The Frick Collection, New York)* (detail), ca. 1928. Oil on canvas, 17½ × 22 in. The Frick Pittsburgh

Fig. 1. The Overholt Homestead, n.d. The Frick Collection / Frick Art Reference Library Archives

Fig. 2. Henry Clay Frick, ca. 1870–75. The Frick Collection / Frick Art Reference Library Archives

Fig. 3. Workers drawing coke from the Connellsville coke region, ca. 1880–90. The Frick Collection / Frick Art Reference Library Archives

Fig. 4. View of the Pinkerton barges from across the Monongahela River, fifteen minutes after they were set on fire, 1892. Photo B. L. H. Dabbs. The Frick Collection / Frick Art Reference Library Archives

Fig. 5. Henry Clay Frick and Adelaide H. C. Frick, taken in Boston during their wedding trip, 1882. Photo James Notman. The Frick Collection / Frick Art Reference Library Archives

Fig. 6. Adelaide H. C. Frick with her children, Childs, Helen Clay, and Martha Frick, 1888. Photo Napoleon Sarony. The Frick Collection / Frick Art Reference Library Archives

Fig. 7. After Ferdinand Victor Léon Roybet, *The Musical Party*, 1885. Photogravure on satin, 10¾ x 8¼ in. The Frick Pittsburgh

Fig. 8. Jean-François Millet, *Shepherd Minding His Sheep*, ca. 1863–66. Pastel, conté crayon, and pen and ink on dark buff wove paper, 14¾ × 19 in. The Frick Pittsburgh

Fig. 9. Charles Lockhart's gallery, ca. 1880

Fig. 10. Andrew W. Mellon, 1905. Glass negative. Photo Harris & Ewing. Prints & Photographs Division; Library of Congress, Washington

Fig. 11. George Hetzel, *Landscape with River*, 1880. Oil on canvas, 45 × 30 in. The Frick Pittsburgh

Fig. 12. Top row, William Nimick Frew, Joseph Woodwell, Henry Clay Frick; middle, Margaret Woodwell, Emily Frew, Adelaide Frick; bottom, Marika Ogiz, Helen Clay Frick, Virginia Frew, ca. 1900. The Frick Collection / Frick Art Reference Library Archives

Fig. 13. Narcisse-Virgile Diaz de la Peña, *The Pond of Vipers (La Mare aux Vipères)*, 1858. Oil on canvas, framed 33⅝ × 41¼ in. The Frick Pittsburgh

Fig. 14. Théobald Chartran, 1898. The Frick Collection / Frick Art Reference Library Archives

Fig. 15. Théobald Chartran, *Henry Clay Frick*, 1896. Oil on canvas, 49¼ × 39½ in. The Frick Pittsburgh

Fig. 16. Théobald Chartran, *Andrew Carnegie*, 1895. Oil on canvas, 46¼ × 35⅜ in. Carnegie Museum of Art, Pittsburgh; Gift of Henry Clay Frick

Fig. 17. Henry Clay Frick (left), A. A. Hutchinson (top left), Frank Cowan (top right), and Andrew Mellon (bottom right) on board the steamer *Abyssinia*, 1880. Tintype. The Frick Collection / Frick Art Reference Library Archives

Fig. 18. Henry Clay Frick with his wife, Adelaide; Andrew Carnegie; and others in Kingussie, Scotland, ca. 1895. The Frick Collection / Frick Art Reference Library Archives

Fig. 19. George Inness, *Spirit of the Night*, 1891. Oil on canvas, 34½ × 49¾ in. Williams College Museum of Art, Williamstown, Massachusetts

Fig. 20. *The Great Loan Collection of Pictures* in the main gallery of the New Carnegie Art Galleries, 1895. Photo B. L. H. Dabbs. Carnegie Library of Pittsburgh

Fig. 21. William Bouguereau in his studio, ca. 1885. Photographs of artists in their Paris studios, 1880–90; Archives of American Art, Smithsonian Institution, Washington

Fig. 22. George Hetzel (front) with John W. Beatty (directly behind him) and Walter Miller, n.d. The Westmoreland Museum of American Art, Greensburg, Pennsylvania

Fig. 23. Postcard from Henry Clay Frick to Helen Clay, commemorating a luncheon hosted by artist Théobald Chartran at his villa on Lake Geneva, August 13, 1904. The Frick Collection / Frick Art Reference Library Archives

Fig. 24. Frits Thaulow, *Steel Mills Along the Monongahela River*, 1898. Pastel on paper, overall 40 × 46 in. Duquesne Club, Pittsburgh

Fig. 25. William Henry Jackson, *Details of Main Entrance to Art Palace* (World's Columbian Exposition, Chicago), 1893. From W. H. Jackson and Stanley Wood, *The White City (As It Was)* (Chicago: White City Art Company, 1894).

Fig. 26. Charles Knoedler, Andrew W. Mellon, and Henry Clay Frick in a carriage, 1898. Photo Pach Brothers. The Frick Collection / Frick Art Reference Library Archives

Fig. 27. Roland Knoedler and Adelaide Frick in Palm Beach, 1904. The Frick Collection / Frick Art Reference Library Archives

Fig. 28. Clayton, ca. 1901. Photo Lewis Stephany. The Frick Collection / Frick Art Reference Library Archives

Fig. 29. Lefebvre et Fils, supplied by Tiffany & Company, *Garniture Set*, ca. 1881. Onyx, enamel, and gilt-bronze mounts, 27½ × 18½ × 7½ in. The Frick Pittsburgh

Fig. 30. The reception room at Clayton, ca. 1901. Photo Lewis Stephany. The Frick Collection / Frick Art Reference Library Archives

Fig. 31. D. S. Hess & Company, *Armchair*, 1883. Mahogany and modern leather upholstery, 39 × 24 × 25½ in. The Frick Pittsburgh

Fig. 32. The dining room at Clayton, designed by Frederick J. Osterling, 1892. The Frick Pittsburgh

Fig. 33. The dining room at Clayton, showing Pascal-Adolphe-Jean Dagnan-Bouveret's *Consolatrix Afflictorum*, 1899. Oil on canvas, 87 × 76 in. The Frick Pittsburgh

Fig. 75. Adelaide Frick's bedroom, 1927. Photo Ira W. Martin. The Frick Collection / Frick Art Reference Library Archives

Fig. 76. Jean-Henri Riesener, *Secretaire*, ca. 1780 and 1791. Oak veneered with various woods, gilt bronze, leather, marble, h. 56⅜ in. The Frick Collection, New York

Fig. 77. Workshop of André-Charles Boulle, *Kneehole Desk*, ca. 1692–95, with later alterations ca. 1770 (before 1777). Oak, fir, and walnut veneered with brass, turtle shell, and ebony; gilt bronze, leather, h. 30¾ in. The Frick Collection, New York

Fig. 78. Pierre Gouthière, after a design by Jean-François-Thérèse Chalgrin, executed by François-Joseph Bélanger, *Side Table*, 1781. Bleu Turquin marble and gilt-bronze mounts, h. 37½ in. The Frick Collection, New York

Fig. 79. Italian (Rome), *Chest or Cassone (One of a Pair)*, third quarter of the 16th century with 19th-century alterations, additions, and restorations. Walnut, h. 28½ in. The Frick Collection, New York

Fig. 80. The north wall of the Enamels Gallery, 1927. Photo Ira W. Martin. The Frick Collection / Frick Art Reference Library Archives

Fig. 81. The Fragonard Room (looking east), 2020. Photo George Koelle. The Frick Collection, New York

Fig. 82. Joseph Duveen sitting for his portrait, ca. 1930. Getty Research Institute, Los Angeles

Fig. 83. Sèvres Porcelain Manufactory, model by Jean-Claude Duplessis, painted by Louis-Denis Armand the Elder, *Pot-pourri à Vaisseau*, 1760. Soft-paste porcelain, with later addition of gilt-bronze bases, h. 17½ in. The Frick Collection, New York

Fig. 84. Jean-Antoine Houdon, *Elisabeth-Suzanne de Jaucourt, Comtesse du Cayla*, 1777. Marble, h. 21¼ in. The Frick Collection, New York

Fig. 85. Chinese, Qing Dynasty (1644–1911), Kangxi Period (1662–1722), *Covered Jars with Blue and White Decoration*, 18th century. Hard-paste porcelain decorated with underglaze blue, h. 10⅛ in. The Frick Collection, New York

Fig. 86. Joseph Keppler Jr., "The Magnet." June 21, 1911. Editorial cartoon from *Puck* magazine, New York, vol. 69, no. 1790. Library of Congress, Washington; Copyright 1911 Keppler & Schwarzmann

Fig. 87. Vecchietta (Lorenzo di Pietro), *The Resurrection*, 1472. Bronze, 21⅜ × 16¼ in. The Frick Collection, New York

Fig. 88. Riccio (Andrea Briosco), *Lamp*, ca. 1516–24. Bronze, h. 6⅝ in. The Frick Collection, New York

Fig. 89. Workshop of Nardon Pénicaud or Jean Pénicaud I, *Triptych: The Way to Calvary, The Crucifixion, The Deposition*, ca. 1520–25. Painted enamel on copper, partly gilded, central plaque 10¼ × 9½ in., wings 10½ × 3¾ in. The Frick Collection, New York

Fig. 90. Hans Holbein the Younger, *Sir Thomas More*, 1527. Oil on panel, 29½ × 23¾ in. The Frick Collection, New York

Fig. 91. Paolo Veronese (Paolo Caliari), *The Choice Between Virtue and Vice*, ca. 1565. Oil on canvas, 86¼ × 66¾ in. The Frick Collection, New York

Fig. 92. Joseph Mallord William Turner, *Harbour of Dieppe: Changement de Domicile*, exhibited 1825, but subsequently dated 1826. Oil on canvas, 68⅜ × 88¾ in. The Frick Collection, New York

Fig. 93. Francisco de Goya y Lucientes, *The Forge*, ca. 1815–20. Oil on canvas, 71½ × 49¼ in. The Frick Collection, New York

Fig. 94. James McNeill Whistler, *Arrangement in Black and Gold: Comte Robert de Montesquiou-Fezensac*, 1891–92. Oil on canvas, 82⅛ × 36⅛ in. The Frick Collection, New York

Fig. 95. Giovanni Bellini, *St. Francis in the Desert*, ca. 1475–80. Oil on panel, 49 1/16 × 55⅞ in. The Frick Collection, New York

Fig. 96. Titian (Tiziano Vecellio), *Portrait of a Man in a Red Hat*, ca. 1520. Oil on canvas, 32¼ × 28 in. The Frick Collection, New York

Fig. 97. Agnolo Bronzino (Agnolo di Cosimo), *Lodovico Capponi*, ca. 1550–55. Oil on panel, 45⅞ × 33¾ in. The Frick Collection, New York

Fig. 98. Edouard Manet, *The Bullfight*, 1864. Oil on canvas, 18⅞ × 42⅞ in. The Frick Collection, New York

Fig. 99. Hans Holbein the Younger, *Christina of Denmark, Duchess of Milan*, 1538. Oil on panel, 70½ × 32½ in. National Portrait Gallery, London; Presented by the Art Fund with the aid of an anonymous donation, 1909

Fig. 100. Bernard Partridge, "Hans Across the Sea?" from *Punch* magazine, May 12, 1909. Punch, or the London Charivari

Fig. 101. Anthony van Dyck, *Marchesa Elena Grimaldi Cattaneo*, 1623. Oil on canvas, 95⅝ × 54½ in. National Gallery of Art, Washington; Widener Collection

Fig. 102. Titian (Tiziano Vecellio), *Diana and Actaeon*, 1556–59. Oil on canvas, 72⅝ × 79⅝ in. Bought jointly by the National Gallery and National Galleries of Scotland with contributions from the Scottish Government, the National Heritage Memorial Fund, The Monument Trust, Art Fund (with a contribution from the Wolfson Foundation), Artemis Investment Management Ltd., Binks Trust, Mr. Busson on behalf of the EIM Group, Dunard Fund, The Fuserna Foundation, Gordon Getty, The Hintze Family Charitable Foundation, J Paul Getty Jnr Charitable Trust, John Dodd, Northwood Charitable Trust, The Rothschild Foundation, Sir Siegmund Warburg's Voluntary Settlement and through public appeal, 2009. National Gallery, London

Fig. 103. Helen Clay Frick (center) visiting soldiers in France during her Red Cross service, 1918. The Frick Collection / Frick Art Reference Library Archives

Fig. 104. Page from Helen Clay Frick's scrapbook, showing Johannes Vermeer's *Girl with a Pearl Earring* (1665), recorded during a trip to France and the Netherlands, 1932. The Frick Collection / Frick Art Reference Library Archives

Fig. 105. The Frick Art Reference Library (now the Frick Art Research Library), 1936. Photo Samuel H. Gottscho. Museum of the City of New York

Fig. 106. Duccio di Buoninsegna, *The Temptation of Christ on the Mountain*, 1308–11. Tempera on panel, 17 × 18⅛ in. The Frick Collection, New York

Fig. 107. Jean-Auguste-Dominique Ingres, *Louise, Princesse de Broglie, Later the Comtesse d'Haussonville*, 1845. Oil on canvas, 51⅞ × 36¼ in. The Frick Collection, New York

Fig. 108. Malvina Cornell Hoffman, *Bust of Helen Clay Frick*, 1919. Plaster, h. 26½ in. The Frick Collection, New York

Fig. 109. Fra Filippo Lippi, *The Annunciation*, ca. 1440. Tempera on panel, left panel 25⅛ × 9⅞ in., right panel 25⅛ × 10 in. The Frick Collection, New York

Fig. 110. Cimabue (Cenni di Pepo), *The Flagellation of Christ*, ca. 1280. Tempera on panel, 9¾ × 7⅞ in. The Frick Collection, New York

Fig. 111. Sassetta (Stefano di Giovanni), *The Annunciation*, ca. 1435–40. Tempera on panel, 9 × 11¼ in. The Frick Pittsburgh

Fig. 112. Elizabeth Shoumatoff, *Childs Frick*, 1952. Oil on canvas, 30 × 25 in. American Museum of Natural History. Image © AMNH

Fig. 113. Chinese, Ming Dynasty (1368–1644), Wanli Period (1573–1620), *Stem Bowl*, 1573–1620. Hard-paste porcelain with underglaze blue, h. 4 in. The Frick Collection, New York

Fig. 114. "Childs Frick with Tusk, Cripple Creek, Alaska, 1938–39." Photo Otto Geist. © AMNH, VPA 108 Frick Laboratory Field Work

Fig. 115. Giovanni Battista Moroni, *Portrait of a Woman*, ca. 1575. Oil on canvas, 20⅜ × 16¼ in. The Frick Collection, New York

Fig. 116. Hans Memling, *Portrait of a Man*, ca. 1470–75. Oil on panel, 13⅛ × 9⅛ in. The Frick Collection, New York

Fig. 117. François Gérard, *Camillo Borghese*, ca. 1810. Oil on canvas, 83⅞ × 54¹¹⁄₁₆ in. The Frick Collection, New York

Fig. 118. Saint-Porchaire ware, attributed to Bernard Palissy, *Ewer*, mid-16th century. Glazed earthenware, h. 9¼ in. The Frick Collection, New York

Fig. 119. David Weber, *Table Clock with Astronomical and Calendrical Dials*, probably 1653. Gilt brass and silver, h. 23⅜ in. The Frick Collection, New York

Fig. 120. Meissen Porcelain Manufactory, after Johann Gottlieb Kirchner, *Great Bustard*, 1732. Hard-paste porcelain, h. 33 in. The Frick Collection, New York

Fig. 121. Du Paquier Porcelain Manufactory, *Ewer*, 1725–30. Hard-paste porcelain, h. 8⅝ in. The Frick Collection, New York

Fig. 122. Nevers, *Platter*, ca. 1660–70. Faience (tin-glazed earthenware), h. 1⅞ in. The Frick Collection, New York

Fig. 123. Pisanello (Antonio di Puccio Pisano), *Leonello d'Este, Marquis of Ferrara* (obverse); *Allegory of the Blessings of Peace* (reverse), ca. 1445. Bronze, diam. 2¹¹⁄₁₆ in. The Frick Collection, New York

Fig. 124. Pierre Reymond, *Covered Tazza (One of a Pair)*, late 16th century. Limoges; enamel on copper, parcel-gilt, h. 8½ in. The Frick Collection, New York

Fig. 125. Maurice-Quentin de La Tour, *Anne-Marguerite Perrinet de Longuefin, Madame Rouillé*, ca. 1738. Pastel on laid paper, 24¼ × 19½ in. The Frick Collection; Promised Gift from the Collection of Elizabeth and Jean-Marie Eveillard

Fig. 126. Gerald Kelly, *Portrait of Mr. Frick in West Gallery*, 1925. Oil on canvas, 48 × 40 in. The Frick Pittsburgh

First published in the United States of America
in 2025 by
Rizzoli Electa, a division of
Rizzoli International Publications, Inc.
49 West 27th Street
New York, New York 10001
rizzoliusa.com

Publisher: Charles Miers
Associate Publisher: Margaret Chace
Senior Editor: Philip Reeser
Production Manager: Alyn Evans
Design Coordinator: Tim Biddick
Copy Editor: Claudia Bauer
Managing Editor: Lynn Scrabis

in association with

The Frick Collection
1 East 70th Street
New York, New York 10021
frick.org

Editor in Chief: Michaelyn Mitchell
Assistant Editor: Gemma McElroy

Designer: Jesse Kidwell

Copyright © 2025 The Frick Collection

All rights reserved. No part of this publication
may be reproduced, stored in a retrieval system,
or transmitted in any form or by any means,
including photocopying, recording, or other
electronic or mechanic methods, without the
prior written permission of the publisher.

A CIP catalogue record for this book is available
from the Library of Congress.
Hardcover edition ISBN: 978-0-8478-4575-0
Paperback edition ISBN: 978-0-8478-7450-7
Library of Congress Control Number:
2024944859

2026 2027 2028 / 10 9 8 7 6 5 4 3
Printed in China

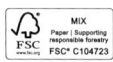

FSC
MIX
Paper | Supporting
responsible forestry
FSC® C104723

Front cover: The Fragonard Room, 2020.
Photo George Koelle

Back cover: Gerald Kelly, *Portrait of Mr. Frick
in West Gallery*, 1925 (fig. 126).

Page 2: Henry Clay Frick and
Helen Clay Frick, 1910.

Page 4: View of the Garden Court,
The Frick Collection, New York, 2015.

Page 10: Walter Gay, *The Living Hall
(The Frick Collection, New York)* (detail),
ca. 1928.